Eighth Edition

Today's

ISMS

Prentice-Hall, Inc., Englewood Cliffs, New Jersey 07632

Library of Congress Cataloging in Publication Data

EBENSTEIN, WILLIAM, (date)
   Today's isms.

   Includes bibliographies and index.
      1. Communism.   2. Fascism.   3. Capitalism.
I. Fogelman, Edwin, joint author.   II. Title.
HN18.E2   1979   335   79-13814
ISBN   0-13-924399-2
ISBN   0-13-924381-X pbk.

Editorial/production supervision and interior design by Joan L. Lee
Cover design by Judith Winthrop
Manufacturing buyer: Harry P. Baisley

PRENTICE-HALL INTERNATIONAL, INC., *London*
PRENTICE-HALL OF AUSTRALIA PTY. LIMITED, *Sydney*
PRENTICE-HALL OF CANADA, LTD., *Toronto*
PRENTICE-HALL OF INDIA PRIVATE LIMITED, *New Delhi*
PRENTICE-HALL OF JAPAN, INC., *Tokyo*
PRENTICE-HALL OF SOUTHEAST ASIA PTE. LTD., *Singapore*
WHITEHALL BOOKS LIMITED, *Wellington, New Zealand*

To the memory of Bill

Contents

2

Fascism, 111

3

Capitalism, 147

4

Socialism, 207

Preface

This eighth edition is dedicated to the original author of *Today's Isms*, William Ebenstein. Untimely death prevented Bill from preparing the new edition himself.

In revising the text I have deleted sections that are no longer topical, updated the factual information, and added a number of new topics, including sections on Chinese communism, Eurocommunism, Spain after Franco, and detente. The basic structure of previous editions has been retained, although the chapters have been reorganized for greater coherence. I have tried to preserve the direct style, specific examples, and broad perspective that have marked the book from the beginning.

During the quarter century since *Today's Isms* first appeared profound changes have taken place within and among the nations of the world. The mid 1950s were a time of economic expansion and international tension; the late 1970s are a time of economic uncertainty and increased international interdependence. The clear-cut confrontations of the Cold War years have given way to a more complex world with a number of competing and diverse centers of power. The growing strength of Western Europe and Japan and the emergence as major international forces of China and the OPEC countries have greatly altered the issues confronting us as well as the context in which these issues must be settled. In some ways it is a safer world, although the nuclear arms race, the proliferation of nuclear weapons, and the instabilities of the international economy pose clear new dangers.

Despite these far-reaching changes, the alternatives discussed in this book—not simply of ideologies but of differing ways of life—are no less pertinent today than they were 25 years ago. Although circumstances and policies have changed, the contrasting ideals and practices of communism, fascism, capitalism, and socialism still dominate our world. Predictions of an end to ideologies and of an impending convergence between opposing systems have proved somewhat premature. Judgments and choices among alternative ideologies and societies must still be made. For this reason clarification of what is at issue among these alternatives is a continuing necessity.

The underlying purpose of *Today's Isms* remains what it has been since the first edition: to aid in this task of clarification. What are the main doctrines of communism, fascism, capitalism, and socialism, and how do societies based on these doctrines actually work? These are the questions the book seeks to answer. Only on the basis of thoughtful answers to these questions can responsible decisions be reached about the great political choices of our time.

Edwin Fogelman

1

Communism

Marxist Theory

THE ECONOMIC INTERPRETATION OF HISTORY

Before Marx, history was interpreted in several typical fashions. Religious interpreters saw history as the working of divine providence and human development as but part of the unfolding of God's design *Religious* of the whole universe. The main difficulties with this interpretation of history are that divine will is unknown and unknowable to man's direct experience and that there are many contrasting human conceptions of God and divine plans for mankind.

A second dominant pre-Marxist approach to the understanding of human history was *political:* Great emperors, kings, legislators, and *heroic* soldiers were viewed as the decisive forces in history; and historical writing was largely the record of kings, parliaments, wars, and peace treaties. This political emphasis tends to exaggerate the relative role that most people assign to government and politics in the total setting of their lives. It is natural that statesmen, politicians, and political philosophers consider politics the most important single element in human relations, and political remedies the most important solution to human problems. But human nature and human problems are more intricate than politics; politics is only one approach—and not always the most penetrating one—among many others.

A third major approach, the *hero* interpretation of history (popularized by Carlyle), is closely related to the political viewpoint: Most heroes are conventionally chosen from great emperors, kings, generals, legislators, founders of new states, pioneering reformers, and revolutionaries. The hero interpretation, however, overstresses the role of the individual at the expense of the larger cultural, religious, social, and economic circumstances that form the background without which there can be no meaningful exercise of leadership. Although it is undoubtedly true that leaders mold events, it is no less true that events mold leaders.

The fourth pre-Marxist approach to the understanding of history was through the impact of *ideas:* Ideas were conceived (by Hegel, for example) to be the principal causes of the historical process. The material conditions (social, economic, technological, military) of society were thought of as essentially derived from, and caused by, the great motivating ideas. This emphasis on ideas often also implied that history was evolving toward the realization of key ideas, such as freedom and democracy. While this theory undoubtedly contains much that is valid, the exclusive emphasis on ideas as the main driving force in history overlooks the fact that ideas not only generate events but also reflect them. Therefore, to isolate ideas as the chief agent of human action is to neglect the framework of circumstances; circumstances, after all, make some ideas possible and others not, and it is circumstances from which ideas derive their vitality and practical impact.

The study of history may also be focused on war; The phenomenon of conflict is present in all phases of human development, and the birth, rise, and decline of states are often directly connected with warfare. The shortcoming of the *military* interpretation of history lies in its failure to recognize war as the result, rather than the cause, of events. There is no doubt that war often marks a turning point in the life of nations and civilizations; yet the dramatic swiftness and decisiveness of war should not draw attention from the multitude of psychological, ideological, and material factors that lead to war and contribute to its complexity.

Marx's analysis of society was set forth through his *economic* interpretation of history: The production of the goods and services that support human life, and the exchange of those goods and services, are the bases of all social processes and institutions. Marx does not claim that the economic factor is the only one that goes into the making of history; he does claim that it is the most important one, the *foundation* upon which is erected the *superstructure* of culture, law, and government, buttressed by corresponding political, social, religious, literary, and artistic ideologies.

Marx describes the relations between men's material conditions of life and their ideas by saying that *"it is not the consciousness of men which determines their existence, but, on the contrary, it is their social existence which determines their consciousness."* In a nomadic society, for example, horses might be considered the principal means of acquiring and accumulating wealth. From Marx's viewpoint, this foundation of nomadic life is the clue to its superstructure of law, government, and dominant ideas. Thus, those who own the greatest number of horses in such a nomadic society would also be the political chieftains who make and interpret the law; they are also likely to receive the highest respect and deference from those tribe members who own no horses. The predominant social and cultural concepts would reflect the dominant economic position of the owners of the horses. Even in religion the impact would not be missing: God might be represented in the image of a swift and powerful rider, and the concept of divine justice and rule would be, in a sense, an extension and magnification of human justice as determined by the horse-owning chiefs.

In a settled agricultural society, the ownership of land would provide the clue to the political, social, legal, and cultural institutions and conceptions. In such a society, according to Marx, the landowning class rules state and society even if another formal organization of authority exists. Similarly, the landowning class would also set the predominant social standards and values.

Finally, according to Marx, *in the modern industrial society of the last two hundred years the ownership of the means of industrial production is the master key:* The capitalists not only determine the economic destiny of society, but also rule it politically (regardless of formal and legal façades to the contrary) and set its social standards and values. The ultimate purpose of the law, education, the press, and artistic and literary creation is to maintain an ideology that is imbued with the sanctity and justice of capitalist property ownership.

Our understanding of history has gained immensely from Marx's economic interpretation. It is virtually impossible to write history today without relating economic forces and conflicts to political, military, and international issues. In pointing out Marx's overemphasis on economics we must not go to the other extreme of denying the importance of economic interests in human affairs. The Marxian theory reduces man to an earthbound beast with no spark of the lofty and divine; some anti-Marxian theories, on the other hand, have raised human beings to the angelic level, having no contact with the earth, nearly divine in goodness. Humans are only too often inclined to dress up their selfish and material aims and actions in high-sounding moral or religious phrases.

Marx's economic interpretation suffers from the same defect that afflicts all theories that pretend to supply the master key to history: *excessive generalization and simplification.* Whenever a single factor (be it the hero, war, religion, climate, race, geography, and so forth ad infinitum) is required to do the work of explanation and illumination that can only be properly done by several factors, its burden proves too heavy. No single factor has been predominant throughout history, and which factor is the most important in a particular situation is a question of empirical inquiry.

In any event or series of events there is always a complicated pattern of many factors, and it is none too easy to disentangle them. It is difficult enough to identify precisely the component motivations of an action of one person, because these actions are often mutually contradictory and logically inconsistent. It is even more difficult to isolate the determinant components in a single action of a small group. And it is virtually impossible to generalize about large-scale collective actions and processes throughout the whole of history.

To take a practical illustration: the Marxist interpretation holds that *imperialism* is caused primarily by economic interests and rivalries, that it is an essential aspect of capitalism, and that war in the capitalist era is the inevitable result of such imperialist rivalries among capitalist states. There have undoubtedly been examples of imperialism in history, ancient as well as modern, whose origins can be traced to economic factors—some of the colonial acquisitions of advanced capitalist nations like the Netherlands, Britain, and France in the eighteenth and nineteenth centuries can be attributed chiefly to economic forces. On the other hand, contemporary Western Europe and Japan provide examples of flourishing capitalist societies without empires or imperial ambitions.

Conversely, the Soviet Union and (to a lesser extent) China show that there can be imperialism without capitalism. The Soviet Union annexed three Baltic countries (Estonia, Latvia, Lithuania) in 1940, and helped itself to portions of Poland, Czechoslovakia, Romania, Finland, Germany, and Japan during or after World War II. More recently, Soviet imperialism has become firmly entrenched in the Near and Middle East. Russia has followed a policy of imperial expansion before the coming of capitalism, during the capitalist era, and now in her postcapitalist stage of development. Thus communist imperialism cannot be explained in Marxian economic terms, according to which imperialism is the last phase of an advanced capitalist economy with an abundance of capital that it seeks to invest in less-developed areas. The Soviet Union, and even more so China, suffers from scarcity of capital rather than its abundance. Their imperial ambitions are motivated, as the imperial ambitions of other nations in the past and present, by a mixture of economic goals and noneconomic forces of national interest and expanding spheres of influence.

Similarly, the Marxian economic explanation of *war* is neither wholly true nor wholly false, and can account for only part of the historical reality. There have undoubtedly been some wars that have been primarily caused by economic interests and conflicts. The economic interpretation, nevertheless, misses the core of the great and vital conflicts of history.

The Greeks fought the Persians 2500 years ago not primarily to protect Athenian investments and trade interests in Asia Minor, but because they knew that a Persian victory would mean the end of Greek civilization. Although a Persian victory would undoubtedly have entailed serious economic and financial losses for the Greeks, the main effect would have been the destruction of the Greek way of life, its devotion to the search for truth and its appreciation of human values.

To take more recent illustrations, the core of the conflict in the two world wars was not the protection of British investments in Africa or of American loans to Britain and France, but the more fundamental issue of whether totalitarian militarism was to rule the world. Again, there is no doubt that a German victory in either war would have entailed profound economic losses for the vanquished, but the economic effects would have been relatively minor compared with the effects of forced reversion to a way of life based on a denial of the Western liberal tradition.

What the Marxist-communist interpretation misses in the analyses of major conflicts is, first, the element of *power* (which is often the cause rather than the effect of economic advantage) and, second, the clash of *value systems*, which are frequently more important to people than economic interests, whether the values concerned are specifically political, religious, intellectual, or—in a wider sense—the symbolic expression of a whole way of life.

In fact, when conflicts of interest are primarily economic, compromise will usually be relatively easy. It is when more deeply felt values —individual liberty, freedom of religion, or national independence— are at stake that compromise becomes more difficult.

Before Marx, basic social change was thought to result from the work of great political leaders, legislators, and pioneering reformers. Marx rejects the traditional emphasis on the force of personality as the principal agent of important social change and looks instead for an explanation in impersonal economic causes. The two key concepts that he uses in approaching the problem of basic social change are, first, the *forces of production* and, second, the *relations of production*. The clash between these two is the deeper cause of basic social change:

> At a certain stage of their development the material productive forces of society come into contradiction with the existing productive relationships, or, what is but a legal expression for these, with the property relationships within which they have moved before. From forms of development of the productive forces these relationships are transformed into their fetters. Then an epoch of social revolution opens. With the change in the economic foundation the whole vast superstructure is more or less rapidly transformed. (Marx, *Critique of Political Economy,* 1859)

The Marxist conception of the forces of production expresses man's relation to nature and is essentially what we would call today technological and scientific know-how. Marx's notion of the relations of production expresses man's relation to man and encompasses all that we would include today under the term *social institutions.* Seen in these more modern terms, what Marx roughly suggests is that in every social-economic system there is at first a balance between knowledge and social organization, but gradually a disequilibrium or lag develops between available scientific knowledge and existent social institutions. *Our scientific knowledge grows faster than our social wisdom.*

This lag is the more modern, and broader, version of Marx's imbalance between the forces of production and the relations of production. Since the economic aspects of society are, for Marx, its chief determining factor, it is not surprising that he reduces the general phenomenon of the lag between knowledge and wisdom to the more specific lag between forces of production and relations of production.

Thus, when new productive forces developed within the productive relations of the feudal system, social revolution was, according to Marx, inevitable because the productive relations of feudalism (property relations, market controls, internal customs and tariffs, monetary instability) did not permit the utilization of the newly developing productive forces of industrial capitalism.

6

The capitalist system, having run its cycle, now shows the same tendency to rigidity, Marx holds, and it is due to meet the same fate when its productive forces (the capacity to produce) have outstripped its productive relations (law of private property, production for private profit). Like the social systems preceding it, capitalism will eventually stand in the way of scientific knowledge and will not permit technological resources to be fully employed.

What has doomed all historically known forms of economic organization, according to Marx, is the fact that when new productive forces develop, the existing productive relations—that is, the existing social institutions—stand in the way of their proper utilization. Each system thus eventually becomes wasteful in terms of the creative potentialities that have developed in its womb but are not permitted to be born and to grow. Only public ownership of the means of production can, according to Marx, bring into existence a new system of productive relations based on production for common use rather than for private profit that will match the tremendous forces of production actually or potentially known to man. In other words, man's capacity to produce will find full expression only in a social system in which production is only limited by scarce resources and incomplete knowledge, and not by such faulty social institutions as production for private profit based on the private ownership of the means of production.

Marx's insight that man's knowledge of physical nature ("forces of production") grows faster than his wisdom in creating social institutions ("relations of production") is highly important in understanding a vital source of tension and conflict both between and within nations. In international affairs, our capacity to produce hydrogen bombs is far ahead of our institutional arrangements for harnessing nuclear energy for peaceful purposes. Within advanced industrial nations, poverty testifies to the fact that our capacity to produce goods and services surpasses our wisdom to create institutions through which wealth can be more equitably distributed.

What distinguishes Marx from non-Marxists is his insistence that basic social change—caused by the excessive lag between advanced scientific knowledge and retrograde social institutions—can be brought about only by *violent revolution;* non-Marxists, on the other hand, affirm that the necessary changes can be effected by peaceful means.

REVOLUTION: THE ONLY WAY OUT

In the *Communist Manifesto,* Marx explains why violent revolution is the only method of basic social transformation. When technological know-how ("forces of production") begins to outstrip the existing social, legal, and political institutions ("relations of production"), the owners of the means of production do not politely step aside to allow history to run its inevitable course. Since the ideology of the ruling class reflects the existing economic system, the owners of the means of production sincerely believe that the existing system is economically the most efficient, socially the most equitable, and philosophically the most harmonious with the laws of nature and the will of God.

Marx penetratingly denies that the individual feudal landowner or industrial capitalist obstructs social change out of selfish greed: The resistance of the ruling class to change is so obstinate—making revolution finally inevitable—precisely because it identifies its own values with universally valid ones. The ruling class will, therefore, mobilize all the instruments of the legal, political, and ideological superstructure to block the growth of the forces that represent the potentially more progressive economic system. For this reason, Marx states early in the *Communist Manifesto,* the "history of all hitherto existing society is the history of class struggles."

Marx could find no instance in history in which a major social and economic system freely abdicated to its successor. On the assumption that the future will resemble the past, the communists, as the *Communist Manifesto* says, "openly declare that their ends can be attained only by the forcible overthrow of all existing social conditions."

This is a crucial tenet of Marxism-Leninism and the one that most clearly distinguishes it from democracy.

Marx had no clear-cut notion of how the political transformation from capitalism to communism would come about. Though in the *Communist Manifesto,* as throughout most of his other statements on the problem, he believed in the need for revolution, he was occasionally less dogmatic. Speaking in 1872 at a public meeting in Amsterdam, Marx conceded that the working class can travel on different roads in its quest for power: "We know that we must take into consideration the institutions, the habits and customs of different regions, and we do not deny that there are countries like America, England, and—if I knew your institutions better I would perhaps add Holland—where the workers can attain their objective by peaceful means. But such is not the case in all other countries."

Marx never fully pursued the implications of this distinction, and the orthodox opinion of Marxism-communism has remained that fundamental social and economic change is impossible except by class war, violence, and revolution.

In the early 1830s there occurred two major revolutions that Marx failed to appraise properly. In 1832, the passage of the Reform Act in England meant that the government of the nation would thenceforth be shared by the aristocracy and the middle classes, with the weight shifting in favor of the latter.

At about the same time, the Jacksonian revolution in the United States effected a similar peaceful shift in class power by bringing the men from the backwoods into American politics and successfully challenging the supremacy of the gentlemen from Virginia and New England who had treated the government of the United States as their political preserve.

These changes in Britain and the United States were more than just political victories: They inaugurated a permanent shift in the distribution of social and economic power in both nations, the kind of basic change that Marx had in mind. When revolution swept over Europe in 1848, England was spared because the aims of the revolution of 1848 —winning for the middle class its proper share of social and political power—had already been peacefully obtained by the British middle class in 1832.

If Marx had given the political factor its due weight, if he had fully grasped the importance of the Reform Act in England and the Jacksonian revolution in the United States, he might have realized that socialism, too, might be accomplished without violence in countries that possessed democratic traditions strong enough to absorb far-reaching social and economic changes without resorting to civil war. A recognition of the cultural and political factors in the equation of social change, however, would have amounted to a virtual abandonment of the central position of Marx: History is the arena of class wars, and ruling classes always defend their positions to the bitter end.

When Marx allowed, occasionally, that in countries like England, the United States, or the Netherlands violent revolution would be unnecessary in transforming capitalism into the classless proletarian society, it was obvious that what the three countries had in common was *political democracy,* providing the means for peaceful social change. Whether the range of Marx's exceptions should now be enlarged thus depends on whether democracy has spread in the world since his death.

In any case, Marx's concession that in a few politically advanced countries revolution might be unnecessary has always caused communists a good deal of headache. Lenin took up the question in *State and Revolution* (1918), his best known and most influential political tract, claiming that by 1917 "this exception made by Marx is no longer valid" because England and the United States had developed bureaucratic institutions "to which everything is subordinated and which trample everything under foot." Between 1872 and 1917, both England and the United States broadened the suffrage and moved steadily in the direction of more political and social reform. In 1884, only one year after

Marx's death, a British Liberal leader, Sir William Harcourt, said, "We are all socialists now," indicating that all parties accepted basic social and economic reform.

Since the historical record of the years 1872–1917 seemed plainly to contradict Lenin's dogma, it was necessary to rewrite history. Far from admitting that England and the United States had moved toward more political and social democracy since 1872, Lenin maintained that both countries had become more repressive, authoritarian, and plutocratic.

Since 1917 the United States has seen the peaceful revolution of social reform, which started early in the century with Theodore Roosevelt's Square Deal, was continued by Woodrow Wilson's New Freedom, and culminated in Franklin D. Roosevelt's New Deal.

In Britain, Lloyd George's "People's Budget" of 1909 gave the propertied classes a taste of things to come. In 1945, the victory of the Labour party at the polls was more than a mere electoral triumph. Just as 1832 meant the incorporation of the middle classes into the government of the nation, 1945 meant the same thing for the working classes in Britain. Whether the Labour party is henceforth in office or in opposition, the British working class will remain an active partner in the business of governing the nation.

The communist insistence on revolution as the only way of basic social change violates Marxist doctrine at one central point. According to Marx, the conditions of man's existence determine his consciousness, and social change is, therefore, not the product of mere will and free choice. Where the conditions of society permit peaceful change from private to public ownership of the means of production, the use of force is, in a deeply Marxian sense, un-Marxian.

The communist concept of universal revolution and dictatorship is in harmony with Marx's theory of consciousness only in societies in which the conditions of social and political life have created a general distrust in the possibility of peaceful change; it is out of harmony in nations whose democratic consciousness is the result not of paper constitutions but of the conditions of their existence. By insisting on universal revolution and dictatorship as the one and only method of change, communists in fact proclaim the un-Marxian doctrine that, regardless of historical, cultural, social, economic, and political conditions, a uniform consciousness—the creed of communism—can be imposed everywhere by sheer force.

There is a similar, reverse dogmatism maintained by anticommunist adherents of free enterprise who would like to see it practiced in the whole world. They, too, violate elementary common sense and historical experience. Whether a society is likely to operate a capitalist economy is not a matter of pure logic and choice, but the result of historical environment, cultural heritage, social institutions, and political ideologies. Thus, in 1900 it would have been reasonable to predict that basic changes in Britain or the United States would occur without revolution, and that such changes would be accompanied by violence and revolution in countries like Russia or China.

At present, it is often possible to predict whether change will be possible with or without violence. Yet there are countries, such as Brazil or India, where prediction is difficult because the balance of democratic versus undemocratic habits and traditions is not easy to define. Clearly, because such borderline countries do exist, no general prediction based on dogma—be it communist or anticommunist dogma—is likely to be accurate. Every prediction is a question of investigating each particular situation rather than of applying preconceived universal laws of development.

MARX'S HUMANISM AND THE CONCEPT OF ALIENATION

Marx's emphasis on class struggle and violent revolution as the conditions of basic social change has in recent years proved a liability to the spread of Marxism in both communist and noncommunist countries. In communist countries, the experience of Stalinist totalitarianism has shown more sensitive people, particularly in the younger generation, that a doctrine of hatred easily leads to the practice of brutality, and that no true community can be founded on the perpetuation of hostility and violence. In noncommunist countries, the experience of far-reaching social change in the direction of the welfare state has convinced many that Marxian class war and revolution are not only morally questionable but also practically unnecessary, and that therefore the desired changes of capitalism can be accomplished better through gradual amelioration based on social cooperation than through sudden, fundamental changes based on revolutionary violence and class struggle.

In their search for a humanist basis of Marxian communism, liberal-minded writers in both communist and noncommunist countries have concentrated on Marx's early thought, particularly his *Economic and Philosophical Manuscripts,* written in 1844 when he was 26. Interest in this early writing has been greatly stimulated by the fact that it focuses on the concept of "alienation" (estrangement), a concept which has become fashionable in contemporary thought as a result of highly popular works of social psychologists and existentialist philosophers. The concept of alienation has many roots. In its Judeo-Christian origin, alienation signifies the separation of man from God through sin. In early nineteenth-century German philosophy, Hegel formulated a more secular version of alienation which, though still tinged with religion, emphasized man's separation from his essence, spirit, the absolute. Marx rejected the concept of alienation as developed by the religious tradition, particularly in its Protestant Calvinist version, as well as in Hegel's metaphysical version, since both approaches seemed to him too abstract, too divorced from man in his concrete reality.

Finally, the romantic doctrine of alienation greatly influenced the young Marx. Although in the early nineteenth century romanticism was primarily a worldwide literary movement, its manifestation in Germany also had strong social and philosophical elements. In its social outlook, romanticism was basically a protest against the spread of industrial civilization. The romantics felt that industrialism was destroying the natural and organic bonds of life that characterized preindustrial, medieval Europe. They lamented that man in industrial society was becoming "alienated" from nature, from his fellow men, from family and nation, and—most important of all—from himself. In despair, some romantics felt that the only escape from the evils of industrial civilization was the return to agrarian life—a highly impractical proposal.

In his *Economic and Philosophical Manuscripts,* Marx shared the romantics' concern about alienation, but he arrived at a different conclusion because he saw the problem of alienation in a different perspective. Marx had the genius to see that industrialism was here to stay, and that it should be welcomed as the only hope of liberating mankind from the ills of material want, ignorance, and disease. Whereas the romantics saw the evil in industrialism, Marx perceived alienation as the result of *capitalist* industrialism. Under capitalism, Marx said in the *Manuscripts,* man is alienated from his work, the things he produces, his employers, his fellow workers, and himself. The worker does not work, Marx writes, in order to fulfill himself and his creative potential, for his work "is not voluntary but imposed, *forced* labor." His work does not satisfy the worker's needs, but is merely a means of satisfying the needs of others—the capitalist employers who use him as an instrument for making profits. Capitalism thus dehumanizes the worker, who "sinks to the level of a commodity," and produces palaces for the rich, but hovels for the poor. The worker is alienated from the employer, who appropriates the products of his labor and enjoys pleasures and freedoms denied the worker. He is also alienated from his fellow workers, with whom he competes for employment and favors bestowed by the employer. Money is the most visible symbol and expression of alienation under capitalism, the "visible deity" that transforms all human relations— including love and friendship—into monetary relations. Marx specifically affirms the need for a society in which love cannot be bought, but can "only be exchanged for love."

Marx shows in his *Manuscripts* that man's predicament included ethical and psychological as well as economic elements. Postulating communism as the only solution to the human alienation engendered by capitalism, Marx defines communism in the *Manuscripts* without reference to hatred or class war: "Communism is the *positive* abolition of *private property,* of *human self-alienation,* and thus the real *appropriation* of *human* nature by and for man. It is, therefore, the return of man himself as a *social,* that is, really human, being, a complete and conscious return which assimilates all the wealth of previous development. Communism as a fully developed naturalism is humanism and as a fully developed humanism is naturalism." In ambitious language born of youthful confidence, Marx also says that communism "is the solution to the riddle of history and knows itself to be this solution."

Yet this phase of Marx's humanistic and ethical concerns did not last long. In a crucial change of outlook, influenced perhaps by his growing familiarity with the living conditions and struggles of the working class, he quickly abandoned the humanistic and ethical elements in his conception of communism. In *The German Ideology,* written jointly with Friedrich Engels in 1846, the ethical socialists were attacked for talking of "human nature, of Man in general" rather than of man as a member of the proletariat, the working class. The individualistic leanings of the *Manuscripts* were increasingly replaced by the concept of *class,* and the ideal of love and fellowship was replaced by that of class struggle.

In the *Communist Manifesto* of 1848, Marx specifically ridicules the philosophical socialists who talk about "alienation of humanity" or about the "philosophical foundations of socialism," conveniently forgetting that he himself had defined communism in the *Manuscripts* as "the true solution of the conflict between existence and essence, between objectification and self-affirmation, between freedom and necessity"— ali terms taken directly from Hegel's philosophical vocabulary. In the *Communist Manifesto* Marx also attacks the ethical socialists as "utopians," because they reject revolutionary action and "wish to attain their ends by peaceful means, and endeavor, by small experiments necessarily doomed to failure and by the force of example, to pave the way for the new social gospel."

Marx was aware that in his *Manuscripts* of 1844 he had expressed ideas which were similar to those of the ethical and philosophical socialists. He therefore decided not to publish what he later considered an insignificant juvenile aberration. In fact, the *Manuscripts* were not published during Marx's life, and after his death his literary executor,

Engels, also refrained from publishing the *Manuscripts.* They were finally published in German in 1932; an English translation appeared nearly three decades later. Since then, the *Manuscripts,* particularly because of their focus on the fashionable concept of "human alienation," have been used for diverse purposes. In communist countries, particularly among more liberal Marxists, the *Manuscripts* have served as a weapon to discredit totalitarian attitudes of orthodox communists. While more liberally oriented thinkers in Eastern Europe cannot explicitly propagate "liberalism" by name, they can advocate some of its substance under the protective cover of the "young Marx." Some Yugoslav Marxists have argued, for example, that the replacement of a capitalist economy with a state-run economy does not in itself solve the problem of alienation, and that state property should therefore be transferred to groups of workers on the basis of self-management, that is, by more democratic participation in the decision-making process. Without using words like "liberalism" or "democracy," such liberally oriented Marxists affirm the basic principle that no socialism or communism deserves that name unless it has the political element of democratic self-government.

In noncommunist countries, the *Manuscripts* have served the goal of making Marxism respectable, since Marx is then presented as a humanistic socialist and liberal individualist primarily concerned with man's self-realization through love and free cooperation in a classless society without force and oppression. Such interpreters of Marx stress his humanistic goals, particularly as expressed in his early writings, and treat less the means for basic social change he advocated from the *Communist Manifesto* to the end of his life—class struggle, revolution, and the dictatorship of the proletariat. By focusing on Marx's ultimately humanistic goals, these Western interpreters seek to make him the descendant of the humanistic ideals of Jefferson rather than the ancestor of Lenin's dictatorial methods.

Whatever the merits of these political efforts in communist and noncommunist countries—to make liberalism respectable in the former and Marxism in the latter—from the analytical and historical viewpoint Marx cannot be transformed into a basically liberal humanist, since from *The German Ideology* (1846) on, he saw in the humanistic, ethical, and liberal socialists the most dangerous enemies of communism. Most of Marx's polemical writings were directed not against avowed opponents of communist doctrines, but against socialists who happened to disagree with him on what socialism meant and how it was to be achieved. This attitude of Marx was later repeated by Lenin and other communists, and to this day communists consider democratic socialists of the British Labour party type as more dangerous and damaging to the cause of communism than the conservative parties of a capitalist society.

ECONOMIC CONTRADICTIONS OF CAPITALISM

The end of capitalism will be brought about, Marx argues, not by "subversive conspiracies" of professional revolutionaries, but by the same inexorable laws of social development and change that destroyed previous systems. Marx uses, first, the "gravedigger" theory: The more capitalism succeeds, the more capitalist enterprise is organized in large-scale units. As a result, large numbers of workers are in constant and close association and mutually reinforce their status as proletarians. Big Labor inevitably follows Big Business.

The capitalist class has no way of escaping the dilemma of rearing its own destroyer as it goes along: The *law of the falling profit rate* (which is not to be confused with the absolute amount of profit) makes such escape impossible. Marx's prediction of the declining profit rate was based on the assumption that, under the capitalist system of production, the entrepreneurial class would steadily accumulate more and more capital; the greater abundance of capital would inevitably be reflected in the decline of the price (interest) and return (profit) of capital.

There can be no disagreement—because the facts speak too plainly —that the absolute amount of profits has risen immensely since Marx and is constantly rising.

What about Marx's prediction that the *rate* of profit (and of interest) would go down because capital would become more abundant? Here, too, the prediction has not come true. During the Depression of the 1930s, the rates of profit and interest were low and seemed to confirm Marx's forecast. Yet in the 1950s, 1960s, and 1970s, as in earlier periods of prosperity, the rates of interest and profit again reached new highs.

The facts of economic history do not support Marx's law of the falling profit rate. Marx's prediction was erroneous because he looked primarily at the *supply* side of capital: More and more capital is constantly created and accumulated in the capitalist system, and increased supply of a commodity (in this case capital) leads to a lower price— provided the demand remains the same. Yet this did not happen. The reason for the high interest rates (price of capital) in the 1950s, 1960s, and 1970s, the highest in a century, is that, despite an all-time abundance in the supply of capital, the *demand for capital has grown even faster,* since too many companies simultaneously want fresh capital for the improvement, expansion, and building of productive facilities.

The price of capital (interest) or return of capital (profit) are subject to supply and demand and not to any Marxian law of predetermined constant decline. Whenever the demand for capital outruns the supply, the rate of interest goes up, and the price of capital behaves like any other price.

The reason Marx overlooked the importance of the demand side in the capital market was his expectation (and hope) that the capitalist system would gradually lose its vitality and growth, thus requiring less new capital for investment. This, however, has not happened.

Finally, Marx underestimated the role of technological progress. Capitalism constantly produces not only more capital, but *more efficient capital*. More available capital need not lead to lower rates of profit if the capital is more efficient.

In a stationary economy in which there is little or no technological innovation, more capital might automatically lead to lower rates of profit and interest. In a progressive economy in which the productivity of capital is constantly raised, profits and the rate of profit may go up although the absolute amount of available capital is also rising.

Moreover, technological innovation strengthens the demand side in the capital market because new technologies require large capital investments, thus counterbalancing the effects of increased capital on the supply side. The current capital investment needed to create a new job in the average American industry is well over $25,000, and it is much higher in the mining, chemical, and petroleum industries. Therefore, as long as capitalism continues to progress technologically, the effects of increased capital resources will not, as Marx assumed, depress either the absolute volume of profit or the rate of profit.

Marx's main objection to capitalism was its inefficiency as well as its injustice. Here again, experience has contradicted his forecasts. Per capita consumption in Western Europe is more than double that in the Soviet Union, and in the United States it is three times greater. As to technological innovation, the capitalist countries still are in most cases the creators, and the communist countries, except in space science and technology, the borrowers and imitators.

Marx also stated that capitalists would seek to stem the impact of the law of the falling profit rate in two ways: First, they would constantly seek to "rationalize" industry, or make it technologically more efficient. This would eliminate the less efficient enterprises and would lead to concentration of economic power, large-scale industrial organization, and increasing proletarianization. Second, they would invest capital in underdeveloped countries, where the return for capital (profit) is still very high. Marx points out that this device delays, but does not avert, the inevitable doom. In the colonial country, too, capital becomes increasingly more abundant, a native capitalist class develops, threatened by its own proletariat, and the law of the falling profit rate makes the imperialist solution of the capitalist dilemma at home unfeasible.

Contrary to Marx, the flow of private investments from industrially advanced nations has been guided not only by the economic consideration of profits, but also by the political consideration of safety and stability. In 1977, American investments abroad were over $137 billion. The western hemisphere, in which American capital has traditionally felt safest, accounts for about 40 percent, and Western Europe accounts for another 40 percent. In Asia and the Pacific, the trend of American investments has been toward Australia, Japan, and the Philippines rather than toward less developed and less stable nations like India and Indonesia. This is a typical illustration of Marx's underestimation of the political factor in economics.

The American investment pattern abroad can also be found in other advanced industrial nations. The main outlet for Canadian foreign investments is in the United States and Western Europe rather than in Asia or Africa, and similar policies characterize British and German investments in other countries.

Another source of tension that undermines the vitality of the capitalist system, according to Marx, is unemployment. In Marx's own time, industry expanded at an enormous rate, and there was a chronic shortage of labor. Yet Marx foresaw that the maldistribution of wealth and income under capitalism would lead to periodic crises of unemployment. The Depression decade of 1929–1939 seemed to confirm his prediction; there was severe unemployment right up to 1939, when the preparation for war gradually eliminated it.

After World War II, the growth of welfare-state policies in the major capitalist countries led to the recognition of full employment as a primary social objective. Among the major Western economies, only the United States has had a serious unemployment problem, averaging between 4 and 5 percent in the 1950s and 1960s, reaching a peak of 8.5 percent in 1975. Other Western nations, such as West Germany, France, Sweden, and Switzerland, have for years had a labor shortage and have brought in large numbers of workers from Spain, Italy, Greece, Yugoslavia, and Turkey. Japan, the second largest capitalist economy in the world, has also increasingly suffered from a labor shortage and has sought to overcome it by recruiting foreign workers and setting up factories in other countries. Oddly—and contrary to Marx's predictions—communist states like Poland and Yugoslavia have suffered from chronic unemployment for many years, and since the middle 1960s even the Soviet Union has admitted the existence of periodic unemployment.

Marx also predicted that two other developments would disinte-
grate the capitalist system: the *concentration of economic power* and,
as a direct result, the *increasing proletarianization* of society. There is
little doubt that, compared with earlier stages of industrial development, the contemporary capitalist economy shows impressive features
of concentration. Yet Marx did not foresee that in highly advanced
capitalist nations concentration of management might be mitigated by
important counterforces: the spreading ownership of industry among
large numbers of persons through the holding of shares of corporate
businesses and the growing control of business managements by government, labor unions, and public opinion.

MARX TODAY

Marx's position as one of the intellectual giants of the nineteenth
century is so secure that he does not need to be approached with
worshipful reverence rather than with critical rationality. Even in his
own time, Marx was so dissatisfied with the vulgarizers and simplifiers
of his thought that he once stated, "I am not a Marxist." A century and
a quarter has passed since the publication of the *Communist Manifesto,*
and nearly a century has gone by since he died. It therefore stands to
reason that the world of the 1870s which Marx analyzed with passion
and acumen is not the world of the 1970s and 1980s. The passage of
time has brought forth new problems and new perspectives of viewing
both old and new issues. Although Marx's ideas contributed to important changes of social reality and analysis, the relevance of his thought
diminishes as the post-Marxian world becomes increasingly different
from the world that Marx knew.

In his economic theories and predictions, Marx assumed—in typically nineteenth-century fashion—that industrialization and economic
growth were the main road toward the liberation of mankind from
misery and ignorance, but that such liberation could be achieved only
if the means of production were publicly owned and managed. Until
recently, non-Marxians agreed with Marx on the desirability of perpetual economic growth, but disagreed on the question of the ownership
of the means of production. Increasingly, the suspicion has been spreading in advanced economies that worshiping perpetual economic
growth may be worshiping a false idol, since the main problem of
perpetual economic growth—the pollution of the natural as well as of
the human environment—has little if anything to do with the ownership of the means of production. The Mississippi and Volga rivers have
been transformed into major sewer lines, impartially polluted by waste

and refuse from privately owned factories in the United States and publicly owned plants in the Soviet Union.

Closely connected with the issue of environment is that of the conservation of resources, an issue which did not exist in Marx's world and concerning which therefore little guidance can be found in Marx's writings. Until recently, mastering and exploiting nature was considered the hallmark of progress both in capitalist and collectivist societies. Gradually, more and more people are startled by the realization that natural resources are limited and that the uncontrolled plunder of nature must be retarded if future generations are to have a chance of living in dignity or even of surviving. The "ecological demand"—that is, human demands on the environment through the extraction of resources and the return of waste—is several times higher than the rate of economic growth, and in this unequal race between the ecological demand and the demand for endless economic growth the reality of the former must eventually win out over the dreams and aspirations of the latter. Here again, it makes little difference whether the plunder of resources is carried out by governmentally owned or privately owned enterprises.

The issue of limited resources is closely linked to that of population. The dramatic and explosive growth of population, particularly in the less developed nations, is considered by many the main threat to peace and stability in the next century, regardless of prevailing political and economic ideologies. Marx did not pay much attention to this problem, since he shared the nineteenth-century optimism that industrialization would solve the challenges of population growth. Between 1950 and 1979 gross national product in less developed countries grew at almost the same rate as in developed countries. However, per capita income has grown much more slowly in less developed countries, since their population growth is more rapid than that in developed countries. As a result, the per capita income gap between developed and less developed countries is constantly widening in the noncommunist as well as in the communist world.

Finally, concern over population growth has also been spreading in the economically advanced countries, such as Japan and the United States. This concern is motivated not only by considerations of dwindling resources but also by the desire to recapture a minimum level of the quality of life, which can be relentlessly destroyed by economic growth necessitated by a growing population. Silence, solitude, and space become increasingly more scarce in a growing population, and the demands for zero population growth reflect the feeling that some values in life cannot be measured by, and must not be subordinated to, quantitative criteria of economic growth.

Industrialization affects not only the physical environment—the relation of man to nature—but also the human environment, or the relations of man to society. Marx lived in an age of small-scale industrial enterprise, which had not yet developed the deadening monotony of the assembly line for the workers or the flattening conformity of the "organization man" for the white-collar and managerial groups of contemporary large-scale industrial corporations. Marx thought that industrialization as a technological and social process could be wholly beneficial once the private ownership of the means of production were replaced by public ownership through a communist revolution. He never considered the possibility that public ownership could be even more oppressive than private ownership if such a collectivized economy were managed by a politically oppressive government. In Marx's conceptual framework there was no room for a system such as Stalinism but what was unthinkable for Marx became the Soviet reality for an entire generation. Marx made the same mistake in relation to public ownership that was made, in reverse, by nineteenth-century defenders of capitalism who were certain that the economic system of capitalism had to be accompanied eventually by a political democracy. Experience has shown that both expectations were incorrect: Private ownership can exist under both democratic and authoritarian political systems, and the same is true of public ownership.

Marx also failed to foresee the problems of large-scale bureaucracy inherent in large-scale economic organizations, whether in a collectivized or in a private-enterprise economy. In the *Communist Manifesto,* Marx predicted that after the communist revolution "political power" would disappear, or, as Engels put it, "the state would wither away." Even Lenin wrote in *The State and Revolution,* before he came to power, that in a communist society there would be no need for a "special machine," since "all would take a turn in management." Experience has shown that large-scale industrial enterprises lead to large-scale organizations, which in turn lead to large-scale bureaucracies, in the face of which the individual feels increasingly impotent, regardless of who owns the means of production. In fact, large-scale bureaucracy is more likely to develop in collectivized than in private-enterprise economies, since the pervasive force of bureaucratization is mitigated in private-enterprise economies by the millions of small businesses and farms that still exist side by side with the large corporations.

Specialization of work existed in Marx's time, but not nearly to the extent to which it was developed after his death, particularly in the form of the assembly line, as pioneered by Henry Ford. In all industrialized societies, workers' complaints about the harsh discipline, boredom, and monotony of the assembly line are becoming louder and have more recently become a significant source of labor unrest and strikes. A high degree of specialization makes the worker more efficient and productive, but as Alexis de Tocqueville perceptively pointed out in his *Democracy in America* (1835–1840), "in proportion as the workman improves, the man is degraded. What can be expected of a man who has spent twenty years of his life in making heads for pins?" If the worker is degraded by such work, it makes little difference whether the pins are produced in a privately or publicly owned factory.

So far, neither capitalist nor communist economies have shown any marked capacity to attain the technological efficiency of the assembly line without the human cost of the assembly line. If solutions to the problem will be found, they will not be in the writings of Marx but in societies in which workers possess considerable political freedom and in which employers are farsighted and imaginative. Sweden is currently the only country in which experiments are being tried out to replace the assembly line. In 1972, a major Swedish automobile manufacturer experimentally organized work teams in which workers switch jobs in building a car, or the individual worker follows the assembly line and carries out various jobs along the way.

Finally, as the nineteenth century moves further away from our own age, Marx can provide little guidance in solving a problem that confronts mankind more starkly today—in the era of nuclear weapons —than ever before: *nationalism.* In Marx's view, national sentiment is but part of the ideological superstructure of capitalism. However, he felt that capitalism itself contributes to the disappearance of nationalism. "National differences and antagonisms between people," he wrote in the *Communist Manifesto,* "are vanishing gradually from day to day, owing to the development of the bourgeoisie, to freedom of commerce, to the world market, to uniformity in the mode of production and in the conditions of life corresponding thereto." This optimistic and cheerful forecast fully reflects the typical outlook of nineteenth-century thinkers —Marxian, non-Marxian, anti-Marxian—who looked at the world through the narrow blinkers of economic theory. In that narrowly economic perspective, the whole world was destined to become one market; commerce would flow freely among nations and continents; and nationalism would disappear as an obsolescent prejudice of the preindustrial age. One world market would mean one world community living in peace and harmony and enjoying progressively rising living standards.

Although trade among nations has expanded enormously since Marx's time, such commercial expansion has not resulted in a corresponding decline of nationalism. Nationalism has shown a remarkable resilience even in politically mature states. In Canada a strong separatist movement has developed in French-speaking Quebec in the last decade; in Belgium the tensions between speakers of French and Flemish have become more intense; in Britain the tragic civil war in Northern Ireland has shown the persistent strength of national sentiments, and less violent affirmations of nationalism have also been expressed by the Welsh and Scottish.

Among communist states, too, there has been no decline of nationalism. Even Stalin seemed to lack the power to prevent Yugoslavia from regaining its national independence in 1948; after Stalin's death, the uprising in East Germany in 1953, the Polish Revolution of 1956, and the Hungarian Revolution of 1956 were all motivated by the desire for national independence and freedom from Soviet domination. Romania has been able to pursue an independent economic and foreign policy by gradual steps, thus avoiding so far the fate of Czechoslovakia in 1968, whose communist leadership sought to regain national independence too rapidly in the view of the Soviet government. It is a remarkable fact in the present-day world that nationalism is much stronger—in contradiction to Marx's analysis—in communist Eastern Europe than in capitalist Western Europe.

Although Marx stated in the *Communist Manifesto* that "the working-men have no country," subsequent events have contradicted that assertion. Before World War I, a number of European Marxist and socialist parties publicly committed themselves not to support their capitalist governments in case of war. But when war broke out in 1914, these declarations were quickly forgotten, and workers in France, Germany, and other belligerent countries supported their governments as loyally and patriotically as did the capitalist bourgeoisie. Some socialist pacifists opposed the war of 1914 on the ground of international solidarity and absolute opposition to any war. More importantly, some hard-line Marxists vigorously denounced any collaboration between the proletariat and the bourgeoisie as "social chauvinism," and held that only one type of war could be justified by Marxists: the war of the exploited working class against their exploiters, the capitalist bourgeoisie. Among these hard-line revolutionary Marxists, a Russian exile living in neutral and liberal Switzerland attacked the European socialist and Marxist parties with particular vehemence for their surrender to nationalism and patriotism. His name was Vladimir I. Lenin.

LENIN'S CONTRIBUTION TO THE THEORY OF COMMUNISM

The nature and deeper meaning of philosophical ideas can frequently be inferred from their appeal and impact. In the countries of Western Europe and North America, the inevitability of revolution as

Karl Marx preached it has had comparatively little impact; the liberal tradition in those countries keeps the door open for peaceful change. Although many social reformers have agreed with some of Marx's indictments of capitalism, they have refused to embrace a philosophy of class hatred and war to remedy social injustices.

In only two major countries did the ideas of Marx take root in the nineteenth century: Germany and Russia. Despite the façade of representative institutions, imperial Germany was in fact an autocracy that did not permit genuine government by the people. The Germans followed the philosophy of Hegel (although Marx claimed that he had turned Hegel upside down). Hegel had asserted that the *state* was an objective reality and that its laws, like those of nature, could be understood, but not changed, by man. Marx followed the cast of Hegel's thought by claiming that the laws of society, in respect to its nature and evolution, have the same scientific validity that Hegel had claimed for those of the state.

By contrast, the liberal philosophical tradition of the West rejects the Hegel-Marx conception that human reason can only understand the laws of the state and society and affirms the possibility of rational control and creative change of social and political institutions. The experience of free government is the psychological background for this affirmative, activist philosophy, whereas the experience of autocratic government in Germany provided the psychological background for the determinism of Hegel and Marx.

In nineteenth-century Russia, conditions for the acceptance of Marxian ideas were even more favorable than in imperial Germany. Whereas Germany paid homage to virtue by at least adopting the forms and formalities of representative institutions, Russian tsarism long recoiled from such hypocrisy on the ground that pretenses, if practiced long enough, might easily turn into second nature.

Of all the major states in Europe, Russia was first in illiteracy, economic backwardness, religious obscurantism, oppression of minorities, political despotism, and social inequality. Marx's prophecy, clothed in the language of scientific concepts, of the eventual liberation of man from bondage and oppression through revolutionary action made a strong impression on Russian radicals. *Das Kapital,* Marx's magnum opus, was translated into Russian before any other language; oddly enough, the tsarist censorship permitted the publication of the work on the ground that it would not be read by many because of its difficult style.

Among the Russian followers of Marx, Lenin (1870–1924) was both the leading theoretician and the most agile and effective practical politician.

Lenin's most important contribution to the theory of communism is to be found in his pamphlet *What Is to Be Done?* (1902): the concept of the *professional revolutionary*.

Marx, reflecting the nineteenth century's respect for man's capacity to think for himself, had assumed that the working class would spontaneously develop its class consciousness in the daily struggle for economic existence and that its leadership would come largely from its own ranks. Lenin had much less confidence in man, even if he belonged to the proletariat. Communist activity, said Lenin, is to be carried on along two lines. First, workers are to form labor organizations and, if possible, Communist parties, operating openly, legally, and as publicly as conditions allow. Side by side with such organizations, there are to be small groups of professional revolutionaries, patterned after the army and the police, highly select and entirely secret. Lenin did not care whether the professional revolutionary was of proletarian origin as long as he did his job well. The organizations of the professional revolutionaries must be highly disciplined and centralized, he went on, and must constantly guide and supervise the communist-led economic and political associations—the labor unions, the party, and the rest.

Lenin also advised the professional revolutionaries to infiltrate and form cells in all existing social, political, educational, and economic bodies in society, be they schools, churches, labor unions, or political parties. Above all, he advised infiltration of the armed forces, the police, and the government.

Lenin's tomb: a communist shrine

Wide World Photos

Lenin made it clear that communists should engage in illegal work even where legal Communist parties are permitted. He thought that legal opportunities should be utilized to the fullest extent, but he specifically advised communist activists to work through front organizations, constantly changing names and officers of organizations and always keeping the ultimate objective in mind: revolutionary seizure of power.

In particular, the secret nucleus of professional revolutionaries is responsible for the recruitment and training of spies, saboteurs, and agents for all other activities relating to intelligence, foreign and domestic. There are bridges between the legal Communist parties and the inner rings of spies and agents of the professional revolutionaries, since necessity often compels the choice of such agents from party ranks; ideally, however, the two sets of organizations are to be kept separate.

FROM MARX TO LENIN

Lenin always thought of himself as a faithful follower of Marx. Yet, as a man of action operating in Russia rather than in Western Europe, he was bound to modify Marxism in its practical revolutionary application. In his concept of the professional revolutionary Lenin consciously introduced a new approach to class war and communist organizational strategy that has permanently changed the nature of Marxism as understood by Communist parties. Other modifications by Lenin have created a body of ideas and attitudes, Marxism-Leninism, which combine some original ideas of Marx with their reformulations by Lenin. Communist thinkers are convinced that the Marxian inspiration and its Leninist modification are always harmonious. Noncommunist thinkers feel that some Leninist positions contradict Marx in spirit if not in letter.

In comparing Lenin with Marx, one is struck by the differences of temperament, background, and outlook. Marx was above all the scholar and polemicist, whereas Lenin was primarily the master organizer and practical politician and leader. Marx sought to change the whole world by his ideas; Lenin had one fixed, and more limited, goal: to seize power in his own country, Russia, and reshape it according to communist principles. Yet the most important difference between the two men is not to be found in explicit fundamental doctrine, but in the different inarticulate and implicit premises of their times. Marx was the product of the nineteenth century, and though he tried to envision and help create the society of the future, he always retained a world view typical of the nineteenth century. By contrast, though born in the nineteenth century, Lenin developed to maturity and stature in the twentieth century, and his deepest attitudes were typical of the twentieth century.

Marx's belief in the *primacy of economics over politics* not only resulted from his economic interpretation of history, but also reflected a typically nineteenth-century bias. The prevailing view in the nineteenth century was one of almost unlimited faith in economic forces as the main engines of social and economic progress. Thus, liberals in the nineteenth century confidently expected that the right economic policies would ensure domestic stability and progress, solve the problem of poverty, and lead to universal peace. Laissez-faire economic policies within nations and free trade between nations made up the magic formula that would lead to a world without force and oppression. Marx's formula was different from that of his liberal contemporaries, but it was nevertheless an economic formula.

By contrast, Lenin, in typically twentieth-century style, believed in the *primacy of politics over economics,* although in terms of explicit doctrine he always considered himself a faithful follower of Marx's economic interpretation of history. Because of his deep commitment to the overriding importance of politics, Lenin spent most of his revolutionary energy in building up an organizational apparatus in tsarist Russia. Although before the revolution he spent 17 years abroad, mostly in Switzerland, he kept in close touch with the day-to-day activities of the Bolshevik group which he led. His ability to maintain his leadership and the discipline of his revolutionary movement from afar for so many years testified to his political acumen and dynamic personality as a leader and organizer.

Because Marx was so committed to nineteenth-century economic thinking, he expected that the first communist revolutions would occur in Western Europe, with its advanced capitalist economies. Marx shared the general conviction of his century that the laws of economic development could not be interfered with, and that each country had to go through the various stages of capitalism before it became ripe for communist revolution. By contrast, Lenin looked at the problem from a more political viewpoint. The task of communist leadership and the professional revolutionaries, Lenin thought, was to attack and destroy the existing social and political system where it was weakest—in the economically less developed areas of Europe, Asia, Africa, and Latin America. Lenin agreed with Marx that communist revolution was inevitable, but he asked: Why wait until capitalism has matured? Why not smash it where it is politically and organizationally weakest—that is, in economically retarded Russia and in areas of Asia and Africa?

As a Russian, Lenin profoundly understood the weak social cohesion and low organizational energy that mark economically underdeveloped societies. In such countries, the mass of the population consists of poor peasants living in isolated villages, with inadequate means of communication. There are few or no independent labor unions and practically no middle class—the backbone of anticommunist resistance in economically more advanced countries. In his own country Lenin noticed that a comparatively small force of army and police could keep control over a vast—but unorganized—mass of people. Lenin therefore believed that with a relatively small but highly disciplined and well-organized counterforce, power could be wrested from the apparatus of the existing system. "Give us an organization of revolutionists," Lenin said in *What Is To Be Done?*, "and we shall overturn the whole of Russia." By 1917, Lenin did have the organization he needed, and he did overturn Russia.

Lenin also had a deep understanding of the importance of the underdeveloped areas in the balance of world power. Marx shared the typical nineteenth-century prejudice that Europe was the center of the world and that underdeveloped areas were merely colonial appendages of leading European powers. As a Russian, with one foot in Asia, Lenin was free from this European conceit. He was the first important political figure in this century to see the world as more than Europe, and, above all, the underdeveloped areas as an increasing factor in world politics. Many people in the West still do not grasp the crucial role of underdeveloped areas; Lenin—with his genius for political analysis and organizational strategy—understood at an early date that communism would first be established in underdeveloped countries before the hard core of anticommunist resistance—Western Europe and North America—could be tackled. A master strategist, Lenin hoped that once the "soft underbelly" of world capitalism had been conquered by communism, Western Europe and North America would not put up too much resistance.

Both Marx and Lenin believed in the inevitable victory of communism throughout the world. Yet this common belief was marked by significant differences. Marx expected that a communist revolution would lead to the *dictatorship of the proletariat,* an essentially economic entity, over the *bourgeoisie,* also a basically economic category. Marx even hoped that in such a temporary dictatorship of the proletariat there would be a variety of parties and groups, all united in the common goal of destroying the last remnants of capitalism but differing on lesser issues. By contrast, Lenin's concept of dictatorship meant, in more political terms, the dictatorship of the Communist party over the proletariat, since he had little faith that the working class had the political understanding or spontaneous organizational ability to secure the existence and expansion of a communist state. In 1904, Leon

Trotsky—then an orthodox Marxist critical of Lenin—predicted that the dictatorship of the party would be replaced by the rule of its Central Committee, "and, finally, the dictator will take the place of the Central Committee." Trotsky's prediction of Stalinism as an inevitable outgrowth from Leninist concepts and organizational practices came true and was tragically confirmed by Trotsky's own experience: In 1929, he was forced by Stalin to leave Russia, and after years of wandering from country to country he was assassinated by a Stalinist agent in Mexico in 1940.

Marx believed that communism in a particular country would be preceded by internal economic crises, and that each country would develop its own revolutionary movements when conditions were "objectively ripe." By contrast, Lenin took a more activist and worldwide view, combining ideological universality with Russian national interests. Particularly after the success of the November Revolution, he saw that Russia would become the base and nerve center from which communist revolutions in other countries could be engineered.

Finally, Marx and Lenin viewed international politics in different perspectives. In nineteenth-century fashion, Marx took comparatively little interest in international politics, since economic forces and tendencies were presumed to determine world affairs. By contrast, Lenin saw every problem in its global perspective, both before and after he seized power in Russia. Even while Russia was still reeling under the devastating impact of military defeat, revolution, and civil war, while millions of Russians were starving, Lenin devoted much of his thought and political effort to organizing centers of communist activity throughout the world, particularly in Asia, which he correctly sensed would be the most fruitful target for communist expansion.

Soviet Communism in Practice

SOCIAL-ECONOMIC CHANGES UNDER COMMUNISM

The first major attack in this century against the established social order occurred in Russia toward the end of World War I. The tsarist regime was overthrown in a bloodless revolution in March 1917, and it seemed that Russia would have the opportunity to develop democratic institutions for the first time in her history.

The majority of Russians wanted political liberty as well as fundamental social change. Inexperienced in the conduct of public affairs, however, and failing to understand the nature and goals of communism, the new democratic government of Alexander Kerensky allowed the Bolsheviks, led by Lenin and Trotsky, to subvert and quickly destroy the new regime.

Between March and November 1917, the Bolsheviks (the party was not known as the Communist party until 1919) used three classical methods of gaining power, methods they were to repeat later in almost identical fashion in other countries.

First, they presented themselves in their propaganda as a people's party dedicated to liberty, democracy, and social justice and opposed to all forms of reaction and social injustice. In an agrarian country like Russia, the communists emphasized the need for agrarian land reform and encouraged the seizure of land by the peasants even before they were in control of the government. A generation later the Chinese communists proclaimed themselves no more than agrarian reformers, thus following the pattern of propaganda established by the Russian communists in 1917.

The second technique the Bolsheviks employed was infiltration of other political parties, trade unions, soldiers' councils, and local government authorities. In particular, the communists managed to infiltrate and gradually disrupt the Social Revolutionaries, the largest party in Russia, dedicated to social reform and especially concerned with the question of the peasants. This technique of infiltration was again employed by the communists during and after World War II when they tried to take over other socialist parties in a number of countries.

The third method used by the Bolsheviks in their revolution was force. In free elections in the summer and fall of 1917, the Bolsheviks polled about one-quarter of the total vote. Though this represented a far from negligible proportion, the Bolsheviks accepted the fact that in a free election they could not hope to win. In November 1917, therefore, the Bolsheviks seized the key positions of power in Petrograd and Moscow, and from there the revolution quickly spread all over Russia. Opposition to communist revolution sprang up in various parts of the country, and a civil war ensued that lasted until 1921.

The ravages of World War I, followed by the devastations of the civil war, made immediate social reform impractical. Lenin was realistic enough to see that the Russian people would starve to death if communist principles were imposed at that time. As a result, he inaugurated in 1921 the New Economic Policy (NEP), which permitted limited private ownership; this policy's main objective was to maintain and increase production on the farms and in the workshops and factories by retaining the old capitalist incentives of efficiency and profit. The application of the NEP for some seven years gave Russia a breathing spell, allowing the new rulers to consolidate their power more effectively and giving the Russian people the temporary illusion that the bark of communism was worse than its bite.

But in 1928 Stalin decided that the time had come to put communist principles into practice, and he withdrew the temporary concessions earlier made by Lenin (who died in 1924). The first Five-Year Plan, starting in 1928, aimed primarily at the rapid industrialization of Russia and secondarily at the collectivization of farming. In 1917 many peasants had sympathized with Bolshevism, not for reasons of theory or ideology, but because the Bolsheviks promised them the land that they and their ancestors had tilled and coveted for centuries.

The reasons that motivated Stalin to force collectivization on the peasants were manifold. First, the communist rulers felt that agricultural production would be increased by mechanization and that this could be more easily effected on large-scale, collectivized farms than on small, individually owned ones. Second, individual ownership and operation of farms denied a key principle of communism, namely, that all means of production be transferred to public ownership. Collectivization would bring agriculture in line with industry, which was developed from the start on the basis of state ownership and operation. Third, the communist rulers saw in continued individual farm ownership a direct political and psychological threat to the acceptance of coercive political direction from the center.

The independent peasant had to be transformed into a dependent agricultural proletarian; as a member of a collective farm, the peasant was constantly working with others, talking to others, eating with others, and could thus be more easily supervised and regimented.

Another reason behind collectivization was the need for labor for the newly developing industries in the cities. The required labor force could be obtained only by mechanizing agriculture and thus saving human labor. Finally, collectivization had an important military objective: In case of war, the collectives were to provide the nucleus for organized resistance behind the lines. In World War II, these military expectations were largely fulfilled: The Germans were never completely able to suppress Russian guerrilla activities behind their lines.

The cost of fundamental social and economic change in Russia was heavy. In the process of collectivizing the farms in the years 1929–1933 about seven million peasants lost their lives. Half of that number died during the "collectivization famine," and the other half perished in slave labor camps in Siberia or the Arctic. To show their resistance to collectivization, the peasants slaughtered as much livestock as they could for their own use, so that by the time collectivization was accomplished, the number of livestock had greatly decreased. The human population thus increased at a much faster rate than the number of cattle and cows.

The Soviet diet still emphasizes starches—cereal products and potatoes—whereas the diet of most Americans is mainly vegetables, fruits, and foods of animal origin. Cereals and potatoes make up well over half the Soviet diet, but only about one-quarter of the American diet. The Soviet diet has considerably improved in recent decades, but its quality is still substantially below the standard of other advanced industrial nations.

The only realistic way to compute the cost of food and other basic items is to measure the amount of working time it takes to buy a given quantity of goods. Moscow working time is 200 to 1600 percent of working time in New York for basic foods, 600 to 1000 percent for basic clothing, and 200 to 800 percent for a few other articles. On the average, the Soviet family spends about one-half of its income on food, whereas the average American family spends only about one-sixth of its income on food.

Looking at the farm picture as a whole, one discovers that the contrast between Soviet and American agriculture is the most striking of all segments of the two economies. In the United States, about 4 percent of the labor force is currently employed in agriculture; in the Soviet Union, the figure is about 30 percent, the same proportion as in the United States 60 years ago. In the United States, therefore, one farm worker feeds himself and 19 other workers and their families on the highest standard in the world, and vast surpluses still accumulate which are sold abroad or given away under foreign aid programs. In addition, the government pays farmers several billion dollars annually for *not* producing foods and fibers. In the Soviet Union, by contrast, almost one-third of the labor force is employed in farming and can barely feed itself and the other two-thirds of the population. Items like coffee and chocolate, part of the ordinary diet of workers in Western countries, are still luxuries in the Soviet Union and cost—as measured in working time—over ten times as much in the Soviet Union as in the United States. Before 1914, Russia was one of the world's leading exporters of farm products; the collectivization of agriculture has turned her into an importer. Canada and the United States have been the main suppliers of wheat and corn, and in 1972 the Soviet Union contracted to buy from the United States and Canada large quantities of grains for a period of three years at a cost of about $2 billion.

In the early years of Soviet collectivization of farming, government-imposed low prices induced many peasants to grow as little as possible and to slaughter much of the livestock for their own consumption. As a result, there was widespread famine in the early 1930s, particularly in the Ukraine, where peasant resistance was strengthened by the force of nationalism.

After World War II, the Soviet government decided to intensify collectivization. Between 1950 and 1970, the 250,000 collective farms were amalgamated into 35,000. The objective was to increase production and at the same time reduce the individuality of the peasant. In addition to these 35,000 collective farms *(kolkhozy),* there are 14,000 state farms *(sovkhozy)* in which the peasant works on a wage basis, just as in a Soviet factory. The peasant in the collective farm still has some share in the success or failure of the whole farm.

The absolute numbers of collective farms and state farms do not give an accurate picture of Soviet farming, for the average state farm employs more workers and has four times as much land as the average collective farm. From the viewpoint of communist ideology, the state farms represent the highest possible form of agricultural organization and production because the peasant has been completely turned into a proletarian dependent on the state for his wage. Communist leaders hope that someday all collective farms will be transformed into state farms, and under Khrushchev's administration state farms were clearly favored over collective farms. His successors have been more realistic, and the Collective Farm Charter of 1969 specifically recognized the collective farm as a basic Soviet institution.

After more than 40 years of farm collectivism, the Russian peasant is still deeply opposed to communism in agriculture. Peasant pressure has forced the government to allow a member of the collective farm to devote part of his time to a small plot of land under his own personal management; he may then sell the products of his own effort on the open market at higher prices than are paid by the government (which is able to buy farm products at artificially low prices bearing little relation to the national forces of supply and demand).

Although the peasant's own piece of land amounts to only an acre or so, it supplies him with nearly half of his income, and these dwarf holdings, amounting to only 3 percent of all Soviet farm land, account for about one-half of all Soviet potatoes, meat, vegetables, and eggs. The peasants sell their personal produce in the farmers' markets found in most Soviet cities. It is not uncommon, however, to see individual peasants, often women, arrive in the center of Leningrad or Moscow with a basket of fresh tomatoes or fruit and sell the produce in a few minutes to an eager crowd of buyers who are always on the lookout for items that are scarce or of inferior quality in state stores. Although the prices in farmers' markets are about double those in state stores, there is a steady stream of customers. The higher prices of privately produced

The author in line to buy fresh fruit in the center of Moscow

produced foods are partly due to their higher quality and partly to the scarcity of roads and vehicles in the rural areas, resulting in serious bottlenecks in storing and shipping foods. Often, the only way to get the privately produced food to the urban markets is for the individual farmer to travel hundreds of miles by bus, rail, or even air to the city and sell there directly to the customer. Long condemned in theory and tolerated only as a necessary evil, farmers' markets finally won official recognition and endorsement in 1972, when the Soviet press stressed their important contribution to the Soviet standard of living.

Yet these peasants—whether in the Soviet Union or in other communist states—are not fanatical individualists. While opposed to collective farms, they eagerly accept cooperative farm institutions, such as Canadian, Danish, and New Zealand farmers have developed. There is a world of difference between collectivism and cooperativism: The purpose of collectivism is to destroy the individuality of the farmer, the aim of cooperativism is to strengthen the individual farm.

Interestingly enough, workers and professional people who have left the Soviet Union have indicated in interviews that they would want to maintain public ownership in only the key industries if Soviet communism should ever be overthrown or radically transformed, but would want to return to private ownership in light industry, retailing, and some of the professions. Where economic activity—as in agriculture, light industry, and retailing—can be performed in the classical pattern of the individual owner-manager-worker, what little uncensored Soviet opinion we have is opposed to the economic changes of communism.

Only where ownership, work, and management are technologically not feasible in one individual unit—as in heavy industry and some public services—does public ownership meet with approval.

In the field of industrialization, progress under Soviet communism has been immense, as was first proved by Russia's ability to withstand the onslaught of Germany in World War II. Though Russia received some strategic supplies from the United States during the war, the bulk of the industrial production needed to defeat Germany came from Soviet workshops and factories. Russian industrialization, from the first Five-Year Plan, has been oriented primarily toward the power of the state. From a Marxian viewpoint, equitable redistribution of income should have been the main objective once the means of producing wealth were transferred to public ownership. However, the Soviet leaders were not only Marxists but also realistic nationalists who regarded Soviet power and prestige rather than distributive egalitarianism as the top priority. As a result, industrialization was focused on heavy industry and military preparedness as well as on specific programs in science and technology in which—as in the space program—Soviet power and prestige are vastly enhanced. Inevitably, the commitment of the Soviet leadership to these policy goals of industrialization has led to considerable neglect of agriculture and consumer goods industries throughout most of the six decades of Soviet rule.

Until the late 1950s, appliances common in the American home were either unknown or extremely scarce in the Soviet Union. Since then, the Soviet economy has made great strides in meeting consumer demands for some basic appliances and durables. However, the supply of such appliances is still way behind other advanced industrial nations, since the latter often import large quantities in addition to domestic production. Moreover, the cost differential of basic appliances and consumer durables in the Soviet Union and the United States should be borne in mind. To purchase a refrigerator, television set, or automobile, the Soviet worker has to put in ten times as many work-hours as the American worker. Also, the range of appliances available in the Soviet Union is limited by Western standards. Color television sets were first produced in 1971 (60,000 as compared with 4.65 million in the United States), and numerous items—such as freezers, electric coffeemakers, dishwashers, clothes dryers, and food mixers—are still in the planning stage or available only in small quantities.

The Soviet Union's growing commitment to the economic needs and goals of a consumer society was reflected in the 1960s in its first program of mass production of a few basic home appliances, such as television sets, refrigerators, and washing machines. The 1970s and 1980s are becoming the first two decades of the automobile—the universally coveted symbol of the affluent consumer society. So far, the Soviet Union has been the only major advanced industrial nation in the world to have remained outside the automobile age. Both Stalin and Khrushchev looked upon the automobile as a typical expression of capitalist frivolity and unrestrained individualism. Ironically, at the very time when the romance of the automobile has begun to lose its glow and glamour in Western nations due to traffic congestion and environmental concerns, Soviet policy makers have decided, in response to intense and persistent consumer pressure, to enter the automobile era. Lacking car manufacturing know-how, the Soviet Union in 1966 contracted with Fiat and Renault—respectively the largest Italian and French automobile companies—to build huge plants in Russia for the mass production of automobiles.

Reflecting rising living standards and the growing pressure of consumer demand, the leadership under Brezhnev and Kosygin has since the mid-1960s experimented with a measure of broadened consumer choice. Until that time, central planners determined what each plant had to produce, how much labor had to be employed, and at what prices the goods were to be sold. Gradually, after the worst shortages of consumer goods abated, the Soviet government found that an increasing number of items (cameras, bicycles, lampshades, sewing machines) remained unsold on store shelves and in warehouses because they were overpriced, defective, poorly designed, or had been produced in unrealistically large quantities. Consumer goods industries were the first to be affected by the "Kosygin reforms." If the reforms did not work out, Soviet production of heavy machinery and military hardware would not be disrupted. After the consumer industries, the Kosygin reforms were gradually applied to light and heavy industries, and by 1970 most of Soviet industry was covered.

As the reforms have been applied to consumer industries, performance in sales rather than in gross output has become the main criterion of enterprise efficiency and profitability. Management now contracts directly with suppliers for materials and sells directly to wholesale and retail outlets. The size and composition of the labor force are now determined primarily by management rather than by central planners. However, central planners still determine the volume of sales to be met as well as the rate of profit in terms of invested capital. If management can fulfill or exceed the planned sales volume, plant managers may receive bonuses of up to 50 percent of basic salary, and production workers, too, receive bonuses. Profits of individual enterprises are thus substantially determined by the orders they receive from stores, and their orders are in turn largely determined by the preferences of consumers.

"I suppose we'll inherit the capitalist headaches—mortgages, crabgrass, buying on credit. . . ."

While these reforms give the consumer more choice than in the past, they should not be exaggerated as a recognition of the free market and of consumer sovereignty or as a return to capitalism. In the capitalist market economy, not only does the consumer determine which make of car he will buy, but the total consumer demand determines *how many* cars will be produced. In the Soviet Union, the government continues to determine the amount of capital and labor resources to be allocated to automobile production. Between 1960 and 1975, the Soviet Union increased automobile production from 140,000 to 1.3 million units annually, but in the same period Japan's annual production of automobiles increased from 165,000 to 4.6 million, since in Japan production was determined, not by the government, but by consumer demand. Similarly, in the Soviet Union the government continues to determine the amount of available materials and manpower to be allocated to construction of heavy industry, space complexes, and military installations rather than of shops, motels, hotels, restaurants, and supermarkets.

The main effect of the Kosygin reforms is thus the reduction of waste through stronger incentives for increased efficiency and profitability rather than the abandonment of the key principle of communist economics. The government will continue to decide how, for what purposes, and in what relative proportions available capital resources and manpower are to be allocated.

Of all the segments of the Soviet economy, services and housing have been the most neglected. Complaints in the Soviet press reveal that it takes three to four months to have shoes repaired, even longer to have a radio or television set repaired, and that it is next to impossible to get any laundering or dry cleaning done. Perpetual shortages of restaurant and hotel facilities not only limit domestic Soviet tourism but also deprive the government of the eagerly sought hard currencies of foreign tourists. Shops and stores of all types are in conspicuously short supply. The Soviet shopper has to stand in line three times to purchase something. In the first line, he finds out whether the item is in stock and what it costs. In the second line, he pays the cashier and gets a receipt. In the third line he exchanges the receipt for the merchandise. A few supermarkets and self-service stores have been opened since the late 1960s, and more are planned, but there is no indication that the traditional methods of retailing will disappear very soon.

The Soviet record in housing is even more unimpressive. In the precommunist Russia of 1914, available per capita living space for the urban population was seven square meters (one square meter is equal to 10.76 square feet). In 1940, after a decade of communist industrialization and planning, per capita living space had dropped to 4.34 square meters. Until 1957, the figure still stood under five square meters. From 1958 on, the Soviet government made a determined effort to improve housing conditions, and by the end of the 1960s urban per capita living space finally reached seven meters again—the level of 1914.

The Soviet government defines nine square meters per person as the minimum "health norm," but at the rate of recent building it is unlikely that this minimum standard will be met before 1980. Current living space per person in the Soviet Union is less than half the space available per person in Western Europe, and less than one-third the per capita space in the United States.

Since housing is perpetually scarce and most available housing is state-owned, the government allocates available space on the basis of social criteria as it perceives them. Thus, the primary consideration is not need but the contribution a person makes to society, as expressed in this manner by a Soviet writer: "We consider it just to provide housing in the first instance to those who do excellent work" (*Problems of Communism*, May–June 1969, p. 7). Outstanding scientists, scholars, artists, high-ranking party and government officials, and military personnel with the rank of colonel and above receive extra space in recognition of their status and work. Need is recognized only in the cases of persons with certain types of illnesses who require some additional living space.

The main benefit for the Soviet citizen in state-owned housing is the low rent, usually amounting to about 5 percent of monthly earnings, as contrasted with 15 percent of monthly earnings which the average American spends on rent or mortgage payments. However, the Soviet citizen lives in cramped quarters, as compared with five rooms per average American dwelling unit. Also, Soviet housing often still lacks the basic conveniences common in other industrial nations. Conveniences in urban housing have been greatly upgraded in recent years, but rural housing has been little changed by over 50 years of communist rule. "Only 15 or 20 miles outside Moscow itself," an American reporter writes (*New York Times,* May 22, 1972), "people are in another world. At the city limits, the sidestreets are not paved, and wooden homes all have outdoor toilets, and elderly women still get water from the community pump."

Since the government has been unable to supply sufficient housing, the occupancy of one apartment by several families—each family living in one room and sharing the kitchen and bathroom facilities—has been one of the most vexing problems. Soviet citizens with more money, initiative, and connections can escape state-owned housing in two ways: through private housing or cooperative housing. If a citizen wishes to build his own house, he must first obtain permission from the government to use a plot of land, since all land belongs to the state. Next, he must obtain construction materials, either legally or through the black market. The maximum size of the house is limited by law to 60 square meters, or the equivalent of five small to medium-sized rooms. Finally, the law generally forbids private building in major urban areas; thus most private home ownership is in smaller towns or rural areas. In the early 1970s, over 20 percent of the urban population and 75 percent of the rural population lived in private houses. In the past, private homeowners were subjected to various forms of bureaucratic chicanery, being denied building materials, water lines, and other facilities, but in 1972 the government came out in support of private homeownership as a practical method of alleviating the perennial housing shortage—the most serious deficiency in the Soviet level of living.

The second method of escaping state housing is cooperative housing. In larger cities, a minimum of 60 members is required, made up generally of fellow workers in a plant or families in a neighborhood who want better housing. In general, cooperative housing—accounting for

10 to 15 percent of new urban housing in recent years—is used mainly by the more affluent groups in Soviet society, since membership requires a large down payment for construction costs and monthly payments that are several times higher than rents charged for smaller and less desirable accommodations in state-owned housing. Also, the tenant in a housing cooperative owns his apartment; he thus enjoys more security than a tenant in state-owned housing, and ownership of an apartment in a housing cooperative may turn out to be a profitable investment.

As in the United States and other Western nations, living in a cooperative apartment house in the Soviet Union is a status symbol of upwardly mobile executives, engineers, and members of the better-paid professions. The Soviet government favors cooperative housing over private housing, since cooperatives fit the communist ideology of collectivism better than does individual homeownership, considered an unfortunate remnant of bourgeois ideology that is tolerated only for practical reasons and for the time being. Also, the higher-ups in the party and government who determine correct ideology happen to be among the more affluent elements in society and prefer the comforts of the better-designed cooperative housing to the austerities of the smaller, mass-produced accommodations in state-owned housing.

The persistent housing shortage in the Soviet Union is reflected in Soviet law. No one is allowed to live in Soviet cities without registering with the police, and the police often reject a request for residence in large cities because housing is not available. Illegal residents in major cities may receive severe prison sentences, particularly if the offender is a person without officially sanctioned means of earning a living.

The Soviet worker is subject to decisive managerial authority such as has not been known in most capitalist countries for more than two generations. The communist promise to liberate the worker from capitalist exploitation has been partially fulfilled—the capitalist has been eliminated—but this has not led to the freedom of the worker, since the place of the capitalist has been taken by the state. The main function of Soviet labor unions—as of labor unions in other communist countries —is to promote maximum production as determined by state planners. In pursuing the goal of maximum production, the Soviet labor union enforces labor discipline within the plant and organizes competitions to increase output. Basic conditions of work—wages and hours—are set by the government and cannot be significantly changed by union pressure, since party members are expected to ensure that labor unions adhere to government policies. In addition to its role as an agent of government policy, the labor union has administrative and social welfare functions: Unions help to enforce safety laws, administer the social insurance system, provide housing for workers, and supervise educational, cultural, and propaganda activities. The character of the Soviet labor unions as "company unions" is underlined by the fact that they include managerial personnel, since the managers directly represent the employer—i.e., the government.

The freedom of job movement of the Soviet worker is limited by various restrictions and disincentives. Until 1956, workers who quit their jobs without official permission were penalized by either salary cuts or prison terms. However, the penalties were increasingly ignored by the middle 1950s, and workers were finally legally permitted to change jobs, particularly since expanding industrialization opened up many employment opportunities in all parts of the country. In 1970, the Soviet government decided that productivity was suffering from excessively frequent job changes, and imposed new restrictions. Workers who quit their jobs more than twice in one year have to accept employment in enterprises selected by government officials and cannot receive higher wages than they earned before. Such "fliers" (as they are called in Russia) also lose various bonuses, vacation benefits, and other emoluments which are linked to seniority at the same enterprise. Another type of limitation on freedom of movement is imposed on graduates of professional, technical, or trade schools on the college or high school level: They are required by law to work for three or four years in assigned areas selected by the authorities.

During the first 15 years of the Soviet regime, an attempt was made to limit inequalities of income to a moderate range of differential; from the middle of the 1930s on, however, with the inauguration of the era of purges, the last vestiges of equalitarianism were wiped out and an entirely new policy was brought into being. Wages based on performance rather than on fixed hourly rates became the policy, a policy that labor unions in Western nations had opposed for two generations as exploitative.

The old-fashioned capitalist appeal for higher production compensated by higher incomes was covered up with slogans like "socialist competition," and workers were driven on to greater production efforts by the policy of Stakhanovism, inspired by the alleged feats of a coal miner named Stakhanov. Whereas the original concern in communist theory had been with problems of just distribution, Soviet policy has in practice concentrated on maximum production. The incentive of higher income rather than service to the community has become the main appeal of Soviet social and economic policy, and equalitarianism has been derided as "petty-bourgeois prejudice," "hostile to socialism," and conducive to "wrong attitudes" toward work.

The twin characteristics of the Soviet economy—strong managerial authority and the competitive incentive principle for workers—seem to have little in common with communism. *Monthly Review,* the leading Marxist journal in the United States, comments editorially on economic communism in the Soviet Union and Eastern Europe as follows: "*The managers operate according to what are essentially capitalist standards.* Their economic thinking and decision-making are directed to the goals of production, productivity, competitiveness in international markets: These are seen as ends, not as means. And the means to these ends are precisely the workers who are to be manipulated by propaganda, incentive schemes, fear of loss of income, dread of unemployment, etc. This not only *resembles* the economic ideology of capitalism, it *is* the economic ideology of capitalism" (*Monthly Review,* February 1971, p. 11).

In line with the Soviet policy of encouraging incentive, personal income taxes are among the lowest in the world. The Soviet government derives the bulk of its revenue from sales taxes and other indirect levies that proportionately hit the lowest income groups hardest. Only a small proportion of government revenue derives from income taxes. In the United States, the picture is the exact reverse: Revenues are derived mainly from progressive income taxes, under which system the tax rate goes up as the income rises. In concentrating on sales and other indirect taxes, the Soviet tax system hits consumption, whereas income taxes in Western nations hit the productive effort.

The group with the highest income level is the same in the Soviet Union as in the United States: business managers and executives. Yet, whereas the income tax in the United States goes up to 70 percent (and is even higher in other Western nations such as Britain and Canada), the top tax rate for Soviet executives is 13 percent. The top inheritance tax rate in the United States is 77 percent; in the Soviet Union, inheritance taxes were abolished in 1942—another bonus to the affluent elements in Soviet society.

According to official claims, the problem of social classes has been solved in Soviet society, because from the Marxist viewpoint there can be no class inequality except on the basis of the private ownership of the means of production.

Yet Soviet reality tells a different story. There are at least three distinguishable classes. In the first group—numbering a few hundred thousand families, perhaps as many as a million—are the top government officials, party leaders, military officers, industrial executives, scientists, artists, and writers. Members of this elite group do not have to share their homes or apartments with other families, many benefit from padded expense accounts for travel and vacation for themselves and their families, some have town and country homes and official or privately owned cars, and a small privileged minority may even enjoy the ultimate in luxury—travel to Western countries. The second class is made up of the intermediary ranks of civilian and military officials, collective farm managers, and some of the more affluent skilled workers and technicians in industry; this group forms the middle class of Soviet society and numbers four to five million families. The third class is made up of the bulk of the population, the mass of workers and peasants, numbering more than 50 million families.

Upward social mobility in the Soviet Union largely depends, as in noncommunist countries, on access to higher education. Such access is unequally distributed in the Soviet Union, and the inequality reflects the reality of the Soviet class structure. Soviet researchers have found that only ten out of every hundred secondary-school graduates from families of collective farmers and state-farm workers continue their education, whereas 82 out of every hundred secondary-school graduates from families of urban white-collar workers and officials receive a higher education.

What is remarkable about social stratification in communist countries is that the income spread between the different classes has remained very wide, while it has been narrowed continuously in the democratic nations of the West through taxation and other measures. Moreover, within the bulk of the population, the working class, the difference between wages of skilled and unskilled workers has been kept at a high level in the Soviet Union, whereas in democratic nations this differential has been systematically reduced, largely by the pressure of free labor unions. The differential between skilled and unskilled workers is about three times greater in the Soviet Union than in the United States.

As Aristotle said over 2000 years ago, the main question is not *who* owns property, but *how* property is used.

In our own day, the experience of communist economic change teaches again that the principal issue is not whether the government owns the means of production, but who owns the government.

SOURCES OF STRENGTH IN COMMUNISM

Communism's most important source of strength is probably the enormous widening of the base from which the elite is recruited. Before World War I, the Russian elite—in government, the army, business, science, and the arts—was drawn from a small social group of upper-class and upper-middle-class background. There was a tremendous gap between the small governing class of Russia, in intimate contact with Western Europe, and the vast inchoate masses of peasants. The communist revolution, particularly in its first impetus, swept away distinctions of class, sex, or nationality and opened up a new world of opportunity for people who had hitherto been excluded from opportunity of any sort. Industrialization, perhaps the most dynamic key in creating new opportunities in science and government as well as in industry, formed a new managerial class, recruited on a wide basis, for which there was no precedent.

A quick glance at the social background of recent top leaders of the Soviet Union gives us a fair idea of the Soviet leadership as a whole:

Leader	Occupation of father
Brezhnev	steel worker
Grishin	railroad engineer
Gromyko	artisan
Kosygin	lathe worker
Kulakov	peasant
Kunayev	office worker
Mazurov	peasant
Podgorny	foundry worker
Polyansky	peasant
Suslov	peasant

These leaders are typical representatives of the men who run Soviet industry, government, and armed forces. Those Westerners who have dealt with them agree that they are able and confident, full of drive and energy. In the United States, these men would be corporation executives, political and military leaders, and top government officials—the very same jobs they hold in the Soviet Union. Because their ideas and aims seem (and sometimes are) so different from Western ideas and objectives, many persons have been blinded to their high technical and executive ability.

The competition for leadership positions in the Soviet Union is stronger than in the democratic world, the premium for success greater, and the penalty for failure harsher. The successful manager who overfulfills his production quota is rapidly promoted and his rewards are—in relation to the rest of the population—more ample than in capitalist countries. The incentive system is more fully developed than in the United States and other Western nations, and generous bonuses are paid to successful executives.

The penalty for failure is also greater than in capitalist countries. Under Stalin, managerial failure could result in slave labor or even execution; in more recent years, the manager who fails in his production job is more likely to be fired or downgraded to a less responsible job.

The less a position in the elite is directly tied up with politics, the more recognition can be given to talent and merit. As long as a leading surgeon, chemist, mathematician, engineer, or industrial executive is politically discreet, he will generally be left alone. The more a position in the ruling group is tinged with politics, the more criteria besides merit and talent become relevant and frequently decisive.

Rapid industrialization is another source of communist strength, in Russia as well as in other communized states. Before World War I, Russia was an overwhelmingly agricultural country; Soviet industrial power ranked behind the United States, Britain, Germany, France, Japan, and Austria-Hungary. After World War II, the Soviet Union moved up to second place, preceded only by the United States.

In absolute figures, industry in the Soviet Union and the other communist states still lags considerably behind the United States and other noncommunist nations. But what is impressive is the rapid rate of industrial growth in the communist states, which considerably exceeds that of many Western nations. Even if it be argued that the communist states have now the initial advantage of underdeveloped countries undergoing rapid industrialization, and that their present rate of expansion cannot be indefinitely maintained, the Western nations will have to step up their own productivity and rate of industrial growth if the present balance of industrial power, still heavily in favor of the noncommunist states, is not to be lost.·

Fast economic growth is not something which automatically comes out of either communism or capitalism but is the result of hard work and know-how. Within the communist group of nations, some have shown faster economic progress than others, as is true of the capitalist world. Specifically, the Soviet Union has no superior record of economic growth as compared with *all* capitalist nations. While it is true that the Soviet Union has, in the period of the 1950s and 1960s, grown faster economically than the United States, other capitalist nations have done better than the Soviet Union. As the following table shows, the growth record of the Soviet Union during 1950–1960 was more impressive than in the 1960s, and the superior performance of Japan as compared with the Soviet Union in 1950–1973 is particularly striking. However, the eyes of the world are focused on the comparative economic growth of the Soviet Union and the United States rather than of the Soviet Union and Japan. During the 1950s, the Soviet rate of growth was more than one and three-quarters that of the United States; during the 1960s, the Soviet growth rate was only slightly above that of the United States. In the 1970s, the focus of attention moved from both the Soviet Union and the United States to Japan. By 1980, Japan (with a current population of 115 million) will pass the absolute size of the gross national product of the Soviet Union (with a current population of 260 million), and by the year 1990 Japan may even exceed the gross national product of the United States (with a current population of 220 million). Real per capita income is already higher in Japan than in the Soviet Union, and may exceed that of the United States in the early 1980s.

In gearing economic policy to the requirements of heavy industry and defense, the Soviet Union has made strenuous efforts to close the production gap with the United States in such key commodities as iron, steel, coal, and petroleum. In 1971 the Soviet Union passed the United States for the first time in steel production, thus becoming the world's foremost steel producer. In the United States, the relative decline of steel production is due in part to the fact that other products (such as aluminum and plastics) are increasingly replacing steel in many uses; also, in an advanced consumer economy like the United States', people are increasingly buying more services, amenities, and luxuries, and fewer goods that use steel. Similarly, the Soviet Union now produces more coal than the United States, yet the production lead of the United States over the Soviet Union in natural gas and electricity in the period 1950–1975 increased. Gas and electricity are both cleaner and cheaper than coal, they are more conducive to labor productivity than coal, and they are also indispensable to an economy geared to numerous household appliances.

The most serious lag of the Soviet economy, in terms of advanced technology and sophistication, is in computers. In 1972, the Soviet Union had six to seven thousand computers as compared with about 85,000 computers in the United States, and also ranked behind West Germany, Britain, and Japan in its computer stock. Moreover, the

Average annual rates of economic growth for seven major economies, 1950–1973

Country	1950–1960	1960–1965	1965–1973
Japan	8.7	10.2	10.8
West Germany	7.9	5.0	4.6
Soviet Union	6.1	5.0	4.8
Italy	6.1	5.1	4.9
France	4.4	5.9	5.8
United States	3.3	4.9	3.5
Great Britain	2.8	3.3	2.5

Source: World Tables (World Bank, 1976).

"Soviet computer stock is on the average about 10 or 15 years behind the West in quality and design" (*The Economist*, December 12, 1970). As to the capacity of the Soviet stock of computers, three top Soviet scientists state, in a document unpublished in their own country, that "the total capacity of our [i.e., Soviet] pool of computers is hundreds of times less than in the USA. . . . We are simply living in a different era" (*Survey*, Summer 1970, p. 162).

Viewed in the long-term historical perspective, the Soviet economic achievement leads to several considerations. First, there is no question that the Soviet Union is now the world's second largest industrial power and the equal, in terms of military power, of the United States. Second, Soviet levels of consumption still trail significantly those of many Western nations and of Japan, and there is no likelihood of closing the gap in the near future. Finally, the Soviet economic achievement, impressive as it is by any standard, does not validate the Soviet claim to having discovered or developed a method of rapid economic growth that cannot be achieved under any other social, economic, or political system. Japan's record of industrial growth from the late 1890s to the late 1930s, and again since 1950, is the outstanding refutation of the Soviet claim, although not the only one. During these periods, levels of personal consumption rose faster in Japan than in Russia between 1913 and the 1960s, and during the half-century of early American industrialization, from the 1870s to the 1920s, American consumption levels also rose at a faster rate than in Russia during its half-century of industrialization. The system of government under which an economy operates is an important factor, but it is only one factor among many. The potential of economic development in each country is related to many factors unique to it; a country that imitates Soviet, Japanese, or American political or economic institutions will not necessarily match Soviet, Japanese, or American economic achievements.

The third major area of Soviet strength is in education and science. The Soviet launching of the first artificial earth satellite on October 4, 1957, came as a bombshell to those who still had the illusion that Russia was largely a country of illiterate peasants. This Soviet first was followed by many others: The Soviets sent the first man, the first woman, and the first team of astronauts into space; they sent the first satellite past the moon and around the moon, and theirs was the first to land on the moon; and they accomplished the first "space walk" by an astronaut and the first link-up in space between two manned spacecraft. Although the successful landing of astronauts Armstrong and Aldrin on the moon in July 1969, the first in history, boosted American morale at home and American prestige abroad, this success does not minimize the importance and quality of the overall Soviet space effort.

Soviet failure to accomplish manned landings on the moon by late 1972—in sharp contrast to repeated successful American manned landings between 1969 and 1972—was probably due to Soviet backwardness in computer technology. Manned spacecraft heading for the moon require vast computerized data-processing centers on earth receiving information from the spacecraft and guiding its course, and they also require microminiaturized computers on board the spacecraft that do not overload its space and weight. By the end of 1972, Soviet computer technology had apparently not mastered either aspect of computerized data processing connected with moon flights.

The Soviet space effort is not the result of a crash program, but of sustained work and planning over many years. The increase in the years 1926–1952 of Soviet professional manpower was as follows: engineers, ten times; teachers, five times; and physicians, four times. Since 1958 the proportion of those age 15–19 enrolled in secondary schools and of those age 20–24 enrolled in institutions of higher learning has been higher in the Soviet Union than in the major Western countries, with the exception of the United States, which still leads in the absolute and proportionate sizes of secondary-school and college students. By the early 1970s, the median number of years of school completed by the Soviet population age 16 and older was about eight years, as compared with 13 years for the same group in the United States.

The intense demand for a higher education or advanced professional training in the Soviet Union is also reflected in the high proportion of fully employed students who receive their training through evening or correspondence courses. In the 1960s, such students outnumbered regular full-time students by a substantial margin. In recent years, the number of full-time students has risen to about one-half the total number of students admitted to institutions of higher learning and professional training.

A breakdown by field of study reveals that, in the four decades since the early 1930s, the Soviet Union has trained more than twice as many engineers than the United States and is continuing to train engineers and scientists at an annual rate about double that of the United States. The total pool of engineers and physicists is now greater in the Soviet Union than in the United States, and the gap is growing year by year. By contrast, the United States has trained three times more graduates in the humanities and social sciences than the Soviet Union, and the American numerical superiority in these areas largely accounts for the continuing overall lead of the total number of American college students over the total enrollments in Soviet institutions of higher learning and training.

In the field of medicine, the Soviet Union has trained more than twice as many physicians than the United States, and in the last several years the annual number of Soviet medical graduates has been double that in the United States, although the Soviet population is only 18 percent higher than that of the United States. Currently, there are 28 physicians per 10,000 population in the Soviet Union but only 16 per 10,000 population in the United States. The shortage of medical training facilities in the United States is the most significant factor in this regard. At present about one in every five doctors admitted to practice in the United States has received his medical training abroad, and of these graduates of foreign medical schools close to one-third are Americans. In American hospitals, about one out of four interns and resident physicians is a graduate of a foreign medical school. Many of the foreign physicians who immigrate to the United States come from developing countries in Asia and Latin America that suffer from an acute shortage of health personnel. The inferiority of health services in the United States is also reflected in the number of hospital beds; in the Soviet Union, there are over 110 hospital beds per 10,000 persons as compared with only 75 beds per 10,000 in the United States. Most important of all, medical and health services in the Soviet Union are available to every Soviet citizen with little or no charge, whereas such services are paid for by the government in the United States only for persons over 65 under federal Medicare and for low-income families (regardless of age) under various state programs.

The Soviet commitment to education as a major goal of national policy is expressed in many ways. With a national income that is less than half that of the United States, the Soviets spend a greater proportion of their national income on education. The Soviet university professor receives five to eight times the wage of the average factory worker, whereas the American professor receives only about twice the American worker's pay. Tuition, textbooks, and medical care are free of charge in Soviet universities and institutions of higher learning, and dormitory quarters—extremely crowded as they may be—cost only a few rubles per month (a ruble equals $1.52). In addition, most Soviet students receive monthly stipends ranging from 30 to 60 rubles—the latter figure is close to the minimum monthly wage of an urban worker. Students in such fields as mining, electronics, and chemical engineering receive the highest stipends, and an additional bonus of 25 percent is given to those students who maintain a consistently excellent record.

Entry into Soviet higher education is through written and oral examinations. These examinations are much more competitive than American College Board tests; currently, about 30 percent of secondary-school graduates in the Soviet Union are admitted to colleges and universities, as compared with about 65 percent of American high school graduates. The Soviet approach—very much like that of other European countries, whether communist or noncommunist—is much more elitist and professional than the American: In the Soviet view, only a highly qualified minority should be given the opportunity for higher education, and such education aims at turning out trained professional man- and womanpower.

Applying objective examination standards for admission to Soviet colleges and universities has created, as in many other countries, social problems of class. Workers' and peasants' sons and daughters are underrepresented in institutions of higher learning. In a study of Soviet education, the education editor of the *New York Times* found that "elite universities, such as Moscow and Leningrad, have a more select upper-middleclass urban enrollment than America's Ivy League" (*New York Times,* October 5, 1967). In recent years, therefore, Soviet educational authorities have set up special remedial and preparatory programs for children of peasants and factory workers—similar to such programs for blacks, chicanos, and Puerto Ricans in the United States—to improve their chances for obtaining a higher education.

Finally, the most direct source of communist strength lies in military power. Although the Soviet citizen consumes less than one-third of the American standard of consumption, and although the whole Soviet national product is less than one-half of the United States', the two countries spend about the same amount on military preparedness. The per capita income in China is about one-fortieth that of the United States, but its armed forces are equal in size to those of the United States, and it has consistently devoted large resources to the development of nuclear weapons, even during the near-famine period of the early 1960s.

The vast expenditures on building up military strength have paid off in territorial expansion. Since the outbreak of World War II the Soviet Union has acquired an area larger than all the New England and Middle Atlantic states, with a population of over 25 million. In addition to these outright annexations, the Soviet Union established, by armed force, communist governments in Eastern Europe, with a combined population of over 100 million. China conquered and annexed Tibet.

Never before in history has imperialistic expansion resulted in the acquisition of so much in so short a time. By contrast, the Western powers have given independence to over 800 million people in former colonies since World War II.

The first source of weakness in communist states is their stress on *conformity*. The most distinguishing quality of a leader is his courage to be different, to have new ideas, to be in a minority, even in solitude. Yet as time goes on, the leader in communist regimes is increasingly being replaced by the bureaucrat, the yes-man. The era of Soviet purges of the middle 1930s marked the conflict between the leaders who had made the revolution and the bureaucrats who administered it. Conformist as prerevolutionary Russia was, it allowed much more diversity than has been tolerated under the communist regime. In precommunist Russia, opposition parties of all types, including radical and socialist parties, functioned openly, and the press reflected all political viewpoints. *Pravda,* which became the official organ of the Communist party after the revolution, began publication in 1912; it suffered occasional harrassments, but it was published.

Lenin, Trotsky, Stalin, and Khrushchev were all products of precommunist Russia. Malenkov, Stalin's immediate successor, was the first Soviet leader who was entirely a product of communist rule. He proved not to possess the qualities of a leader; in 1955, he was removed as prime minister, and in 1957 he was purged by Khrushchev and exiled to central Asia. Brezhnev and Kosygin, who followed after Khrushchev's ouster in 1964, are also entirely products of communist rule. Brezhnev was trained in land surveying and metallurgical engineering, but his main profession became, early in his career, professional party work. Kosygin was trained as a textile engineer and spent most of his career in economic and administrative positions, avoiding involvement in ideological or political controversies and conflicts within the Communist party. As after the deaths of Lenin and of Stalin, "collective leadership" after Khrushchev lasted for about six years. Since 1970, Brezhnev has gradually emerged as the recognized number-one man in the Soviet hierarchy; in 1971, Kosygin was demoted from second to third place in the Politburo, whereas Brezhnev, as the general secretary of the Communist party, retained his party leadership. Brezhnev's preeminence became particularly evident in the area of diplomacy. During President Nixon's visit to Moscow in 1972, for example, the important negotiations over Soviet-American arms limitations and expanding trade relations were carried on between Nixon and Brezhnev; although Brezhnev held only a party position, he was recognized to be, in effect, the top political decision maker in the Soviet Union. In addition to foreign affairs, party control and ideology are Brezhnev's main areas of interest and dominance, whereas Kosygin's principal leadership is in economic matters. In June 1977, Brezhnev's predominance was further recognized when he became President of the Soviet Union.

Both men lack the despotic ruthlessness of Stalin and the colorful flamboyance of Khrushchev. Brezhnev's and Kosygin's rise to power was marked by efficient bureaucratic performance rather than by personal leadership. Instead of Stalin's limitless autocracy and Khrushchev's personal rule with its unpredictable periodic swings from more authoritarian to more lenient attitudes, the Soviet Union may be entering—if Brezhnev and Kosygin reflect a new long-term trend—an era of totalitarian organization men.

In some respects, this type of totalitarianism may be more liberal than under Khrushchev (not to speak of Stalin), as in the approach to the farm problem or in giving greater managerial authority to industrial executives. But in the more fundamental areas of political and intellectual unorthodoxy, the Brezhnev-Kosygin regime has persistently pursued a course of re-Stalinization. In 1956, Khrushchev delivered his famous secret speech on the crimes of Stalin at the Twentieth Party Congress in Moscow, and during his rule he frequently attacked the "era of the cult of personality"—the official Soviet term for Stalinism. By contrast, Brezhnev and Kosygin have sought to refurbish Stalin's reputation, and both have made it plain that they have no use for anti-Stalinist criticism. Khrushchev believed that Stalinism could be disposed of by condemning its excesses as the crimes and mistakes of one man—an aberration from Soviet communism rather than its natural outgrowth. Brezhnev, by contrast, has adopted the more consistently Marxian viewpoint that major social and political developments cannot be explained by the acts of one individual—king, president, or Communist party secretary—but must be perceived in the context of the whole system, that is, Soviet communism. From this viewpoint, intensive de-Stalinization inevitably leads to decommunization, or at least to a loss of faith in the infallibility of Soviet communism and the party hierarchy. Brezhnev's approach has been to ban anti-Stalinist expressions of thought—in fiction and nonfiction—but he has also shrewdly avoided excessive campaigns of praise for Stalin, since they, too, might merely revive the whole issue of Stalinism. Instead, there are occasional positive statements about Stalin, celebrations of his anniversary, a statue here, a museum bearing his name there—just to remind the public in a low key that the Stalin era must be accepted as an essential part of Soviet history.

Khrushchev's ambivalence on repressing or allowing unorthodoxy was clearly shown in connection with the two greatest authors of the Soviet era, Boris Pasternak and Alexander Solzhenitsyn. When, in 1958,

Pasternak was awarded the Nobel Prize in literature for his novel *Doctor Zhivago* (which was banned for publication in the Soviet Union), he was compelled by the Soviet government to refuse the award. In addition, he was subjected to an organized campaign of vehement attacks and threats.

In the early 1960s, the Khrushchev regime relaxed repressive controls of literature, and the high point of this short thaw was marked by the publication of Solzhenitsyn's *One Day in the Life of Ivan Denisovich*. Although this story of life in a Soviet slave labor camp is cast in the form of a novel, the author wrote from personal experience, having spent the years 1945–1953 in such a camp. The novel was published in the Soviet literary magazine *Novy Mir,* known for its more liberal leanings, but to this day *One Day* has not been published in book form in the Soviet Union. Unwilling to produce literature that is "cosmetics," as he put it, Solzhenitsyn has had the courage to plead in strong language for more intellectual freedom. As a result, his published works have been banned in the Soviet Union, and even the issues of *Novy Mir* that carried *One Day* have disappeared from the shelves of public libraries. Apart from *One Day,* three stories by Solzhenitsyn were published in *Novy Mir* in 1963 and a novella in the same magazine in January 1966, but since the latter date Soviet authorities have not permitted any of Solzhenitsyn's work to be published in the Soviet Union. In 1968, two of his major novels, *Cancer Ward* and *The First Circle,* were published in Western countries and immediately hailed as classics in the grand Russian literary tradition. In 1971, his novel *August 1914,* the first volume of a projected trilogy on World War I, was published in France and shortly thereafter in many other Western countries.

Following the publication of *Cancer Ward* and *The First Circle* Solzhenitsyn was expelled in 1969 from the Union of Writers, thus officially depriving him of the opportunity to publish in his own country. Yet in 1970, Solzhenitsyn was awarded the Nobel Prize in literature "for the ethical force with which he has pursued the indispensable renditions of Russian literature." Solzhenitsyn decided not to go to Stockholm to accept the prize in person when the Soviet government refused to assure him that he would be permitted to return to his homeland. Although wounded in World War II and twice decorated for bravery, he was accused of having collaborated with the Germans. His mail was checked, his apartment bugged, his wife lost her job, and his friends were shadowed by the secret police. The Soviet minister of culture, Yekaterina A. Furtseva, said: "Solzhenitsyn is opposed against our entire society, and that is why we treat him the way we do" (*New York Times,* May 25, 1972).

In 1973 Solzhenitzyn authorized publication in the West of *The

Gulag Archipelago, a damning indictment of the Soviet slave labor camps, which had been in existence since the time of Lenin. The book had a powerful impact; it described in detail how the camps were run and who were the victims. For the Soviet authorities this was the last straw. In February 1974, Solzhenitzyn was suddenly deprived of his citizenship and expelled from the Soviet Union. Since then he has travelled and lectured throughout the West denouncing totalitarianism and calling for a return to spiritual values and more vigorous anticommunism.

Other dissenters have been less fortunate. In 1966, two Soviet writers, Andrei Sinyavsky and Yuli Daniel, were sentenced to serve long terms in "strict regime labor camp" for having published "anti-Soviet" works in foreign countries under the pen names Abram Tertz and Nikolai Arzhak. Although the trial was closed to foreign reporters, its proceedings became known abroad. The conduct of the trial—and the official attacks on the two writers before the trial—as well as the sentences (seven years for Sinyavsky and five for Daniel) shocked even communist leaders in some Western countries who publicly warned the Soviet rulers that the trial had done the Soviet Union more harm than the writings of the defendants.

Of many court trials in 1968, two in particular attracted international attention. Early in 1968, four young dissidents were tried in Moscow for having published underground literary magazines. The leader of the group, Alexander Ginzburg, was charged with having committed the additional crime of compiling a record of the Sinyavsky-Daniel trial and sending it abroad. The sentences for three of the accused ranged from two to seven years of labor camp. The mildest sentence—one year—was given to a 21-year-old student who had typed manuscripts for the defendants.

In 1968, the trial of Pavel Litvinov and Larissa Daniel attracted international attention. Litvinov, a 30-year-old physicist and grandson of Maxim Litvinov, Soviet foreign minister under Stalin for many years, had become actively involved in liberal circles. Because of his prominent social background, he was at first treated leniently, the punishment consisting solely in the loss of his prestigious job. But on August 25, 1968, he and several friends, including Larissa Daniel, a graduate in philosophy, unfurled a banner in the center of Moscow protesting the Soviet invasion and occupation of Czechoslovakia. Litvinov was sentenced to five years of exile in a labor camp, Daniel to four years, and several codefendants to three years. Daniel, in poor health, was sent to Siberia, where she was assigned the job of hauling heavy pieces of lumber into a wood-processing factory.

In 1969 Anatoly V. Kuznetsov defected to Britain. Kuznetsov was at the peak of his literary fame at the time of his defection, and at the age of 40 he had a great literary career ahead of him. Yet he chose to leave his mother, wife, and son in the Soviet Union so that he could live in freedom and security. He had received permission to go to Britain for two weeks only after he had informed on fellow writers and had assured secret police that he would continue informing on writers at home and abroad. Once in Britain, he asked for and was granted asylum. Kuznetsov stated that the relations of Soviet writers to the secret police fall into three categories: (1) Writers who enthusiastically collaborate with the secret police "have every chance of prospering"; (2) writers who acknowledge their duty to work for the secret police but refuse to do so suffer numerous disadvantages, including loss of the chance to travel abroad; (3) writers who refuse all advances of the secret police come into conflict with them—"In that case your works are not published and you may even find yourself in a concentration camp" (*New York Times,* August 10, 1969).

From 1970 on, the trials of dissenters multiplied rapidly. One notable case involved Andrei Amalrik, son of a Moscow historian. Amalrik studied history at the University of Moscow, but was expelled in 1963 for expressing unorthodox views on historical subjects. He then wrote five plays and was imprisoned and banished to Siberia on the grounds that his plays had a "patently anti-Soviet and pornographic character" —even though none of his plays had ever been printed or staged. After his return to Moscow, he wrote an account of his experiences in Siberia, *Involuntary Journey to Siberia* (published outside the Soviet Union in 1969) and a short book which attracted worldwide attention, *Will the Soviet Union Survive Until 1984?* (published in Western countries in 1970). In the latter publication, Amalrik pointed out the internal contradictions and social inequalities of the Soviet system and predicted that in 1984 the Soviet Union would become involved in a losing war with China. When asked by the correspondent what he expected next, in a taped interview with a CBS television correspondent in Moscow in the spring of 1970, Amalrik responded: "I think either a camp or exile." The American correspondent was expelled, and Amalrik was tried and sentenced to three years in a labor camp in northeastern Siberia. Amalrik almost died during his long train trip to Siberia; he was repeatedly put into solitary confinement, contracted meningitis, and was finally transferred to a regular prison in Moscow late in 1972, still an invalid and officially recognized as such.

Another case that showed the growing severity against dissenters and also attracted international attention was that of Vladimir Bukovsky in 1972. Bukovsky, the son of privileged Communist party members, was first arrested in 1963 because he had in his apartment two photocopies of *The New Class,* a famous critique of communism by the Yugoslav writer Milovan Djilas. Bukovsky spent the next six years in psychiatric hospitals, insane asylums, labor camps, and prisons. During brief spells of liberty, Bukovsky took an active part in organizing protests and demonstrations against the treatment of fellow dissidents. And Bukovsky had spent considerable time in special psychiatric prisons and insane asylums for political heretics, and he sent documentary evidence abroad that hundreds of sane people are kept in Soviet psychiatric hospitals and asylums for political nonconformity. Bukovsky was arrested again in 1971 and handed over to the Serbsky Psychiatric Institute in Moscow, for in the Soviet Union "if you protest about these things being done to your fellow Soviet citizens, you are liable to find them being done to you" (*The Economist,* January 8, 1972). In 1972, Bukovsky was sentenced to two years in prison and five years in a labor camp, to be followed by another five years of exile in a remote area to be designated by the authorities. His ordeal ended in December 1976, when he was exiled to the West in exchange for the release of an imprisoned Chilean communist leader.

Whereas prison, labor camp, and exile for political dissidents are not the innovations of the Brezhnev regime, it has used these penalties on a much broader scale than was the case under Khrushchev. A new wrinkle, however, is the widespread use of psychiatric hospitals and prisons for silencing political heretics. Although neither Soviet citizens nor the outside world are aware of the extent to which this technique is employed, certainly hundreds of Soviet citizens have been consigned for long terms to such institutions for political reasons. No formal trial is needed for such imprisonment, and the "patient" can be confined indefinitely—until he admits that he was sick when first "admitted" to a psychiatric prison-hospital and disavows the actions that got him there. Only rarely can the tactics of the psychiatric police be foiled—and then it must be at an early stage. On May 29, 1970, Zhores Medvedev, an internationally known biochemist, was kidnaped in broad daylight by two doctors and four police officers and brought to a mental hospital. Medvedev had for years criticized bureaucratic interference in Soviet science and pleaded for greater freedom in international scientific exchange. After being delivered to the mental hospital, Medvedev was diagnosed as having suffered from "incipient schizophrenia" and "paranoid delusions of reforming society."

Some leading Soviet scientists, including Nobel Prize winner Igor Tamm, as well as numerous scientists throughout the world protested against the psychiatric incarceration of Medvedev. Solzhenitsyn issued a statement, circulated privately in Russia and published abroad, in which he branded the "incarceration of free-thinking healthy people in madhouses" as "spiritual murder. . . . It is a fiendish and prolonged torture of those who are to be killed." Bowing to world-wide protests, the Soviet government released Medvedev after 19 days of psychiatric imprisonment—without, however, changing its general policy. The way in which this policy works is analyzed in detail in *A Question of Madness*, written by Medvedev in collaboration with his brother Roy and published in Western countries in 1971.

The Soviet concept of scientists, intellectuals, and writers as belonging to the government was noted by Arthur Miller, until recently one of the most popular American playwrights in the Soviet Union. After a journey to the Soviet Union, in which he met with "cultural officials" and top Soviet novelists and poets, Miller—a man of strong sympathies for the left—concluded that "in the Soviet Union a writer is far more than an individual facing a piece of blank paper alone in a room; he is state property and accountable for his attitudes." Miller also noted that, despite periodic waves of political witch hunting in some Western countries (such as the United States in the 1950s, when he was a target of such attacks), there is a vast difference between noncommunist and communist countries: In the former, publishing is carried on by many competing private companies, whereas "all Russian literature is published by the state and must meet the requirements of the Communist Party" (*Harper's Magazine*, September 1969, p. 42). Shortly thereafter, all of Miller's plays were permanently banned in the Soviet Union.

Adherence to the party line is also demanded in other fields, particularly the social studies and humanities. Even in scientific fields like psychology there is a party line. The fate of Freudian psychoanalysis is a case in point. Until 1930, psychoanalysis was tolerated in the Soviet Union, having attracted considerable attention in Russia long before the revolution. After 1930, psychoanalysis gradually fell into disfavor, and in 1936 the Communist party officially decided that psychoanalysis was incompatible with Marxism-Leninism-Stalinism. After having been branded by the Nazis as false because of its Jewish origin, psychoanalysis was condemned by communists as "the result of the extreme decadence of bourgeois culture" (*Soviet Psychology and Psychiatry*, Fall 1965, p. 45) and was finally assailed as an "ideological instrument of American imperialism."

In the field of pure and applied philosophy, Soviet educational authorities have done much housecleaning too. Their opposition to more conservative thinkers was to be expected, but eventually they took on progressive thinkers also. John Dewey, for example, has been roundly condemned for his pragmatic philosophy, which patient communist research has revealed to be yet another cleverly disguised instrument of American imperialism.

Another method of literary control is through enforced ignorance. Western exchange students are astonished to find that most Soviet students have never heard of John Stuart Mill and never read critical studies of Marx. Even an internationally known writer like Kuznetsov stated after his defection to Britain in an interview with a British reporter: "I didn't even know Orwell's name before I came here" (*Guardian Weekly,* February 13, 1971). Although Soviet libraries contain much of the "forbidden literature," both fiction and nonfiction, most citizens do not dare to request the special permission needed for the perusal of such works. A Soviet student who tried to obtain a copy of Freud's *General Introduction to Psychoanalysis* at the Lenin Library in Moscow was told by the librarian, "There are dozens of patriotic Soviet textbooks that explain everything you need to know about Freud." Then he added, "Why do you want such things in your record? It's not necessary for your development." The student took the hint. (Ivan Epstein, "Portraits from Moscow U.," *Harper's Magazine,* April 1968, pp. 55–56.)

Yet no totalitarian system is as efficient as it claims or as its critics fear. Despite all controls, some more enterprising and courageous persons manage to get hold of forbidden Western books in the social sciences, literary criticism, philosophy, and psychology. An underground black market passes the books along, generally obtaining them from tourists and exchange students. Listening to foreign news is another source of serious information: The news service of the British Broadcasting Corporation holds first place in its reputation for objective reporting and lively scholarly discussions. Like-minded students meet in informal groups and discuss not the dialectics of Marxism-Leninism, but Sartre and Camus. The students know that they are carefully watched by fellow students who report on them to the secret police, but this is considered a fact of life one must accept. More rebellious students and young writers and poets even put out underground magazines, mostly devoted to poetry, literary essays, and social criticism. Since there are no private printers in a collective communist economy, such underground magazines are put out in typescript, circulating in a few dozen or a few hundred copies, often only in a few issues, until the secret police discovers the identity of the editors and puts them into prison.

Of all soviet underground publications in recent years, the *Chronicle of Current Events* has attracted the most attention. Circulated every two months since April 1968, issues are typed and occasionally photocopied. Private citizens cannot buy copying machines, duplicators, or mimeographing devices. Each reader who receives a typed copy of the *Chronical* is expected to type several other copies and pass them on to trusted persons. The circulation is estimated to be small—perhaps a few thousand—but it reaches an influential audience of middle-class and professional people. The success of the *Chronicle* has largely been due to the fact that it avoids inflammatory rhetoric. Instead, it concentrates on a cool, factual presentation of events; activities of the police, courts, and government officials; conditions in prisons, camps, and psychiatric prison-hospitals; and the struggles for human rights in the Soviet Union. The contents of the *Chronicle* indicate a substantial network of correspondents in various parts of the Soviet Union. Internal evidence also suggests that among the contributors are persons with access to information available only to party members and highly placed officials. Some Western observers have wondered whether the *Chronicle* owes its continued existence to the lack of zeal and efficiency of the police, or whether the *Chronicle*—moderate in tone and with virtually no appeal to the working class—has some protectors among influential officials of the government, including possibly the secret police. As so often in the past, both in Russia and under other authoritarian regimes, the illegally circulated literature (called in Russian *samizdat,* or self-publishing) may be the beginning of a broader movement toward constitutionalism and the rule of law.

The government's general policy regarding the circulation of foreign newspapers in the Soviet Union is to permit the sale only of official organs of foreign communist governments and parties. However, even such papers are banned whenever they carry criticisms of Soviet actions or conditions. Yugoslav, Romanian, French, British, and Italian communist papers are thus frequently forbidden, as were Czech papers before the invasion in 1968. Major Soviet libraries subscribe to noncommunist newspapers, but do not display them. A special permit is needed to use them in the library, and such permit is granted only if it is in the interest of the party and government. Chinese communist publications—easily available in American libraries and publicly sold in major American cities—are subject to the most severe Soviet ban. An American tourist can bring into the Soviet Union copies of the *New York Times* or the *Wall Street Journal,* but not of the *Peking Review.*

Censorship of news is also practiced on Western correspondents in Moscow. First, there is physical isolation. Correspondents have to live in apartment houses reserved exclusively for them; police are stationed in front of the buildings to prevent unauthorized Soviet citizens from entering. Next, Western correspondents are not allowed to dig for news on their own. All contacts for news-gathering purposes must first be cleared and approved by the press department of the Soviet Foreign Ministry. Finally, there is the fact of self-censorship of many Western correspondents.

With respect to music and the fine arts, Lenin allowed a lively and varied experimentation in all fields. Under Stalin, the tradition of a party line in the arts was firmly established; in music, for example, the "formalism" of composers such as Prokofiev and Shostakovich was condemned, and composers were urged to make music that is simple, popular, and tuneful. Khrushchev interfered less with music, but asserted his authority more in the areas of painting and sculpture. Under the Brezhnev regime, too, abstract and surrealist paintings are officially disapproved, since such styles violate the canons of "socialist realism," according to which paintings or sculptures must be strictly representational. Socialist realism in art also requires that paintings convey an edifying and inspirational message, which automatically excludes religious themes from art, since religion is considered counterrevolutionary. Artists who persist in officially disapproved styles or subject matter are denied "official status," as a result of which they are unable to exhibit their work in the Soviet Union. However, a number of such "unofficial" painters and sculptors prosper because they are able to sell their work to foreigners or to members of the Soviet scientific or academic community.

One of the basic freedoms most systematically denied by the Soviet government to its citizens is the freedom of movement. The political dissenter may be exiled to Siberia or the far north. The ordinary citizen may be denied permission to take up residence in a city which, in the judgment of the police, is overcrowded. Traveling abroad—a privilege granted by many other authoritarian governments, both communist (Hungary, Yugoslavia) and noncommunist (Greece)—is for the average Soviet citizen still difficult, particularly if travel to a noncommunist country (or a communist country like Yugoslavia) is involved. Would-be tourists to the West must establish a good work record certified by their employers, and their loyalty is closely investigated to weed out potential defectors. Generally, Soviet tourists—particularly when going to the West—travel in groups, always accompanied by secret police representatives, and such privileged tourists have to leave hostages behind —wives, children, parents, or brothers and sisters. Also, the passport fee alone to a noncommunist country is 400 rubles ($608), so that only the well-to-do can afford such trips. Under the constant surveillance of the Soviet secret police, the Soviet tourist in New Delhi or London has to plan carefully how to defect—as the cases of Svetlana Alliluyeva (Stalin's daughter) in 1967 and Anatoly Kuznetsov in 1969 dramatically demonstrated.

When it comes to permanent emigration—a right that was traditionally respected in Russia under tsarist rule—the Soviet citizen generally does not apply, as the desire to emigrate is considered evidence of hostility to the government, often punished by immediate removal from better-paying jobs of the applicant and members of his family. If he vigorously persists in his emigration plans, the Soviet citizen may find himself tried and condemned to several years of imprisonment or service in a labor camp for having "slandered" the Soviet state. If the applicant finally succeeds, he must pay the passport fee plus 500 rubles ($760) for permission to renounce Soviet citizenship—since an emigrant is considered unworthy of Soviet citizenship. To raise these amounts of money—equivalent to a year's earnings for many citizens —the would-be emigrant must sell all his belongings; and by the time he raises the fares for travel abroad for himself and his family he is left with debts to friends and relatives.

Adventurous souls try to leave the country illegally—a dangerous undertaking. According to Soviet law, high treason—punishable by death—includes "fleeing abroad or refusing to return from abroad." Under Stalin, the death penalty often was used in such cases. Under Khrushchev and Brezhnev, the milder punishment of forced labor or prison has been meted out. In 1971, for example, a young Soviet scientist who tried to get out of the Soviet Union by using the passport of a Swiss student traveling there was sentenced to eight years of prison. In the same year, a Soviet seaman who tried to escape from a Soviet ship was sentenced to ten years' imprisonment.

Since 1971, the Brezhnev regime has considerably liberalized its anti-emigration policies with respect to Jews. Numbering about 2.2 million, Soviet Jews are the only one among the 130 nationalities in the Soviet Union who have been denied even minimal expression of their traditional cultural life. No Jewish schools are permitted, and the teaching of Hebrew is forbidden. Official sanctions that originally reflected Stalin's violent anti-Semitism abated somewhat under Khrushchev and Brezhnev, but even in their more moderate forms they have become intolerable to many Soviet Jews. Quotas limit the number of Jewish students in the universities, and virtually no Jews are admitted to military academies and institutes for the training of diplomats. Just as Nazi Germany defined Jews by the racist criterion of "blood" rather than by religious affiliation, Soviet law imposes the Jewish nationality classification even on those Jews who have no ties to the Jewish religion, are completely assimilated into Russian culture, and who would like to merge with the Russian nationality. Inasmuch as Soviet citizens must always carry an internal passport stating nationality and must include a statement of nationality with every application for housing or employment, the provisions of Soviet law open the door to anti-Semitic chicanery on the lowest bureaucratic levels.

Particularly after the Arab-Israeli war of 1967, the Soviet internal and international campaign of "anti-Zionism" was perceived—by Soviet Jews and non-Jews alike—as an endorsement of anti-Semitism. Far from cowing Soviet Jews into submission, the "anti-Zionist" campaign made many Jews more conscious of their Jewishness. A considerable number, running into tens of thousands, made out applications for emigration to Israel. The governmental response at first consisted of dismissing applicants from their jobs and sentencing many to prison terms for "slandering the Soviet state." Yet, as was true of other dissident groups, many Jews persisted in their struggle; some staged hunger strikes and others sent appeals for help to the United Nations and Western governments. Recognizing the reality of anti-Semitism in the Soviet Union, the Soviet government finally relaxed its ban on emigration. In 1971, over 13,000 Jews were permitted to leave for Israel, and in 1972 the number exceeded 30,000.

Late in 1972, the Soviet government sought to stem the tide of emigration of Soviet Jews—whether to Israel or any other country—by imposing special exit fees on applicants according to their level of education. Such fees ranged from $4500 for a holder of a trade school diploma to $37,500 for a holder of a doctoral degree. One purpose of the new punitive exit fees was held to be the discouraging of young Soviet Jews from enrolling in universities. The other purpose was thought to be financial: Since few, if any, Soviet citizens could raise the exorbitant exit fee, such funds would have to be raised abroad, and the Soviet government would thus acquire vast amounts of hard currency.

There is no way of knowing how many Soviet citizens would leave their country if they had the legal right to do so. The case of East Germany, however, throws some light on the extent to which a communist regime makes involuntary prisoners out of its subjects. Between 1950 and 1961, when movement between communist East Germany and noncommunist West Germany was comparatively easy, about four million East Germans—almost a quarter of East Germany's population —fled to West Germany. In 1961, the East German government put up the Berlin Wall and installed barbed wire and mine fields along the intra-German border to stem this mass exodus. Despite such barriers, however, more than 125,000 East Germans managed to get across in the years 1961–1971, although more than a hundred lost their lives in the attempt to escape.

The Communist World

REVOLTS AGAINST SOVIET COMMUNISM

In 1948, Yugoslavia was more completely communized than any other communist state in Eastern Europe. Tito's crime in 1948 was not abandoning communism in favor of capitalism, but rather trying to regain national independence from Moscow for the peoples of Yugoslavia. The Soviet Union mobilized all its resources of propaganda and subversion to overthrow Tito and his brand of national communism. At the time, few people thought Tito could defy Moscow successfully. Yet the unlikely happened, and Yugoslavia is still independent. The Soviet Union has come to realize that an independent Yugoslavia is here to stay and has been compelled by the force of circumstances to achieve a modus vivendi with the Tito regime. Yet Yugoslavia has no illusions about the precariousness of that modus vivendi, and relies on its determination to defend its independence against the Soviet danger. The Yugoslav Constitution of 1963 forbids its citizens and officials to sign any document recognizing capitulation to, or occupation by, another power. On August 21, 1968, President Tito immediately condemned the Soviet invasion of Czechoslovakia as "a grave blow to the socialist and progressive forces in the world." After the Soviet occupation of Czechoslovakia, Yugoslavia made it clear that it would resist Soviet invasion. In addition to regular armed forces of considerable size and quality, Yugoslavia has organized a Territorial Army of three million volunteers—out of a population of 20 million. Ranging in age from 18 to 60, all members are volunteers, and every organization and local community has its units ready to spring into action. Nazi Germany was never able to defeat the Yugoslav guerrillas fighting behind the lines in World War II, and Yugoslavia is confident that its people would be equally successful in fighting Soviet invaders in the same manner.

The break with Moscow in 1948, combined with Yugoslavia's determination to defend its independence against all Soviet threats, has led to considerable liberalization in political and economic affairs. The peasants were given the option of returning to individual farming, and the overwhelming majority chose to abandon the collective farms. Workers in industry have the right to strike and enjoy a substantial amount of "self-management," and privately owned enterprises employing fewer than five people are permitted and do a flourishing business, particularly in the repair, service, and handicraft industries, tourism, transport, and retail stores. About one-half of all restaurants, for example, are privately run, and over half of all houses built in recent years are privately owned. Even independent publishing companies are permitted, an important concession in a sensitive area. Economic aid from Western countries since 1945 has amounted to over $7 billion, and in more recent years French, Italian, and West German investments in various industries have been encouraged.

Yugoslavia is well on the way to becoming a consumer society, with cars, household appliances, credit cards, television commercials, and imported luxury goods. Foreign newspapers and magazines—from

Pravda to *Playboy*—are freely sold at newsstands, and authors forbidden in the Soviet Union, such as Pasternak and Solzhenitsyn, enjoy enormous popularity there. Foreign movies, too, are freely shown, and Western plays are performed on the stage. Foreign tourists visiting Yugoslavia run into the millions, and millions of Yugoslavs annually travel abroad, mostly to neighboring Austria and Italy.

Yugoslavia's is also the only communist government which allows its citizens to emigrate and work abroad. Unlike other communist states, Yugoslavia admits a serious unemployment problem, and many hundreds of thousands of its workers have been encouraged to seek employment in other countries. The main labor-importing countries— West Germany, France, and Sweden—have set up recruiting offices in Yugoslavia, and the Yugoslav government pays the emigrating worker's travel costs. Aside from ideological liberalization, the Yugoslav government favors such policies for two practical reasons: Yugoslavs employed abroad send their families funds in hard currency, and during their employment abroad workers acquire advanced industrial skills that are common in West Germany, France, or Sweden but still scarce in developing Yugoslavia. In the early 1970s, about a million Yugoslavs (out of a population of 20 million) worked in Western countries.

Yet the communist leadership in Yugoslavia reminds the people from time to time that there are limits to freedom in a communist state. The fate of Milovan Djilas is a case in point. Djilas was a lifelong friend of Tito and one of his closest aides both during and after World War II. But in the early 1950s, Djilas began to express democratic ideas. He urged a free press and free public discussion, and he suggested that Yugoslavia be permitted to have more than one party. Djilas was tried in 1955 and sentenced to three years in prison. In 1957, a book by Djilas entitled *The New Class* was smuggled out of Yugoslavia and published in New York. In it, Djilas exposed communism as an instrument of the communist ruling class (the "new class") for the exploitation and domination of the Yugoslav people. A new trial followed in which he received another seven years' imprisonment. Released from prison in 1961 for reasons of health, Djilas went to work on another book, *Conversations with Stalin,* describing the talks he had had with Stalin in the years 1944–1948. After the book was published in 1962 in New York, Djilas was tried again, this time receiving a sentence of nine years. Although released for reasons of ill health on December 31, 1966, Djilas was placed under the restriction of making no public statements for five years. Yet he defied the ban by publishing *The Unperfect Society: Beyond the New Class* in Western countries in 1969. A communist from early boyhood, Djilas had spent three years in prison under the anticommunist regime in Yugoslavia before World War II. Under communism, he found out how much more repressive is communism than the system he had helped to destroy.

After Tito's break with Moscow in 1948, the next major explosion took place on June 16 and 17, 1953, in East Germany. Food conditions had steadily deteriorated under Soviet and East German communist management, and there was less food available than during World War II. Even bread and potatoes were scarce.

The spark which fired the smoldering resentment of the people was a government announcement on May 28, 1953, that workers' wages would be cut further unless they produced at least 10 percent more than in the past. On June 16, building workers on Stalin Avenue in East Berlin staged a spontaneous strike and marched on government headquarters. The strike spread quickly throughout East Germany on that day and the next, and in many communities the workers were in command of the situation, occupying police offices, liberating political prisoners, and setting government and Communist party buildings on fire. Many members of the police force either took a wait-and-see attitude or even went over to the rebels. Before long, the rebels demanded, in addition to more tolerable living conditions, free elections, free labor unions, and the end of Soviet domination.

Hesitating at first to intervene directly, when the Soviet government realized that the communist regime would soon be overthrown completely thousands of Soviet tanks moved into the major strongholds of rebellion, suppressing it in a few days. Several hundred Germans died in the uprising, hundreds were wounded, and about 50,000 were imprisoned.

Three years after the uprising in East Germany the Poles revolted. On June 28, 1956, thousands of workers of the Stalin Steel Works in Poznan went on strike early in the morning and marched toward the center of the city, chanting "Bread, bread, bread," singing Polish national songs, carrying the old Polish national flags, refusing to disperse despite the tank formations quickly brought into the city by the communist authorities. Before long, the striking workers occupied the Communist party headquarters and the radio station and set the city prison on fire after freeing the prisoners. In the ensuing battle with army and police, a battle that lasted for several days, about 200 Poles lost their lives, thousands were wounded, and many more thousands were arrested.

Militarily, the rebellion was successfully repressed, but politically it unleashed a chain of events which is still playing out. In October 1956, Wladyslaw Gomulka was elected first secretary of the Polish Communist party. This announcement came as a bombshell, because Gomulka was known as the leader of Titoism or "national communism" in Poland and had spent several years in prison for that crime.

For a while, the Soviets considered establishing full-scale occupation of the country and the reestablishment of Stalinism by force. But the Poles stood their ground, and Poland had won, for the time being, its struggle for some degree of national independence, although its government continued to be communist-dominated.

One of the most popular moves of the new government under Gomulka was to permit the peasants to dissolve collective farms and return to private farming. As a result, food production rose, leading to improved living conditions for the urban population as well. In industry too, harsh controls over workers were relaxed, and industrial production moved steadily forward from its previous low. Private enterprise in business and trade was permitted on a moderate scale, such as in the case of bakers, tailors, plumbers, repairmen, and skilled craftsmen in the building and tourist trades. In addition to these internal measures aiming at the improvement of its economy, Poland also benefited from American economic aid.

In 1957, the Polish government released from prison Cardinal Wyszynski, the symbol of Catholic resistance to the communist regime, and permitted religious instruction in public schools for the first time. This new attitude of greater tolerance was also extended, for a few years, to literature and the arts, during which time Western books and papers first became available. Arriving in Warsaw from Moscow, one is amazed to see large quantities of French, English, and German books on display in the windows of bookstores—a sight one cannot dream of in the Soviet Union.

From the middle 1960s on, the Polish government under Gomulka gradually nibbled away at these liberties. Censorship of the newspapers was tightened, liberal magazines were banned, and the Catholic church was increasingly harassed. In 1968 and 1969, the government purged the university faculties and student bodies of "revisionist" (liberal) elements, and a pattern of re-Stalinization arose that followed closely that of the Brezhnev regime in the Soviet Union. Increased bureaucratic pressures on peasants and workers led to worsening economic conditions.

In December 1970, the government announced steep increases in food and fuel prices. Within a few days, tens of thousands of workers in Gdansk and other cities along the Polish coast of the Baltic stopped working and started mass demonstrations. Communist party headquarters were set afire and party officials were seized by the demonstrators. The government called in large contingents of army and police forces, and pitched battles ensued, while a Soviet warship lay at anchor outside the port of Gdansk. Hundreds of persons on both sides were killed or injured. Within a few days, Gomulka resigned and was replaced by Edward Gierek. Gierek made some concessions to the workers and peasants, but in essence his policies were "Gomulkaism without Gomulka," thus foreshadowing more popular resistance in the future. Whereas in 1956 the workers in Poznan and other cities rose against Soviet control of Poland, the riots of 1970 reflected a deep-seated protest against Polish communist rule, which ultimately had to rely on guns against the rebelling workers. As a French writer put it: "The police and the army do open fire on the workers in industrial societies, just as Marx predicted. But it is in the communist countries that this happens. There was East Berlin in 1953, Poznan and Budapest in 1956, Prague in 1968, and Gdansk in 1970" (*Le Monde,* Weekly English Edition, November 13, 1971).

The events in Poland in 1956 immediately raised hope and passion in Hungary. On October 23, 1956, university students, quickly joined by thousands of industrial workers, held a mass meeting in Budapest's Parliament Square. Expressing their sympathy for the Polish fight for freedom and independence, they put forward a series of demands, including: the evacuation of Soviet troops from Hungary; free elections; free labor unions and the right to strike; revision of workers' wages and a complete reorganization of the economy; the immediate release of political prisoners and the return of Hungarians deported to the Soviet Union; removal of statues of Stalin; and, finally, reorganization of the compulsory system of farm collectives.

The political police turned a peaceful meeting into rebellion by firing on the students and workers. The fighting quickly spread throughout the country. The workers declared a general strike, and the freedom fighters were soon joined by the regular Hungarian army and police. On the communist side, the Hungarian political police were joined by powerful Soviet tank forces. Yet the incredible happened. The freedom fighters won their struggle, and on October 29, 1956, Hungary was free. Political authority was exercised by the representatives of popular organizations, and almost at once dozens of democratic newspapers began publication. Communists were nowhere to be seen, statues of Stalin were publicly burned, political prisoners were set free —among them Cardinal Mindszenty, who had been imprisoned since 1948.

However, this period of Hungarian freedom and independence lasted for only five days. On November 3 close to 200,000 Soviet troops and 5000 tanks moved into Hungary to suppress Hungarian freedom. After a week of heavy fighting, the revolution was put down. Prime Minister Nagy was kidnaped by the Russians and later executed. Over 35,000 Hungarians were killed in the fighting, and many more wounded. Many thousands were deported to Siberia, while more than 200,000 managed to escape to Austria. The physical destruction of the towns was worse than that suffered by Hungary in World War II, when she was a major battleground for many months.

During the first years after the crushing of the Hungarian Revolution, many people inside and outside Hungary thought that the heroic effort of the nation had been in vain. The communist dictatorship was harsher than before the revolution, and for a while it seemed more Stalinist than the government of the Soviet Union itself. In the end this reasoning—an implied defense of inert submission to communist totalitarianism—proved wrong. The very fact of the revolution encouraged tendencies toward more national independence in other communist states. Even Albania has been able, from the late 1950s on, to defy the Soviet Union by enthusiastically siding with China in its conflict with the Soviet Union.

In Hungary itself, the harsh government installed by the Soviet army after the repression of the revolution in 1956 gradually realized that Soviet tanks were not enough if the country was to regain some measure of political stability. Throughout the 1960s, the movement of relaxing the most oppressive controls gathered considerable momentum; thousands of political prisoners were released under a general amnesty, and the government eased its stringent controls in industry and farming. Writers and artists were given greater freedom of expression, and noncommunists were appointed to important positions. Whereas the previous slogan had been "He who is not for us is against us," the new official slogan became "He who is not against us is with us."

In 1968, Hungary embarked on a major reform of her economy, with the objective of creating market competition and incentives for managers and workers. Rigid centralized planning was relaxed in favor of more autonomy for individual enterprises, enabling them to decide what to produce and where to sell and allowing them to keep a greater share of the profits. Instead of governmentally fixed prices for all goods and services, a new three-tier system was introduced: fixed prices set by the government, controlled prices allowed to fluctuate within a predetermined upper and lower limit, and entirely free prices set by the enterprise in accordance with competitive market forces. In addition, the government began to encourage private small-scale enterprise in the home building, retailing, services, and handicraft industries. More imports of consumer goods were allowed, supplemented by direct foreign investments in tourism and other industries. As a result of these economic reforms, relations with Western countries greatly improved, travel to foreign countries was permitted on a larger scale, and the political environment in the country moved in the direction of cautious liberalization. By the early 1970s, Hungary seemed, next to Yugoslavia, the most liberal communist state in Eastern Europe.

Romania, until the early 1960s held up as a model and docile satellite of the Soviet Union, has in recent years increasingly asserted its national independence. A Latin island in a Slavic sea, Romania has returned to its historic cultural ties with the West. In 1963, the government abolished the compulsory teaching of Russian in grade and high schools and closed the official Soviet Russian Language Institute and Russian bookstore in Bucharest. In 1969, according to official statistics, 55 percent of university students taking a foreign language chose French, 33 percent chose English, and only 10 percent took Russian. Foreign authors are published and widely discussed, and Franz Kafka's works—considered by many to be the most penetrating critique of totalitarianism—are popular among the young avant-garde intellectuals.

In the economic field, Romania has led the opposition inside COMECON against the Soviet concept of "integrating" Eastern Europe for the benefit of the Soviet economy. In particular, Romania is intent on developing its industry and refuses the Soviet-assigned role of being a perpetual supplier of raw materials for the other communist states. Also, Romania is eager to break out of the confining limits of COMECON and to expand its trade with noncommunist states. In 1956, only 29 percent of Romania's trade was with noncommunist nations; in the early 1970s, Romania's foreign trade outside COMECON exceeded one-half of her total trade. Under its revamped economic policies, Romania's gross national product has grown at a faster rate than that of the other Eastern European communist states, and its government therefore insists that its economic reforms are guided by pragmatic considerations rather than by ideological criteria. In the early 1970s, Romania strengthened her economic ties with Western countries by encouraging foreign investments, particularly by French, West German, American, and British companies. The industries involved—transportation, earth-moving equipment, chemicals, and electronics—are vital to the growth of the Romanian economy, and under this new approach in international economic policy Romania has also been able to obtain loans and licenses for advanced technologies from leading Western nations.

In its foreign policy Romania has shown the highest degree of independence of all members of the Warsaw Pact countries (Soviet Union, Poland, East Germany, Hungary, Bulgaria, Czechoslovakia, and Romania) with respect to Soviet policy. Although Romania continues its membership in the Warsaw Pact alliance, its policy has, in fact, been one of strict neutrality. Romania maintains active ties with both China and Albania and has refused to be a party to Soviet-led efforts at condemning China in its conflict with the Soviet Union. When Sino-Soviet border clashes are reported, the Romanian press—in the time-honored style of neutrality in wartime—publishes the official Soviet and Chinese communiqués, giving equal space to each side. In its relations with the West, Romania was until 1972 the only member of the Warsaw Pact alliance—other than the Soviet Union itself—that maintained full diplomatic relations with both West and East Germany. At the outbreak of the Israeli-Arab war in 1967, all Warsaw Pact countries except Romania broke off diplomatic relations with Israel; Romania has not only refused to join the other Warsaw Pact countries in their anti-Israel campaign but has maintained friendly relations with both Israel and the Arab states and has quietly allowed over three hundred thousand Romanian Jews to emigrate to Israel. In 1972, Romania challenged the Soviet Union's anti-Israel policy by inviting Israeli Prime Minister Golda Meir on an official state visit to Bucharest, where she conferred with President Ceausescu and other Romanian political leaders.

Romania was the only Warsaw Pact country that refused to contribute troops to the Soviet-led invasion of Czechoslovakia in 1968, or to condone the act. Only a week before the invasion, President Ceausescu of Romania had pointedly visited Prague and signed a treaty of mutual help and assistance with the liberal Dubcek government there. After the invasion of Czechoslovakia, Ceausescu warned the Soviet Union that no foreign troops would be allowed to enter Romania and ordered the immediate creation of a "people's militia" of workers, peasants, and intellectuals for "the defense of freedom and independence" of his nation. Ceausescu bluntly condemned the Soviet aggression as "a grave mistake and a serious danger not only to peace in Europe but to socialism throughout the world, too."

When Romania invited President Nixon to visit Romania on August 2, 1969, it took a calculated risk in its relations with the Soviet Union. Although the Romanian government tried to keep popular manifestation at a low key, the enthusiasm of the people went beyond the boundaries of the planned low key. A few days later, the Soviet representative at the Romanian Communist party congress in Bucharest attacked "bridge building" (as exemplified in the Nixon visit) as a "perfidious tactic" that was undermining the cohesion of the communist countries of Eastern Europe. Yet the Romanians stood their ground, and President Ceausescu announced that the "people's militia" would continue to defend Romanian independence against "imperialism." "He did not say what 'imperialism,'" an American observer of the party congress reported, "but the delegates' wild applause at his announcement made it obvious that it was not the imperialism of the United States he had in mind" (Tad Szulc, "Letter from Bucharest," *The New Yorker*, September 6, 1969, p. 118). A year later, President Ceausescu returned the

Nixon visit by coming to the United States and conferring with the American president. Addressing the United Nations' General Assembly in New York during his visit, the Romanian president stressed the central position of his country's foreign policy—that relations between states must be based on independence and noninterference. Without mentioning the Soviet Union, it was clear which country President Ceausescu had in mind as a threat to his nation, and it was considered particularly significant that he reiterated his position in New York.

SOCIALISM WITH A HUMAN FACE

Communist rule in Czechoslovakia was established in 1948 through a coup of the Communist party aided by threats of Soviet military intervention. Czechoslovakia was the only country in central Europe, apart from Switzerland, that had had a genuine democratic and libertarian tradition in politics, economics, and religion, and its standards of education and industrial skill compared favorably with those of its neighbors. The communization of Czechoslovakia in 1948 shocked the Western nations into a renewed awareness of Soviet imperialism, and the creation of NATO was the most significant response to that shock. From 1948 to the early 1960s, the communist regime in Czechoslovakia was rigidly Stalinist in its internal policy and docile in its relations with the Soviet Union.

From the middle 1960s on, a new generation of communist leaders began to reappraise the effects of communist rule on Czechoslovakia. In the economic field, the country had fallen behind as a result of both domestic and foreign policy. Domestically, rigid central planning and bureaucratic routine had stifled the traditional initiative and enterprise of the highly skilled Czechs. In its foreign economic policy, the Czech economy had to adapt to the role assigned to it by the Soviet-led COMECON. The Czech economy had to neglect the industries in which it had developed world-renowned skills and profitable markets in the West, such as textiles, glass, china, leather goods, and jewelry, and had to concentrate on basic industries for which it was not suited. As a result, the growth record of the Czech economy was unimpressive— even as compared with the other communist states in Eastern Europe. In politics, the democratic habits of the people increasingly reasserted themselves among workers, students, and intellectuals, as well as among growing numbers of Communist party leaders. In January 1968, Antonin Novotny—the leader and popular symbol of Stalinist communism—was replaced by Alexander Dubcek, a liberal communist, as first secretary of the Czech Communist party. Under Dubcek's leadership, communism in Czechoslovakia embarked on a unique experiment in the history of communism: the transformation of totalitarian communism into *socialism with a human face* by peaceful means, that is, by the combination of public ownership in the economy with political democracy in government.

One of the first acts of the Dubcek leadership was to release from prison more than 30,000 victims of the Novotny regime and to abolish the secret police. Prominent victims of Czech Stalinism executed in the 1950s were rehabilitated posthumously. Old-line Stalinist communists were dismissed from their positions, but the new government was careful not to use force against them. This treatment, in line with the new emphasis on the rule of law, grew out of the conviction that the popular condemnation of Stalinist communists was so profound that no other penalties were needed. All travel restrictions on Czechoslovaks wishing to leave the country or foreigners wishing to visit it were lifted. This freedom to travel was an indirect blow at the Berlin Wall, since East Germans could visit Czechoslovakia and from there make their way to West Germany.

The freedom of speech, of the press, and of assembly spread spontaneously as the government did nothing to discourage them. In fact, the government finally abolished all censorship of the press. Noncommunist papers were freely published, and criticism of communism itself was expressed. In the most famous document of the period—"2000 Words," a manifesto of intellectuals and workers—the following passage appeared: "The Communist party, which after the war possessed the great trust of the people, gradually exchanged this trust for offices, until it had all the offices and nothing else." The signers of the manifesto declared their commitment to socialism, but it had to be a socialism regenerated by democracy: "The regenerative process introduces nothing particularly new into our life. It revives ideas and topics, many of which are older than the errors of socialism." What many Czechoslovak communists wanted for their country was Marxism without Leninism. Some publicly stated that Leninism might be suitable for a country like Russia, but not for Czechoslovakia in its advanced stage of political and economic development.

Finally, the Dubcek leadership allowed the formation of noncommunist clubs and associations, and Wenceslas Square in the center of Prague became the Hyde Park of Czechoslovakia in which groups and individuals could freely express their views. The extent of the freedom enjoyed during the spring and summer of 1968 can be seen in the fact that a public opinion poll was taken on the question of allowing opposition parties. On June 27, 1968, the official daily of the Communist party reported the results of the poll: *90 percent of noncommunists favored the creation of opposition parties, and even more than half of the communists polled did so.*

During the spring and summer of 1968 the Dubcek leadership was warned by Brezhnev and Kosygin to give up the experiment in "socialism with a human face." The main fear of the Soviets—supported principally by East German and Polish leaders—was that the process of liberalization would undermine the monopoly of the Communist party in Czechoslovakia and that an opposition, once given freedom of organization and expression, might provide an alternative government some day. The Czechoslovak leaders defended themselves by arguing that they were fully confident that liberalization under communist leadership would strengthen the cause of communism, and that no political groups would be allowed that challenged the economic principles of public ownership of the means of production. In the area of foreign policy, the Dubcek leadership repeatedly reassured the Soviet leaders that Czechoslovakia would continue its membership in the Warsaw Pact. If the Soviet leaders had permitted the people of Czechoslovakia to continue the experiment of combining public ownership with a high degree of political democracy under the leadership of the Communist party, we should have been provided with an answer to the question of whether a communist society can maintain itself by processes of consent or whether it must rely on political prisons and the secret police.

The Soviet leaders were unwilling to accept either possible outcome of the experiment: If the experiment led to the gradual elimination of communist influence in Czech politics and economics, it might provide an example for other communist countries that communist rule is not a dead end and that a return journey to a noncommunist society is possible—even under liberal communist leadership. Conversely, from the Soviet viewpoint, should the experiment in Czechoslovakia succeed and the party maintain itself in a place of leadership by moral authority rather than by force, the repercussions of such a success might be disastrous for the communist regimes in the Soviet Union and other communist states that relied on prisons and labor camps for the maintenance of communist rule.

The Soviet leadership decided that the experiment in Czechoslovakia had to be ended by armed force, since a voluntary return to Stalinism in Czechoslovakia was out of the question. On August 21, 1968, 200,000 troops, mostly Soviet but including East German, Polish, Bulgarian, and Hungarian contingents, invaded and occupied Czechoslovakia. There was sporadic individual fighting and a few dozen people were killed, but the Czechs had decided not to resist the invasion with their armed forces. Swastikas were painted on Soviet tanks, and numerous inscriptions on buildings explained to the Soviet "liberators" that, to the people of Czechoslovakia, German Nazism and Soviet communism were the same.

Entering Prague during the night, the Soviet invaders did not waste any time. Unmarked cars carrying secret police raced through Prague and arrested known liberals. At 4 A.M., Soviet airborne units surrounded the headquarters of the Communist party, and Dubcek and three other top government leaders were removed by Soviet soldiers and civilians. Then "the four men were led to a Soviet transport plane, pushed with rifle butts. . . . They were treated harshly and insulted. As Premier Cernik was to tell the Cabinet later: 'I feared for my life and that of my comrades.' " (New York Times, September 2, 1968). The four top leaders were flown to the Soviet Union and kept prisoner. President Svoboda of Czechoslovakia flew to Moscow on August 23, 1968, and he made it clear to the Soviet government that he would not participate in any negotiations until the imprisoned leaders had been freed. He reportedly even threatened to commit suicide in the Kremlin if the imprisoned leaders were killed—as had happened to Imre Nagy in Hungary. The Soviets freed Dubcek and his colleagues, and the Czechoslovak leaders surrendered the independence of their country to the Soviets on August 26, 1968. As Josef Smrkovsky, president of the National Assembly of Czechoslovakia and a member of the delegation, later explained, the Czechoslovaks had negotiated "in the shadow of tanks and planes." Soviet troops were to stay indefinitely on Czechoslovak soil—to make sure that totalitarian communism of the Soviet type would prevent any recurrence of the virus of "socialism with a human face."

By the early 1970s, Czechoslovakia was effectively subjected to a Brezhnev-type regime of spiritual and physical coercion. Writers, artists, teachers, and managers were induced or compelled to state publicly that they welcomed the Soviet military occupation of their country. Many formerly liberal communists were dismissed from their positions, and some were tried and sentenced to prison terms. The result, as a liberal communist leader who escaped abroad put it, was inevitable: "Of all Eastern European countries, the deepest depression, frustration, and feeling of hopelessness prevail in Czechoslovakia" (Eugen Loebl, "Spiritual Genocide," New York Times, September 23, 1972).

Whereas the 1948 communist coup in Czechoslovakia was hailed by other communist states and parties as a victory of the cause of Marxism-Leninism, the Soviet occupation of Czechoslovakia in 1968 fragmented the communist world more profoundly than ever before. Three communist states—Yugoslavia, Romania, and China—sharply denounced the Soviet action, but the governments of Poland, East Germany, Bulgaria, and Hungary—who had themselves participated in the aggression—defended the Soviet Union. Not a single Communist party leader in Western Europe defended the Soviet move, and the large Communist parties of Italy and France were particularly outspoken in their condemnation.

Seeing the disintegration of communist unity even in its own backyard, Eastern Europe, the Soviet leadership determined that its policy of coercion in relation to other communist states had to be raised from the level of practice to that of principle. Speaking on November 12, 1968, at the congress of the Polish Communist party in Warsaw, Brezhnev made it plain that the action in Czechoslovakia was not an isolated incident, but the application of a broader principle, since then known as the "Brezhnev Doctrine." Under this policy principle, the Soviet government reserves to itself the right to use military force in any communist country where, in its judgment, a threat emerges to the cause of communism, "a threat to the security of the Socialist Commonwealth as a whole." Significantly, Brezhnev did not confine the applicability of his new doctrine to Warsaw Pact countries, but spoke of "any socialist country"—including, presumably, such states as Yugoslavia and China.

The dilemma posed by the Brezhnev Doctrine to the noncommunist world and to the concept of coexistence between East and West was aptly formulated by the London *Economist:*

> Mr. Brezhnev was saying that once a country has got a communist form of government it will never be allowed to get rid of it; and this, presumably, even if the majority of its people say they want to try something else. The Russians are inviting the Western world to take part in a competition in which, on the principle of democratic choice, noncommunist countries are allowed to go communist but, on the principle of the socialist commonwealth, communist ones are forbidden to make the return journey. Heads we win, tails you lose. It is an odd way to invite people to play ball. (December 7, 1968, p. 18.)

THE SINO-SOVIET CONFLICT

The most explosive conflict between communist states is yet to come: China against the Soviet Union. Basically, it is a struggle over power, but like every power struggle it has other elements as well.

First, there is the issue of nationalism—Chinese against Russians. For more than 300 years, Russia has expanded her empire in Asia, frequently at the expense of China. Russia has, therefore, traditionally feared the prospect of a strong and united China ruled by an effective central government, the kind of government that communist rule has established in China since 1949. From the traditional Chinese viewpoint, the Russians are meddlesome troublemakers, imperialist expansionists, and—by the standards of ancient Chinese civilization—a horde of crude barbarians. In the eyes of the Chinese, Russians are not (as they appear to some Westerners) semi-Asiatic or semi-Oriental, but full-fledged Europeans and, as such, barbarians by definition.

Even during Stalin's rule, Titoism showed that the force of nationalism is stronger than that of "international proletarian solidarity and fraternity." If the nationalism of little Yugoslavia could prevail against Stalin, the nationalism of a great power like China, the Chinese feel, is even more destined to prevail against a mere Khrushchev or Brezhnev. Marx or no Marx, more than 800 million Chinese will not forever accept the idea that the 245 million people of the Soviet Union are the leaders of the communist world. The Chinese cite the Confucian saying, "When two men ride on a horse, only one can sit in front." The Chinese are determined that they, not the Russians, will sit in front.

Closely connected with the traditional force of nationalism is the issue of population and resources. More than 800 million Chinese inhabit a densely populated area, with an annual increase in population running about 12 million people. By contrast, the 245 million inhabitants of the Soviet Union live in a much vaster territory, and the annual increase in population is only about three million. On the Soviet side of the common border, the land is empty and the population sparse; on the Chinese side, the land is overcrowded. This growing gap between the Soviet ratio of people to resources on the one hand and the Chinese ratio on the other may someday lead to Chinese expansion at the expense of Soviet territory.

In particular, the Chinese have publicly proclaimed in recent years that they do not recognize past imperialist treaties and conquests at the expense of China. This is of particular concern to the Soviet Union, since Russia took more territory from China than any other imperialist power. The major areas in dispute include vast Far Eastern stretches of land, from the mouth of the Amur River down the Pacific coast of Siberia and reaching west almost as far as Lake Baikal. Today, this area of untold natural riches is inhabited by 9 million Soviet citizens. The Chinese feel that, with more intensive cultivation of the soil, at least 100 million Chinese could live there—albeit with a lower Chinese standard of living. Next, China desires the "liberation" of formerly Chinese territories in Soviet central Asia, covering an area of about half a million square miles and ten million people. This is rich land with a great

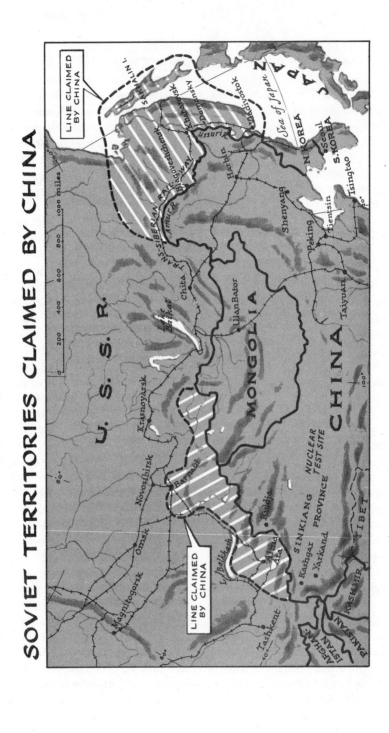

SOVIET TERRITORIES CLAIMED BY CHINA

great potential in food and fibers. Finally, there is Mongolia, with over half a million square miles and only 1.2 million population. A Chinese province from 1686 to 1911, it became a Russian protectorate in 1912–1919 and again a Chinese province in 1919–1921. In 1921, Mongolia became an independent state in form, but in fact it was closely linked with Moscow. China has tried to gain a foothold in Mongolia, playing on racial affinity and historical ties, but Soviet influence has so far remained uppermost. One of the main reasons for the Soviet Union's success is the fact that she has been giving considerable economic aid to Mongolia—about $200 million or more annually, one of the highest per capita foreign aid expenditures of any country anywhere. In 1966, the Soviet Union and Mongolia concluded a military security treaty, giving the Soviet Union the right to station troops in her ally's territory, thus bringing Soviet armed forces right up to the Chinese border. More recently, the Soviets also introduced rocket and missile forces into Mongolia, only a few hundred miles from China's major nuclear installations. Should the Soviet Union decide on a preemptive strike against China, knocking out these nuclear plants would be one of the first objectives. Peking, too, is much closer to Mongolia than to any point in the Soviet Union.

While the Soviet leaders have repudiated many of the internal policies of the tsars, they are not willing to give up the fruits of tsarist conquest, be it in favor of the Chinese or anyone else. So far, the Chinese have publicly stated that they wish to settle the issue of these disputed areas not by force but by peaceful negotiation at "the appropriate time"—in other words, when China is strong enough to bargain effectively with the Soviet Union. Chinese maps now indicate the area of the country before and after the foreign imperialist grabs of Chinese territory. Russia always appears in these maps as the foremost imperialist, helping herself to more Chinese territory than any other imperialist state of the past. Since such maps are published in the officially prescribed schoolbooks in China, a whole generation is growing up eager to regain the lost territories. But when China published a new geographical atlas of the world in 1972, Soviet spokesmen ridiculed the "absurd demands" for territorial changes reflected therein, accusing China of "fanning hostility between the Chinese and Soviet peoples." In addition, the Soviet government has warned China on numerous occasions that "any attempt to encroach upon the Soviet frontier will meet with a crushing rebuff." The Chinese persistently maintain that Soviet occupancy of large tracts of Chinese territory is part of a "huge colonial empire," and that Soviet imperialist ambitions are doomed to fail because the world is "in the era when the imperialist system is heading for collapse" (*Peking Review,* June 16, 1972).

Far from dismissing the territorial ambitions of the Chinese in these areas as idle speculation, the Soviet government has taken them seriously. In the 1960s, the Soviet government began a drive to double the population of the disputed areas in the East and supplemented this campaign with detailed economic plans designed to attract and provide for a rapidly growing population. Even if this project of doubling the population of the Soviet Far East were to succeed, the Chinese population is multiplying so much faster than the Soviet that it is doubtful whether the Soviets can ever match the Chinese population pressure by transferring its own people in sufficiently large numbers. In the meantime, the Chinese have embarked on an intensified settlement program at two crucial frontiers with the Soviet Union: northern Manchuria and Sinkiang. The Soviet authorities are aware of this Chinese pressure on their borders, and Soviet border guards in the Far East and central Asia are on constant alert against "enemy violators." Border clashes have occurred on numerous occasions, each side blaming the other for the intense military activities on the 4500-mile frontier. Since the late 1960s, border incidents have escalated sharply in intensity and duration, and major battles between border troops have resulted in hundreds of casualties. The combined armed strength of the Soviet Union and China along their borders currently exceeds one million men, and the leaders of both countries have publicly stated that they are ready for both conventional and nuclear war. The airport at Omsk in western Siberia has been transformed into one of the largest military airports in the world, and the Soviet Union has developed an extensive delivery system of nuclear weapons close to China's borders. The Chinese possess massive manpower, but are no match for Soviet airpower and nuclear capability. The prospect of a major Sino-Soviet war has become a matter of such concern to Soviet leaders that they have tried to transform the issue from an intracommunist dispute into one that is, or should be, of concern to all nations. War between the Soviet Union and China, *Pravda* editorialized on August 28, 1969, "what with the existing weapons and lethal armaments and modern means of delivery, would not spare a single continent."

Soviet fears of a resurgent China have also been seen in the economic field. During the first years of the communist regime in China —from about 1950 to 1957—Soviet aid and advice were significant in the total economic planning of China. After 1957, as tensions gradually developed, the Soviets began taking measures against China where they could be most painful—in the economic sphere. In 1959, the first repatriations of Soviet advisers, experts, and other technicians took place; by 1960, nearly all Soviet citizens had left China. In some instances the departing Soviet technicians even took with them the plans for the projects they were engaged in, as was the case with the huge Sammen Narrows Dam on the Yellow River. Trade between the Soviet Union and China has also slumped, dropping from more than $400 million in 1964 to less than $50 million, out of total Soviet foreign trade of about $25 billion per year. Soviet trade with China is currently less than with any other communist country—even less than with Mongolia, a nation of 1.5 million people. To make up for the loss in trade with the Soviet Union and the Eastern European communist states, China has greatly intensified its commercial relations with Japan, Western Europe, and, since the Nixon visit to China in 1972, with the United States.

Diplomatically, too, the Soviet Union and China have different— and conflicting—interests, for reasons of geography. For the Soviet Union, the problem of Germany and the specific issue of Berlin are among the key problems in Europe—in both of which China has shown very little interest. By contrast, China's foremost goal in Asia is the eventual incorporation of Taiwan—a matter which is of little concern to the Soviet Union. During India's border conflict with China in 1959 and during the Indian-Pakistani war in 1970, the Soviet Union openly sided on both occasions with India, supplying her with weapons and industrial equipment and supporting her diplomatically in every possible way. Such close relations between India and the Soviet Union were formally expressed in their 20-year treaty of cooperation signed in 1971. From the Chinese viewpoint, the purpose of the treaty was to enable the Soviet Union to "control India and 'Bangla Desh' and infiltrate into the regions of the Indian Ocean and the south Asian subcontinent so as to expand its spheres of influence and contend for hegemony. The aggressive design of social-imperialism knows no bounds" (*Peking Review,* September 1, 1972). The Chinese frequently call the Soviet leaders "social-imperialists," since in the Chinese view the Soviet leaders are "socialists in word and imperialists in deed."

Elsewhere, in Southeast Asia, China apprehensively watches growing Soviet influence in Indonesia, Vietnam, Thailand, Malaysia, and Singapore. China is particularly worried over seeing the waning American presence in Southeast Asia replaced by expanding Soviet influence in areas that it has traditionally considered within its own sphere of influence. From the Chinese viewpoint, Soviet meddling in Southeast Asia is even more offensive and intolerable than that of the United States or of a resurgent Japan. Considering Soviet power to be the main threat to its international position and even to its existence, China therefore embarked on a new course of closer relations with the United States, highlighted by President Nixon's visit to China in February 1972. In September 1972, China renewed diplomatic relations with Japan and began to strengthen economic relations with that country.

Shortly after, on the occasion of the twenty-third anniversary of the establishment of communist rule in China (October 1, 1972), Chinese spokesmen stated that after President Nixon's China visit "the gate to friendly contacts between the people of the two countries is now open," although still expressing some low-key criticisms of American foreign policy. By contrast, vehement criticisms were leveled at the Soviet Union, which was labeled "even more deceitful than old-line imperialist countries, and therefore more dangerous." Rapprochement between China and the United States moved forward decisively in 1979. The Peking government was formally recognized instead of the Republic of Taiwan, and Chinese Deputy Premier Teng Hsiao-ping visited the United States for an extended tour.

The competition between China and the Soviet Union is taking

Drawing by Donald Reilly; © 1972 The New Yorker Magazine, Inc.

"I'm as aware of the evils of communism as anyone, but good God, when you think of eight hundred million Chinese in terms of franchises . . ."

place on all continents, within communist states as well as within Communist parties in noncommunist states. In Europe, Albania, the poorest of the communist states, has come under the influence of China. In Asia, Africa, and Latin America, China portrays herself as the true leader of the poor, have-not nations, whereas the Soviet Union is pictured as being too busy with keeping what she has, and no longer dedicated to world revolution. The Chinese also charge that the "Soviet revisionist renegade clique" (as the Soviet government is consistently termed in the Chinese press) is working for the restoration of capitalism, and that "stinking egoism" has replaced the communist morals of Lenin and Stalin in the Soviet Union. In Asia, Chinese influence is strong in North Korea and Cambodia, whereas Soviet influence is paramount in the communist regime of North Vietnam. Among the Asian communist movements, Soviet influence is dominant in Ceylon, Japan, and India, although in all three cases there are strong pro-Peking factions.

Many Asian Communist parties have deliberately adopted a stance of nonalignment in the Sino-Soviet conflict in order to obtain greater freedom of action by playing one side against the other. Some of the Asian, African, and Latin American parties are truly neutral regarding Moscow and Peking; others are nonaligned but favor one side or the other to some degree. In some cases, the local Communist parties have been rent by internal dissension over the Sino-Soviet issue to such an extent that factions and splinter groups have developed, threatening the unity of the movement as a whole.

In the last decade, the Chinese communists have played on one major theme in their conflict with the Soviet Union, a theme that has particular relevance in the developing countries: color. A mockery of anything even remotely related to Marx or Lenin, the theme of race and color may well become the most powerful weapon in the hands of the Chinese against the Soviets. Fully aware that the majority of the world's people are nonwhite and that in most developing countries the nonwhites vastly outnumber the whites, China is trying to create the image of the Soviet Union as another white imperialist power, seeking to impose its will on the poor, nonwhite masses of the Third World. Thus, when the Soviet Union signed the partial nuclear test-ban agreement with the United States and Great Britain in 1963 and the limited nuclear-arms agreement with the United States in 1972, China refused to join, because she was eager to go ahead with her own atomic weapons program. The Chinese leaders consider such Soviet agreements as evidence that the Soviet Union is joining with the white imperialist "haves" against the "toiling masses" of the nonwhites throughout the world.

The struggle between the Soviet Union and China has shown that, in their practical conduct, communist states follow Lenin's emphasis on political power rather than Marx's "laws" of economic development. However, the doctrine and practice of political power are not the novel contributions of Lenin and communism, but have existed throughout history. Similarly, other communist states and Communist parties have been guided in their attitudes toward the Soviet Union and China by considerations of *national interest*. This emphasis on national interest is an important stage in the process of denuding Marxism and Leninism of one of their fundamental doctrinal elements: faith in internationalism and the universal brotherhood of mankind. At first, the Sino-Soviet conflict was minimized as a mere ideological controversy between two fraternal proletarian parties. Later, the dispute was recognized as a quarrel between two states, two systems of power. Today, the Sino-Soviet conflict is viewed everywhere as the most important potential threat of nuclear war between any two major powers in the world.

Chinese Communism After Mao

Among the major revolutionaries of the twentieth century—including Lenin, Trotsky, Mussolini, and Hitler—none had so long-lasting and far-reaching an effect on his country as Mao Tse-tung. Lenin died in 1927, during the formative years of Soviet communism, warning from his deathbed against the scheming and ruthless Stalin; Trotsky founded the Red Army, which won the civil war that followed the Russian Revolution, but he was exiled from the Soviet Union in 1929, a victim of Stalin's enmity; Mussolini led his March on Rome in 1921, pledging to restore the glories of the Roman Empire, but he was executed ignominiously in 1945 amid the ruins of a lost war; and Hitler's promised Thousand Year Reich ended in flames after little more than a decade.

For his part, Mao Tse-tung helped found the Chinese Communist Party (1921), guided it through two civil wars and a foreign invasion, led it to power in a national revolution (1949), and then for more than a quarter of a century, until his death in 1976, presided over the reconstruction and transformation of Chinese society and politics. For 40 years, from the time he became Chairman of the Party in 1935 until he died at the age of 83, the person of Mao Tse-tung and the cause of Chinese communism were inseparably linked. His prescriptions for how to think and act, published as *The Thoughts of Mao Tse-tung,* became for millions of Chinese a modern equivalent of the ancient *Sayings of Confucius.* Until his death he remained the predominant theorist, leader, and symbol of Chinese communism.

Proclamation of the People's Republic of China on October 1, 1949, was the culmination of a long and arduous journey for Mao and the Chinese Communist Party. When the journey began China was weak and divided, poor and semifeudal, prey to periodic famines, ruled by reactionary warlords, at the mercy of foreign powers who exacted economic and political concessions from an ineffectual central government. When Mao died China was unified and independent, rid of the excesses of political corruption and mass starvation, moving toward economic development, a world power wielding nuclear weapons and serving as a base of support for other communist regimes as far away as Albania. The achievements have been prodigious, but the costs have been enormous. If Mao can be credited with extraordinary achievements, he is also responsible for the exceptional costs.

THE EARLY YEARS OF CHINESE COMMUNISM

Mao was born in 1893 into a relatively comfortable "middle peasant" family that provided him with the basic education that was essential for further advancement. By his own account he was in continual conflict with his father, whom he regarded as harsh, unreasonable, and philistine. At the age of 16 Mao defied his father by leaving his native village to attend school in a nearby town. His studies there were interrupted by the Revolution of 1911, which overthrew the reigning Manchu dynasty and inaugurated the Chinese Republic welcomed enthusiastically by Mao. After a brief stint in the pro-Republican army, he entered the Teachers' Training School in Changsha, capital of his native province of Hunan. During the five years he spent at this school (1913–1918) Mao encountered the personalities, ideas, and activities that soon launched him on his revolutionary course.

Mao's revolutionary impulses turned toward communism after he moved to Peking University to work as an assistant in the library. There he joined a Marxist Study Group and took part in the momentous May 4th Movement (1919), a violent demonstration against the government's acquiescence in territorial concessions to Japan. This explosive display of nationalist fervor was later celebrated as the beginning of communist activity in China. Observing the condition of China during these years, Mao felt deep disillusion over the results of the Revolution of 1911, a feeling shared by his radical teachers and fellow students. The leader of that revolution, Sun Yat-sen, was a Western-educated doctor who had been agitating for years against the corrupt and ineffective rule of the Manchus. In 1905 he formulated his program as the Three Principles of the People: People's Rule (nationalism), People's Authority (democracy), and People's Livelihood (socialism). These principles, always ambiguous and never directly applied to the specific problems of the time, became the main ideological guide for reform groups until Mao himself adapted Marxism-Leninism to the conditions of Chinese society.

Dr. Sun's efforts bore fruit in 1911 when, with the aid of the influential general Yuan Shih-k'ai, the boy Emperor was deposed and a Republic proclaimed. For Mao, as for all progressive-minded Chinese, this was an exciting time. But hope soon turned to bitter disappointment as General Yuan, now President of the Republic, betrayed the Revolution. He aimed to install himself as a new emperor, which he hoped to accomplish through alliances with provincial warlords whose military power would be the basis of his government. Yuan died in 1916, before his plans could succeed; he left as his legacy, and thus as the legacy of the Revolution of 1911, a divided country ruled by autonomous warlords.

The ensuing period was a time of intense intellectual ferment and equally intense political frustration. Reforms of all sorts were proposed and attempted, but it became increasingly clear that without some fundamental change in the governmental structure no permanent progress could be achieved. The violent demonstration of May 4, 1919, was an expression of growing dissatisfaction.

The revolutionary forces that won an inconclusive victory in 1911 produced two heirs: the Nationalist party, later renamed as the Kuomintang (National People's Party), and the Communist party, founded in 1921 by a small group of Marxists, including Mao, in the main industrial city of Shanghai. For a time the two parties worked in collaboration, thanks largely to the urgings of the Soviet advisers who counseled and aided both groups. This collaboration culminated in the successful military campaigns of 1926–1927, in which the warlords were defeated and China seemed on the verge of reunification. But even during the years of collaboration a serious rift was developing between the Kuomintang, now led by Chiang Kai-shek, and the Communists. In 1927 the struggle broke into open civil war.

The sources of this rift, which was to have the most fateful consequences for the future of China, were deep-rooted. At issue were alternative visions of the way to a modern China. Although he had started out as a nationalist revolutionary, Chiang's views and policies grew increasingly narrow and conservative. Consolidation of power in the hands of the Kuomintang became his primary purpose, overriding a concern for major economic and social change. Married to a daughter of the wealthy and westernized Soong family, he converted to Christianity and moved closer to the propertied urban merchants and rural landlords who provided his main support and whose interests he protected. Instead of basic political and social reform, he advocated traditional Confucian morality and rigorous military discipline. In a critical decision he determined to make extermination of the communists his first priority, before turning either to domestic reform or to the looming menace of Japanese aggression. Mao, on the other hand, envisioned a fundamental transformation in the entire base of agricultural China. His early major work of social analysis, "Report on an Investigation of the Peasant Movement in Hunan" (1927), revealed both the unorthodox bent of his communist theory—he placed primary emphasis on the revolutionary potential of rural peasants rather than urban workers—and also the very radical implications of his call for revolution in the countryside. China was overwhelmingly an agricultural country, and Mao was attacking the fundamental institutions of traditional Chinese society.

Chiang's war against the communists went well; before long his Kuomintang armies controlled most of the country. Assaulted in their main base in east-central China (Kiangsi province), the communists resolved on a daring escape to a remote region of the northwest (Shensi province) where they would be safe against attack. The Long March 1937? (1927) became a legend in the history of Chinese communism. The tortuous route covered nearly 7000 miles; of some 100,000 people who began the march less than 30,000 survived to the end. But this remnant, which became the core of victorious communist armies a decade later, consisted of tough, disciplined, dedicated cadres, politically united under their newly-elected Chairman, Mao Tse-tung.

MAO'S DOCTRINES

During the period Mao spent in the north at his capital of Yenan he formulated his theoretical views and initiated the policies that would later be imposed throughout the country. Mao's theories are not always internally consistent, nor do they remain the same through the years. On the contrary, his thought underwent many modifications, even in basic emphasis. Although he was a self-proclaimed disciple of Marxism-Leninism, and important parts of his thought are orthodox Leninism, from the very beginning his views reflected the special conditions of Chinese society as well as the particular circumstances of his own rise to power. A number of themes emerge which are distinctly Maoist:

(a) Cities are secondary to the countryside
(b) Mass action is secondary to the Red Army
(c) Technical expertise is secondary to revolutionary fervor
(d) Objective realities are secondary to subjective forces

(a) Cities are secondary to the countryside

Mao's first efforts as a communist organizer were spent in the villages of his native Hunan, and this experience opened his eyes to the revolutionary potential in rural areas. Lenin too had recognized the revolutionary role of peasants in underdeveloped countries as allies of the industrial workers, but his belief that the more active part would be taken by the better-organized urban proletariat was closer to Marx's original view that the leading revolutionary force in capitalist society was the industrial working class. At first Mao may also have shared this belief; however, he became convinced that the peasants must act not merely as an ally but as the main force in the revolutionary struggle, and that leadership in the struggle must also come from the peasants. Although Mao's view accurately reflected Chinese realities, it was a significant step beyond Lenin.

Mao's determination to base the communist movement in the countryside rather than the cities was confirmed during the Long March. Not only had earlier attempts by the Red Army to capture Kuomintang-dominated cities failed, but in their long trek northward the communist forces found welcome aid in the villages along the route. By the time Mao reached Yenan he was convinced that control of the countryside was the key to success. With the active or at least passive support of the local peasants the communist forces could operate effectively in the countryside, interrupting communication and supply routes, choosing favorable occasions to engage and defeat the troops sent against them, and eventually reducing the cities to submission. Guerrilla warfare became Mao's overall strategy: Communist armies would move through the countryside like fish in the sea ("The People are the Sea, We are the Fish"), ultimately to encircle and conquer the major urban centers. It was a strategy applied by Mao and his trusted comrade-in-arms, General Lin Piao, to the revolutionary struggle—both internal and international. Just as control of the countryside would lead to conquest of the cities, so control of former colonial areas would lead to strangulation of the capitalist heartland in Europe and America. In both respects Mao had reversed the original Marxist priorities: Revolution would succeed in the countryside before the cities, and in underdeveloped countries before the industrialized centers. Mao was adapting Marxism to the conditions of the Third World.

(b) Mass action is secondary to the Red Army

The success of Mao's strategy depended not simply on the support of the local population but first of all on the effectiveness of the Red Army as a military organization. Protracted revolutionary warfare, ex-

86

tending over decades, could not be won by the people; only the army could win such a struggle. This is the basis of Mao's statement that "viewed from the Marxist theory of the state, the army is the chief component of the political power of a state. Whoever wants to seize and hold on to political power must have a strong army."

In fact, military and communist party operations were virtually indistinguishable throughout these years. Mao and his most faithful lieutenant, Chou En-lai, were generals before they assumed key political and administrative roles in the People's Republic, and the same was true of other major leaders from the older generation. The Red Army had played an active part in the revolution since 1927, when General Chu Teh founded the People's Liberation Army by leading a rebellion of troops against the Kuomintang in the city of Nanking. General Chu and his troops subsequently joined Mao on the Long March. The survivors of this ordeal formed the nucleus of the armies which fought first against the Japanese invaders (1937–1945) and then for four years more against the Kuomintang forces. After the People's Republic was established in 1949, the military continued to play a vital role in Mao's regime, both internally and internationally. At the outset the victorious armies served as the de facto administrative units for the entire country; then in a series of military operations they proved themselves as defenders of Chinese security and independence. They fought against the United States in Korea (1950), against India on the borders of Tibet (1962), and against the Soviet Union on the borders of Mongolia (1969). The most dramatic intervention of the military in internal politics came with the Cultural Revolution (1966–1969). Mao made exceptional use of the army during this period, first in moving the groups of youngsters who were the agents of the Cultural Revolution from one part of the country to another, and then in suppressing these same groups when their organizations of Red Guards proved uncontrollable.

Thus, from the early years of communist activity and throughout Mao's reign, the Red Army was a direct partner of the Communist party as revolutionaries and rulers. Unavoidably the partnership suffered periodic strains as struggles for power developed within the leadership. The proper relationship between the army and the party, as Mao saw it, was that "political power grows out of the barrel of a gun. Our principle is that the Party commands the gun; the gun shall never be allowed to command the Party." Although the army, wielder of the gun, is the foundation of the communist state, ultimate control must lodge with the Communist party, if only because the party has the final say in applying communist ideology to new conditions. The supremacy of the party is a fundamental tenet of Leninism, which Mao embraced wholeheartedly and which is presumably endorsed by all loyal communists, including the generals who are themselves members of the party.

But ideology is one thing, and the urge for power is something else. A major challenge to Mao's leadership was exposed in 1971, with the mysterious death of General Lin Piao, Mao's chosen successor.

The Lin Piao affair illustrates the special difficulties of China-watching. Government control of information and travel is so complete that significant events can be entirely concealed, as in the death of General Lin. When the official report was made almost a year after the event, it was so sketchy that some of the most troublesome questions remain unanswered to this day. General Lin had been one of Mao's oldest and closest comrades; his military exploits were renowned; he made contributions to Maoist ideology; as Minister of War he reorganized the army according to Mao's directives and published the famous *Little Red Book,* containing the thoughts of Mao, which became required reading throughout the army and the country; he helped facilitate and then terminate the Cultural Revolution; and finally in 1969 he was named as successor to the aging Chairman Mao. The long-term collaboration between Lin and Mao seemed to confirm the partnership between the army and the party which Mao had celebrated in his writings. But Lin was ambitious and impatient. According to subsequent accounts he organized a conspiracy to assassinate Mao, and when the plot was uncovered he attempted to fly to Russia. The plane crashed, and Lin was dead. The official story leaves many loose ends, but the undeniable conclusion is that Mao had perceived a threat to his rule and acted decisively to end it. Nonetheless, despite the death of General Lin the army remained a dominant force in the regime. To this day military officers are a privileged elite in China. The gun out of which political power grows is well-polished.

*(c) Technical expertise is secondary
to revolutionary fervor*

Mao's vision of communism extended beyond changes in ownership of property, class relations, and social institutions. He envisioned the emergence of a new type of person with distinctive attitudes, motives, and behavior. According to Mao, a genuine communist is not removed from but directly involved with the masses, listening and responding to their needs, participating in their work and culture. Mao held up an egalitarian and communal ideal in which the usual divisions between rural and urban, worker and manager, citizen and official, thinker and doer, elite and mass would be obliterated. All would join the same activities, share the same values, follow the same morality, enjoy the same art. To create such a truly communal society was the revolutionary goal toward which communists must actively strive. Mao expressed the ideal of a close and continuing interaction between leaders and masses in his doctrine of *the mass line:* "In all the practical work of our Party, all correct leadership is necessarily from the masses, to the masses."

But implementation of this revolutionary ideal encountered serious obstacles, which Mao repeatedly denounced and resisted. One obstacle was the all-too-human reluctance of individuals who have achieved some success and influence to share the ruder life of factory and farm. Like people elsewhere, many Chinese preferred the perquisites of higher office to the rigors of physical labor. The ambitious goals of reconstruction, development, and social mobilization which Mao set for China posed immense organizational challenges—affecting the army, economy, schools, communications, government, and the party itself— that could only be met by growing specialization, stratification, and bureaucratization. Well-trained, competent people would only work efficiently in an atmosphere of personal security, institutional stability, and material incentives, in short, in conventional stratified organizations. In every sector of society leaders emerged who welcomed the tendency toward specialization and stratification as the necessary conditions for effective performance of the great tasks that needed to be done. But this tendency went directly counter to Mao's revolutionary ideal of a communal society. The problem came to be expressed as the contradiction between "Red and Expert."

Expert referred to those individuals with special skills or knowledge who remained preoccupied with their work instead of turning to the masses as Mao prescribed. They were less concerned with Maoist ideology than with doing a competent job, whether as scientist, teacher, engineer, or factory manager. Mao derided these people with choice epithets such as "formalists" and "bureaucrats." The individual who came to personify the tendency toward Expert, and who became the main victim of the Cultural Revolution, was Liu Shao-Ch'i.

Liu was a long-time associate of Mao's whose special province was the organization of the Communist party. It was Liu who supervised recruitment of new members, promotion of party officials, and internal administration. He was, together with Lin Piao and Chou En-lai, one of the preeminent leaders next to Mao himself. But unlike Mao, Liu was far more a practical administrator than a revolutionary zealot. He saw the need for building stable institutions rather than instigating further radical change. This attitude, exemplified by Liu but of growing importance in all major sectors of society, posed a threat to Mao's supremacy as ideologue and perhaps also as political leader. Mao prepared the ground carefully, and when the time was ripe he struck against Liu and all the other Experts.

The "Red and Expert" issue is one aspect of a more general problem that has plagued all communist societies: the emergence of what the Yugoslav communist Milovan Djilas called "The New Class." Despite their commitment to egalitarian ideals, communist societies past the first generation of revolutionary leaders have produced a distinctive ruling class based on inequalities in status, privilege, and power. Djilas formulated his heretical view after observing developments in Yugoslavia, but it has particular significance in China, since traditional China was the home of one of the most enduring and distinctive of all ruling classes: the mandarins. The mandarins comprised an elaborate hierarchy of governing officials in the Chinese empire. They were recruited through an arduous process of formal examinations, which produced a self-conscious elite remote in education, attitudes, social position, and even language from the ordinary population. The mandarins were about as far removed from "the mass line" as any ruling class can be. Mao was well aware of this historic phenomenon in Chinese politics, and his emphasis on revolutionary fervor, which exploded in the Cultural Revolution, was ultimately directed against the reemergence in China of another such ruling class. As events since his death suggest, he failed.

(d) Objective realities are secondary to subjective forces

The most distinctive element in Maoism is its emphasis on the possibility of achieving revolutionary change through the application of character, will, and "correct thought" in a variety of historic circumstances. The voluntaristic element in Marxism—that is, the view that change is the result of intentional human actions rather than objectively-determined social conditions—had been developed by Lenin, but Mao carried it much further, as is apparent in his discussion of which groups in society could become part of the revolutionary movement. Marx's position on this central question was based on his rather clear-cut analysis of class relations and the role of particular classes in successive periods of history. Each period revealed a progressive class whose interests and actions would advance the course of social development and a reactionary class which resisted this development. Under capitalism the progressive class was the proletariat, whose actions would "redeem mankind," while the reactionary class was the bourgeoisie, whose opposition to the socialization of private capital must be overcome through revolution. With Mao the Marxist analysis of classes gives way to a far more ambiguous categorization of groups—including poor peasants, middle peasants, rich peasants, farm laborers, rural vagrants, enlightened gentry, landlords, and liberal bourgeoisie, as well as the proletariat. In the end he appealed not to a particular social class but to the "People," which could include individuals from the most diverse social origins, united by their support of communism and adherence to the Thought of Mao. In 1949 he wrote, "Who are the people? At the present stage in China, they are the working class, the peasantry, the urban petty bourgeoisie, and the national bourgeoisie" ("On the People's Democratic Dictatorship"). Mao's net was cast wide.

In the last decades of his life, when he was venerated as the "Great Helmsman" and his *Thoughts* were revered as gospel, Mao became less a communist theoretician and more a Confucian sage. His prescriptions for how to be a good communist touched upon all matters of personal conduct and positive thinking. But ideological flexibility and personal exhortation were always a central part of Mao's approach. In a youthful essay on physical education Mao remarked, quoting a line from Confucius, "When one's decision is made in his heart, then all parts of the body obey its orders. Fortune and misfortune are of our own seeking. 'I wish to be virtuous, and lo, virtue is at hand.' " Perhaps this was Mao's most enduring belief.

Despite his adaptations and modifications of Marxism-Leninism, Mao remained an orthodox Leninist in at least two basic respects: his emphasis on the role of the Communist party and on the importance of the dictatorship of the proletariat (or People's Dictatorship). For Mao, as for Lenin, the party was the central dominating organization, first in carrying out the revolution and then in governing the country. He stated just before the final communist victory: "If there is to be a revolution, there must be a revolutionary party. Without a revolutionary party, without a party built on the revolutionary theory and style of Marx, Lenin, and Stalin, it is impossible to lead the working class and the broad masses of the people to defeat imperialism and its running dogs. . . . The Communist Party of China is a party built and developed on the model of the Communist Party of the Soviet Union." In the late 1950s, under Liu Shao Ch'i's direction, the party had moved away from Mao's control, and in the Cultural Revolution of the late 1960s Mao instituted a far-reaching purge of the party that threatened to destroy the entire organizational structure. But afterward, the party was restored to its central position, and since the death of Mao many of the old figures have reappeared.

Dictatorship—People's Democratic Dictatorship—was also a firm Maoist tenet. In 1949 he wrote, "Our present task is to strengthen the people's state apparatus—mainly the people's army, the people's police, and the people's interests. . . . The people's state protects the people. Only when the people have such a state can they educate and remould themselves on a countrywide scale" ("On the People's Democratic Dictatorship"). In fact, Mao presided over the institutionalization of a remarkable totalitarian system. The goal was not only to suppress opposition but to indoctrinate the entire population into prescribed ways of thinking and acting. Not force and terror but self-criticism, public confession, brainwashing, and social pressure were the instruments of control. Despite some notable reverses, Mao pursued this goal to the end. He created in China, a country long renowned for the colorful diversity of its regions, a society marked by striking uniformity and conformity—at least outwardly.

THE COMMUNIST VICTORY

During the lean years in Yenan, safe from the conquering armies of the Kuomintang, Mao instituted the policies that became the basis for his popular support. These policies included agrarian reform, nationalist appeals to resist foreign invasion, mass recruitment to the communist cause, and intensive political training.

During these difficult years Mao displayed tactical flexibility and a lack of dogmatism. He adjusted his policies to fit the circumstances. For example, his program of agrarian reform was moderate and cautious, so as not to antagonize the peasant small-holders whose support he needed. He recruited soldiers for the Red Army and members for the Communist party wherever he could find them, even among vagrants whom Marx would have dismissed as social flotsam. He insisted that his troops treat the local population with scrupulous honesty, a sea-change from the plundering and corruption of the warlords, the Japanese, and the Kuomintang. Goods taken by the soldiers were always paid for— with script that would be redeemed after the revolution. In this way a large part of the rural populace developed at least an indirect interest in a communist victory.

To mold his diverse recruits into a unified force, Mao relied on two potent forces: appeals to nationalism, and intensive political training. While Chiang denounced the communists as his main enemy, Mao warned against the danger of foreign invasion. This nationalist appeal won wide support among people of all social classes. When the Japanese invasion came, Mao was ready to join with the Kuomintang in a war of national defense. At the same time he also made strenuous efforts to train and indoctrinate new party members as effective cadres, that is, as dedicated and disciplined party activists. When discipline and dedication seemed to wane, Mao instituted a purge of the party—a practice he came to employ periodically in maintaining control—in which officials were transferred to remote areas, denounced for ideological deviations, or expelled from the party.

With the defeat of Japan in sight, the old struggle between the Kuomintang and the communists resumed. This time the communists were in a much stronger position than before; they were in control of large territories in northern China, with experienced guerrilla armies, tested strategies and policies, and broad popular support. China was in effect divided in two, with two armies, two governments, and two contending leaders. Into this difficult situation the United States, formally allied with Chiang's Kuomintang government, sent a mediation mission headed by General George C. Marshall. The two sides came together under Marshall's auspices, but their meetings only confirmed the depth of the conflict between them. Chiang insisted that the communists recognize his position as the legitimate ruler of all China; the communists demanded participation as equal partners in a coalition government and a unified army. General Marshall left, unable to resolve the impasse. In 1946 violence again erupted in the war-weary country. Within two years the Kuomintang forces had collapsed and Chiang retreated to the island of Taiwan, to preserve there the remnant of resistance to communist rule.

Mao's decisive military victory over the Kuomintang produced a traumatic effect in the United States. Chiang was a wartime ally, he had influential friends both inside and outside the government, and he had relied on American aid and encouragement in his anticommunist struggle. Now in the United States the bitter question was raised: Who "sold out" Chiang and "lost" China? A search for the guilty began. In the harsh atmosphere of the deepening Cold War a grim hunt got under way for communists and communist sympathizers in the State Department, the media, the universities, and liberal groups. Congressional investigations were launched, loyalty programs were enacted, accusations of treason were made and repeated—all fueled by frustration over the loss of China. In retrospect it is clear that no traitors were to blame; only a thorough reorganization of the entire Kuomintang governmental structure, leadership, doctrine, and policies could have saved China from the communists. We would learn a similar lesson, at far greater cost, in Vietnam.

THE PEOPLE'S REPUBLIC

In the years between the founding of the People's Republic in 1949 and Mao's death in 1975, Chinese domestic policies underwent striking alterations and reversals, reflections of Mao's ideological commitments as well as changing economic conditions and shifts in power among the leaders. Achievements during some years were notable, but the failures at other times were no less remarkable.

The initial tasks facing the new regime were to establish a national administrative structure and restore the war-shattered economy. The object was to put China back on its feet as a first step toward the more ambitious goals of development and socialization. The approach during these years (1949–1952) was pragmatic rather than ideological. Land reform policies that had been tried in Yenan were extended throughout the country; planning agencies were established to direct economic activity on a national scale; industrial production was revived, in many cases to pre-1949 levels. At the same time, the first of the nationwide mass propaganda campaigns was introduced. These campaigns were to become a characteristic communist method for introducing new policies and mobilizing popular support behind particular programs and leaders. The ground was being readied for the next stage of industrial expansion and collectivization of agriculture.

In the first Five-Year Plan (1953–1957) China began to move in earnest toward industrialization and collectivization. The model for this effort was the Soviet Union. The Chinese adopted a number of practices familiar from Soviet experience: highly centralized economic planning, with strict controls over all phases of production, distribution, and consumption; priority on industry rather than agriculture, and on heavy industry rather than consumer goods; significant differentials in income as incentives for a maximum effort toward economic growth; collectivization of agriculture as the means to control investment, production, and marketing in the agricultural sector. The Russians provided not only an example but also substantial aid, in the form of development loans and technical assistance, for which the Chinese were obliged to pay heavily in their trade with the Soviet Union.

Results of the first Five-Year Plan were impressive. China had taken a major stride toward industrialization, and had achieved a significant rate of economic growth. But the forced pace and direction of development also led to serious problems, which became a source of controversy among the leaders. Some problems were obvious: lagging agricultural output, growing urbanization and urban unemployment, balance of payments deficits in foreign trade. Beneath these overt economic difficulties were deeper issues of the underlying social and ideological implications of Soviet-style development. Although Mao himself launched the program of rapid industrialization and collectivization, against the advice of other leaders who urged a more gradual course, he came now to oppose many of its consequences. Centralized planning reduced local initiative and popular participation in decision making; differential incentives produced inequalities of income and status; bureaucratic agencies spawned a new stratum of technicians and "experts," removed from mass attitudes and experiences; Soviet assistance led to growing dependence on Russian personnel and technology. The distinctive features of Mao's vision of a communist society were being undermined in the reality of an industrial, bureaucratic, materialistic system increasingly removed from egalitarian and communal values. In a momentous decision Mao resolved to abandon the Soviet model of development and strike out along a new and radically different path. The result was the Great Leap Forward.

The Great Leap Forward (1958–1960) involved a reversal of earlier policies and the introduction of a whole series of innovations in industry, agriculture, and administration designed to solve the problems of the first Five-Year Plan and at the same time to set China on a distinctive Maoist path. As he would do again a decade later, in the Great Proletarian Cultural Revolution, Mao intervened in the name of revolutionary ideology to impose a set of policies which were highly controversial, strongly resisted by other leaders, deeply disruptive of existing practices, and largely damaging to further development. The Great Leap was part of a cycle of alternating tendencies that characterized the entire era of Mao's rule: radicalization versus moderation, ideological fervor versus practical flexibility, mass mobilization versus elitist bureaucratization, "politics in command" versus "economics in command," Red versus Expert. In the Great Leap Forward Mao initiated many untried practices which proved unworkable as a basis for sustained economic growth, and in so doing opened the door to his own temporary political eclipse. In a few years of far-reaching and ill-conceived innovations Mao inflicted severe suffering upon the Chinese people.

Among the many innovations of the Great Leap Forward several are especially noteworthy: in overall strategy the policy of "walk on two legs," or emphasis on agriculture as well as industry; in agriculture, introduction of the Communes as a new institutional structure for organizing the entire rural sector of society; in planning, decentralized decision making with broad initiative at the local and provincial levels; in incentives, reliance on ideological motivations rather than material inequalities; in the general organization of economic activity, intensive utilization of cheap labor in place of expensive technology and expertise; and in the development of the country's resources, self-reliance rather than dependence on foreigners. An example that in some ways epitomized the entire Great Leap experiment was the backyard blast furnaces, a quixotic attempt to produce steel not in complex, technologically sophisticated, competently managed steel mills but in rudimentary furnaces tended by ordinary people in their own neighborhoods.

The backyard blast furnaces, like other ambitious but ill-considered policies of the period, were a disaster. Combined with a series of bad harvests, the Great Leap Forward resulted in a giant step backward for Chinese economic development. The years that followed were spent repairing the damage from Mao's innovations.

One other innovation deserves special mention: the Communes. Introduction of the Communes—large-scale organizations to plan and manage the whole range of economic, educational, and political activities on a communal basis within county-wide territorial units—was a triumph of ideology over practicality. Communes were viewed as a higher stage of social organization, in which all private, self-interested behavior would be replaced by community-oriented, socially-beneficial, planned activity. The Commune movement was an attempt to implement literally the ideal "from each according to his ability, to each according to his need." The peasants' ownership of small private plots was a particular target. Although private holdings amounted to only a small part of the total land in production, they accounted for most of the actual output. This survival of private enterprise was eliminated in the Communes, where all land was held in common. People were expected to work hard not for private gain but for the common good, and in return to receive from the community whatever they needed, including free food. But the Chinese peasants were not ready for this experiment in altruism: They gladly ate the free food, but avoided the hard work. It is still unclear which contributed more to the shrunken harvests of those years—the natural disasters of floods and drought, or the manmade disaster of the Communes.

The years 1961–1965 were a time of readjustment in which the failed innovations of the Great Leap were undone and the country moved toward recovery. The pendulum swung from ideology back toward practicality. Private plots were restored, and the Communes disappeared in all but name; material incentives were reintroduced, and technical expertise was rewarded; technological innovation was emphasized rather than mass mobilization, for example by intensive use of chemical fertilizers; central planning was revived, and extreme decentralization reversed. Mao's policies, and Mao himself, gave way to the more conventional approach of the Experts.

The readjustments had their effects: Despite continuing problems, such as high population growth, the economy recovered. Moreover, the recovery was achieved without Soviet aid; self-reliance had become a reality. But Mao had still to be reckoned with. Behind the scenes he began preparing the most radical of all attempts to revolutionize Chinese society: the Great Proletarian Cultural Revolution.

Although the Cultural Revolution (1966–1969) broke like a bomb-shell on the outside world, within China it was the outcome of a political struggle that had been going on for several years. Factions in both the party and the army had been jockeying for power, but not until 1966 did Mao feel strong enough to launch his new campaign. When it came the shocks were felt throughout Chinese society. While the Great Leap Forward had its principal effects in the economy, although innovations were also attempted in other areas, the Cultural Revolution aimed at transforming all major sectors: the party, army, government, factories, schools, culture, arts, family, and the role of Mao himself.

The heart of the Cultural Revolution was the politicization of all social activities, so that no place—schoolroom, laboratory, office, work-shop, concert hall, temple, library, or household—was immune from intrusion and interruption in the name of the people's revolutionary consciousness. The initial personification of this consciousness were swarms of teenage youths whom Mao unleashed as the agents of social transformation. These youths, transported from place to place by the army, converged on cities and towns, confronting teachers in their classrooms, bureaucrats in their offices, managers in their factories, writers in their studies, demanding adherence to revolutionary egalitarianism. Mao got more than he bargained for. The youths, orga-nized into brigades of Red Guards, took over government agencies, terrorized the cities and foreign legations, and started battles among themselves. Mao had to replace them, first with revolutionary commit-tees of adults and eventually with many of the same officials who had been removed in the first place. But the teenagers were reluctant to give up their newfound power. To put the genie back into the bottle Mao again called upon the army, this time to disband the Red Guards and disperse their members throughout the country.

A primary target of the Cultural Revolution were the agents of socialization—those institutions that directly shape people's values and beliefs. Some of the most radical effects occurred in the schools and universities. Conditions sometimes dreamed about by students in their fantasies became reality: no standards for admission to college, no de-manding academic requirements, no discipline in the classroom, no examinations, no failing grades. The result was a nightmare: Teachers could not teach and students would not learn. Aside from the loss to society as a whole—it is estimated that during the Cultural Revolution China lost a million potential doctors, engineers, teachers, and other professionals—one can only imagine the personal misfortune for those

97

young people who instead of embarking on promising careers were left ill-educated and ill-trained in an increasingly modernized society, victims of Mao's devotion to revolutionary egalitarianism.

Although dramatic effects were felt in education and the arts, the most politically significant changes occurred in the party itself. Mao instituted a massive purge of the party which came close to destroying the entire structure which he himself had forged over a period of 30 years. In cities and provinces long-term party officials were vehemently denounced, removed from office, and sent far from home. They were replaced by inexperienced but ardent youngsters who were often incapable of managing the party's tasks. Mao was creating an organizational vacuum in which the army would become the dominant political institution. For a time this actually happened, but with the death of General Lin Piao in 1971 the threat of a military coup was thwarted. The party was gradually rebuilt and restored to its central role.

The Cultural Revolution was Mao's last great effort to transform Chinese society according to his egalitarian and communal vision. Dismayed at the trend toward bureaucratization and elitism which seemed the unavoidable accompaniment of political stability and economic development, Mao intervened decisively, like the Chinese emperors of old, to change the course of his regime. He drastically disrupted the conventional practices and regular personnel in every sphere. The resulting chaos set back the clock in many fields, from the arts to the economy. Moreover, the process got out of hand even for Mao, and he was forced to suppress the very people he had first enlisted in his cause. Although many extreme practices of the Cultural Revolution were subsequently modified, and many individual victims returned to their former positions, its effects continued for years. Until Mao's death, China remained in the shadow of the Cultural Revolution.

CHINA AFTER MAO

Mao Tse-tung died on September 9, 1976. His death had been preceded within the year by the deaths of Chou En-lai, who was the chief executive of the government departments, and Chu Teh, founder of the Red Army who was formally chief-of-state. Thus, a triumvirate of founding fathers passed from the scene together. An era had truly ended.

The death of Mao brought into the open a struggle for power within the party that had been smoldering beneath the surface during the last years of his rule. Several factions vied for dominance: the radicals, led by Mao's widow Chiang Ch'ing, consisting of young cadres who had emerged during the Cultural Revolution dedicated to a continuation of

Mao's uncompromising revolutionary program; the moderates, of whom the most prominent was Teng Hsia-ping, consisting of established party and government officials who had been victims of the Cultural Revolution but were regaining their positions; and a "center-left" faction somewhere between the other more extreme groups, led by Hua Kuo-teng, the prime minister and newly-appointed chairman of the party. Similar factions were present also in the army, and it was to the center-left elements in the army that Premier Hua owed much of his strength. Before Mao's death the radicals seemed to gain the upper hand, deposing the moderate leader, Teng, from his government post and conducting a vigorous campaign against the "capitalist-roaders." Violence erupted as the radicals moved to secure control of the party organization. But they were not strong enough, and the tide began to turn. Teng was rehabilitated, and a new campaign was begun against the radicals themselves—the notorious "Gang of Four" (Chiang Ch'ing and three other leading radicals).

The inability of the radicals to win control of the party cleared the way for Teng to consolidate his position. The "Gang of Four" was denounced, subjected to a campaign of vilification, and finally arrested. The radical challenge had been crushed.

Relief at the demise of the "Gang of Four" swept across the country. Far more was involved than a struggle for power among ambitious individuals: The character of the regime and the direction of future policy was at issue. In the campaign against the "Gang of Four" accusations were made covering a broad range of basic domestic and foreign policies. The arrest of the Four signalled a repudiation of the main thrust of the Cultural Revolution and a reaffirmation of the more conservative approach against which the radicals had struggled. Official endorsement was again given to private plots in agriculture, strict standards in education, traditional discipline in the army, technical competence in the economy, diversity in the arts, seniority in the party, moderation in foreign policy, expansion in foreign trade—to political stability rather than ideological fervor, and to economic development rather than egalitarian idealism. In short, Mao was dead, and Expert had won out against Red.

The transformation of China since the communist revolution of 1949 has been a notable historic achievement. In presiding over this transformation Mao was driven not only by a patriotic passion to unify and develop the country but also by an overwhelming urge to remain in power and an intense zeal to remold Chinese society according to his egalitarian and communal vision. These personal and ideological motives led Mao to institute policies that impeded China's economic growth and hindered its basic institutions. His legacy is one of enormous constructive accomplishment combined with extraordinary episodes of disruption and suffering. Mao's successors have chosen a more cautious course: While his memory is still revered, his revolutionary vision has been set firmly aside.

Eurocommunism

The most important political and ideological development within the communist movements of Western Europe since World War II has been the emergence in the 1970s of Eurocommunism as a major alternative to both the Soviet and Chinese versions of Marxist doctrine and practice. While the Soviets and Chinese reaffirm their rejection of "bourgeois democracy" and vie for supremacy as the dominant communist power, the communist parties of Western Europe claim to have struck out on a path of their own. That path is Eurocommunism.

THE IDEOLOGY OF EUROCOMMUNISM

As an ideology Eurocommunism owes most to the thought of Antonio Gramsci, a founder of the Italian Communist party (in 1921) whose writings began to reach a wide audience only after World War II. Gramsci's achievements are all the more remarkable since he died young (he lived from 1891 to 1937), was always in frail health, and spent the last 11 years of his life in jail, a victim of Mussolini's fascism. Yet he accomplished a great deal: Besides organizing and leading the Italian Communist party, he founded an influential newspaper, was elected as a communist deputy to the national legislature, and following his arrest in 1926 worked diligently on the voluminous "Prison Notebooks," which contain an important reinterpretation of Marxist theory.

Several themes are stressed by Gramsci in his "Notebooks" and other writings: the need for an alliance of all political groups against the threat of fascism; the need for socialist consciousness to permeate the entire society, without which seizure of power in a dictatorship of the proletariat cannot result in true communism; and the need for a broadly-based Communist party as the agent of social change, rather than the elitist party envisioned by Lenin. As Gramsci wrote, "No mass action is possible unless the mass itself is convinced of the ends it wants to reach and the methods to be applied" ("The Southern Question," 1926). Seizure of political power from above will not create a new society; only a revolutionary transformation from below can succeed. To prepare the way for such a transformation was the abiding purpose of Gramsci's life and thought.

Like Lenin and Mao, Gramsci adapted Marxism to new social realities unforeseen by Marx himself. Just as Lenin interpreted Marxism in light of conditions in an underdeveloped country, so Gramsci interpreted Marxism in relation to the more mature capitalism of the twentieth century. Gramsci experienced personally the oppression of fascism, which arose on the ruins of Italy's parliamentary regime, so he knew at first hand that in the twentieth century there is a fate worse than capitalism. Unified opposition to fascism, and preservation of democracy as the political environment in which communism can ultimately thrive therefore became a primary objective. He also understood that support for a mature bourgeois society is not confined simply to a narrow class of property owners but extends throughout all the major institutions—including schools, churches, the mass media, and the bureaucracy. Consequently, any attempt by communists to seize power without first instigating a widespread change of attitude would encounter such resistance that the result could only be a new form of repression. Finally, he saw how politically isolated the communists are as a narrow "vanguard" party without the active support of the working class as a whole, poor farmers, and the educated leaders throughout society. To mobilize these diverse groups for a true social revolution must be another communist objective in twentieth-century bourgeois society.

From the standpoint of orthodox Leninists, these notions are another expression of that heretical "opportunism" which has beset revolutionary Marxism almost from the beginning. In his program of political action Marx called for revolution as the necessary means for transforming capitalist society into socialism. This call for revolution remains at the heart of Marxism-Leninism, which provides a justification for the violent seizure of power whenever a communist party, organized along the elitist "centralist" lines prescribed by Lenin, is able to do so. Yet even at the time they appeared, Lenin's views were challenged by other Marxists, notably by a leader of the German socialist movement, Rosa Luxemburg. If she had not been murdered by right-wing officers in Berlin in 1919, Rosa Luxemburg would undoubtedly have been a preeminent figure in the European communist movement of the interwar years. She was a tireless and influential organizer, teacher, and writer for the communist cause in three countries. At issue between Luxemburg and Lenin was not the need for revolution—both agreed that revolutionary action was necessary to destroy capitalism—but the nature and conduct of the revolution. (Other socialists, the "revisionists," went further and rejected revolution itself in favor of a gradual reform of the capitalist system through the usual practices of democratic politics.) Whereas Lenin saw revolution as the work of a disciplined elite, the vanguard of the proletariat, Luxemburg called for revolution by the masses of workers themselves. She foresaw only too clearly that without direct participation by the masses the revolution would degenerate into the depotism of the party. The ultra-centralist party demanded by Lenin she denounced as "not at all positive and creative, but essentially sterile and domineering." She liked to quote the slogan of the revolutionary Spartacus League: "The emancipation of the working class must be the work of the working class itself."

POLITICAL PROGRAM

The ideology of Eurocommunism has roots in the Gramsci-Luxemburg Marxist tradition. But the importance of Eurocommunism is political as well as ideological. Three major political issues are uppermost: the independence of West European communist parties from domination by the Soviet Union; the commitment of European communists to democratic politics; and the willingness of communists to form alliances with other prodemocratic parties of the left or center.

Independence from Soviet domination

The relationship between the Soviet Union and the communist parties of other countries has been a key issue in communist theory and practice since the Bolshevik revolution of 1917. Lenin had expected that in the wake of the Russian revolution communist uprisings would spread throughout Europe, and he believed such uprisings were necessary for the success of communism in Russia itself. In 1919 an international organization was formed in Moscow, known as the Comintern or Third International, to coordinate and encourage revolutionary activities on a worldwide basis. The failure of the German communist revolt in March of 1921 signaled the end of Lenin's hopes. But the Comintern, the international communist organization, continued to exist, though with a different purpose. Under Stalin the Comintern became the instrument for bringing the communist parties of other countries under Soviet control. Consistent with his doctrine of "socialism in one country," Stalin insisted that unswerving loyalty to the Soviet Union was the primary obligation of communists everywhere; it was at the heart of party discipline. Through the agents and directives of the Comintern Stalin kept a tight rein on communist parties around the world.

Subservience to the Kremlin proved costly for national communist parties outside Russia. Stalin's object was not to promote the best interests of other national parties but to further Soviet foreign policy. Party discipline required the parties to follow policies which often lost popular support in their own countries. The extreme instance came during the Hitler-Stalin Pact of 1939–1941. Stalin decided that Russian security could best be served by concluding a nonaggression pact with Germany. Communists throughout Europe, who had denounced and fought the Nazis in one crisis after another, suddenly were forced to accept Hitler as an ally and to aid him in waging war against their own countries. The traumatic shock of this about-face not only split the parties internally but also led to their suppression. Only after the German invasion of Russia did communists again reverse themselves and rejoin the common struggle.

Following World War II Stalin resumed his effort to control the communist parties in other countries. Although the Comintern had been dissolved in 1943 as a gesture toward Allied cooperation, it reappeared in 1947 as the Cominform, or Communist Information Bureau. The purpose was the same: to assure that communist parties throughout the world faithfully followed orders from Moscow. But the world had changed, and the Soviets soon encountered severe and successful challenges to their supremacy.

The most important of these challenges have already been described: the break between Tito and Stalin in 1948; the east German uprising of 1953; the Polish defiance of 1956; the Hungarian revolt of 1956; the Sino-Soviet split of 1964; the Czechoslovakian challenge of 1968. This last event—the Soviet-led invasion of Czechoslovakia—had especially profound repercussions among the communist parties of Western Europe. Under the leadership of Alexander Dubcek the Czechs had instituted a number of reforms which, among other things, would have lessened their dependence on the Soviet Union. The Russian response was to depose Dubcek by force. The fate of Dubcek aroused Western communists, who denounced the Soviet intervention. At an international conference of Communist party leaders held the following year in Moscow (1969), the West European representatives clearly affirmed their claim to national autonomy in direct defiance of the Brezhnev doctrine which justified Soviet intervention in Czechoslovakia or any place else where a pro-Soviet communist regime was in jeopardy.

The main advocates of Eurocommunism in the 1970s have been the communist parties of France, Italy, and Spain. In all three countries a generation of communist leaders has emerged who espouse similar views of their parties' contemporary role. These new leaders include George Marchais in France, Enrico Berlinguer in Italy, and Santiago

Carillo in Spain. The willingness of these men to criticize Soviet domestic and foreign policies, to reject Soviet ideological pronouncements, and to steer their own course as national leaders independent of Soviet directives marks a possible new stage in relations within the communist world.

Independence from the Soviet Union has special importance in relation to policies bearing on the future of the North Atlantic Treaty Organization and the European Economic Community. Both have been objects of intense Soviet opposition: NATO because it is directed against the threat of Soviet military expansion; EEC because it participates in the international economic network of the capitalist world. Preservation of these arrangements goes directly counter to the most basic Soviet objectives. Yet the Eurocommunist parties have promised support for both organizations. Rather than withdraw from NATO and EEC, they now propose to work within these institutions toward the goals they seek—through NATO toward further detente, and through EEC toward more effective control of multinational corporations.

Commitment to democracy

Besides independence from the Soviet Union, Eurocommunists also pledge to preserve democracy in their own countries and elsewhere—in victory or defeat. A comprehensive statement of their position was contained in a joint declaration issued in 1975 by the communist parties of France and Italy, subscribed to also by the Spanish party. The declaration affirmed "all the liberties which are the result of the great bourgeois democratic revolutions," including the traditional rights of speech, assembly, and religion. French communists were well aware that these rights are denied in the Soviet Union, for they specifically condemned the imprisonment of Soviet dissidents in psychiatric hospitals. In addition, the declaration supported "democratic institutions fully representative of popular sovereignty"; approved "a plurality of political parties, including the right of opposition parties to existence and activity." The final political arbiter is "the verdict of universal suffrage."

The ideological implications of these assertions were made plain at the beginning of 1977 by Marchais, the French communist leader, when he explicitly repudiated the doctrine of the dictatorship of the proletariat. "We disagree," he said, "with the Soviet Communist Party about socialist democracy." The dictatorship of the proletariat "does not correspond to the realities of our policy." "Today the word 'dictatorship' does not correspond to what we want. It has an intolerable significance, contrary to our aspirations and our theses. Even the word 'proletariat' is no longer suitable, for we want to rally the majority of salaried workers, as well as the working class." Following Marchais' recommendation, the phrase was dropped from the statutes of the French party.

Repudiation of the dictatorship of the proletariat was intended to dramatize the Eurocommunists' departure from Leninist principles. For Lenin, as for Mao, proletarian dictatorship and party centralism were key elements of communist theory and practice: They express an unswerving rejection of liberal notions of political democracy and tolerance for opposition. In abandoning a basic Leninist principle, the French communists emphasized their willingness to accept the democratic values of political competition, majority rule, and peaceful change. In light of this newly proclaimed adherence to democracy it may well be asked in what sense the Eurocommunists are communists at all. Haven't they simply revived the doctrines of revisionism—epitomized in the title of Eduard Bernstein's classic revisionist argument, "Evolutionary Socialism"—which has been the ideology of European social-democracy? The Eurocommunists say they have not. In distinguishing their revolutionary program from the reforms advocated by social democrats, Eurocommunists emphasize the scope and rapidity of the economic and social changes they seek to achieve: "The communists are revolutionaries, because they want not the modification but the transformation of society, the replacement of capitalism by socialism." The methods are moderate, but the goals are radical. A vote for Eurocommunism, then, is a vote for revolutionary change, although carried out by democratic means.

Political alliances and coalition government

The most immediate practical expression of Eurocommunism is the willingness of communists to form alliances with prodemocratic parties of the left and center and to join with these parties in coalition governments. As stated in the declaration of 1975, "broad alliances" are necessarily based on "solid and lasting cooperation between Communists and Socialists," and include also the "popular forces inspired by Christianity." In Italy these alliances were part of the "historic compromise" under which the Communist party entered the national cabinet after World War II. In 1973, Berlinguer, leader of the Italian party, called for a revival of this "historic compromise," and offered to participate with the Christian Democrats in a coalition government. The French communists concluded a formal alliance with the socialists in 1972; the two parties contested subsequent elections as a single bloc. In terms of policies, the alliance led the communists to abandon their doctrinaire insistence on socializing all forms of capital, as well as their call for violent revolution. They declared that "small and medium peasant property, handicrafts, and small and medium industrial and commercial enterprises will be assigned a specific role in the construction of socialism"; moreover, as the French party announced, "revolution is not synonymous with violence."

Alliances with the communists always arouse uneasiness, for there are precedents, and they are not reassuring. The practice of collaborating with nonrevolutionary groups in order to infiltrate and subvert them has been a longstanding communist tactic. The notion that communists would join a political alliance on the basis of genuine equality, without attempting to dominate the alliance for their own purposes, may seem farfetched to anyone with a recollection of history. In fact, as soon as the French communists recognized that the main beneficiaries of the Alliance were not themselves but their socialist partners, who might now be in a position to win the presidency, they began to reconsider the entire arrangement. By late 1977 they decided to sever the electoral tie in order to fight the presidential elections (March 1978) on their own, especially in opposition to the socialists. Instead of a unified bloc, the Left was again split by the longstanding antagonism between communists and socialists, which allowed the more conservative parties to win.

The tactic of joining coalition governments also has a history: In the past it was known as both the United Front and the Popular Front. The United Front was proposed by Lenin following the Bolshevik Revolution as a way of splitting socialist parties under the guise of supporting their demands; the Popular Front was promoted by Stalin during the 1930s as a way of combating the threat of Hitler, until Soviet interests changed and the Front was undermined. Participation by the Spanish communists in the pro-Republican Popular Front did not stop them from a campaign to liquidate their supposed allies. Under the circumstances, some skepticism about communist offers of "solid and lasting cooperation" is understandable.

Whatever qualms their new-found partners may feel, the posture of accommodation has brought clear political gains to the communist parties of France and Italy. Since their shift toward independence, democracy, and collaboration, both parties have enjoyed a marked growth in membership: In 1975 the Italian party added 150,000 new members, for a total of nearly 1,800,000; in the same year the French party admitted 93,000, for a total of about 500,000. The Italian party also gained strength at the polls: In regional elections during 1975 it received 33 percent of the vote. Granted their willingness to join coalitions at the national level—an attitude that has yet to be tested in practice—these electoral results mean that it will become increasingly difficult to exclude the Italian communists from government office.

FUTURE OF EUROCOMMUNISM

The claims of Eurocommunism raise thorny questions in both the East and West. One nagging question is obvious enough: Can a leopard change its spots? Eurocommunists insist they have embarked on a historic new course. They explain the historic departure as a response to the novel conditions of contemporary Western societies. In such societies, characterized by deep-rooted democratic traditions, it is essential for the Communist party to win widespread popular support in order to achieve its goals. Principles and practices that may have worked in Russia or China are not applicable to economically advanced, politically democratic countries. Thus a new road must be tried. As disciples of Marx, Eurocommunists claim they have discarded outmoded precepts by adapting their ideas and actions to existing realities, meaning that the experience of other times and countries may be found wanting under new conditions. Moreover, the record of the Soviet Union in both its domestic and foreign policies has produced disillusionment with Moscow as the leader of the communist world. Repression at home and military intervention in other communist countries have discredited Soviet claims to predominance. For these reasons, Eurocommunists argue, they have abandoned the Leninist and Maoist methods of conspiracy, violence, and dictatorship in order to compete within the terms of democratic politics. They have also declared their independence from both Moscow and Peking in order to follow the path appropriate to their own nations.

These declarations have been taken seriously by communists and anticommunists alike. But the question remains whether they can be accepted at full face value. In fact, the political situation of each of the three parties—the French, Italian, and Spanish—is quite different, and the actions of each have varied accordingly. The Spanish party is much smaller than the others, and its main task is to regain the confidence of Spanish workers who remember its disruptive tactics during the Republic of the 1930s. In addition, Spanish communists have watched closely the fate of their comrades in neighboring Portugal. When the Salazaar dictatorship came to an end, the Portuguese party followed a hard Leninist line, aiding an abortive coup against the moderate transitional government; as a result the communists were politically discredited, to the benefit of their socialist rivals who undertook to rule the country. The lesson has not been lost on communist leaders in Spain. In the immediate future their best chance to bolster the party is to follow a course of moderation.

The Italian party is the largest of the three, and the opportunity to gain power by democratic means is almost within grasp. Moreover, communists have already won elections in a number of cities and provinces. With a national victory in sight, the party is not likely to jeopardize its chances by adopting an intransigent position. As evidence that their democratic professions are genuine, Italian communists point to the cities and provinces in which they have governed without suppressing constitutional rights or provoking a counterrevolution. But these examples do not settle the question of whether they would remain equally scrupulous if a communist were commanding the national police or the armed forces. Nor do they settle whether communists would safeguard the military plans of NATO or even their own government if they were members of the national cabinet.

The French party has been in the most uncertain situation, and its actions are least predictable. The party expected greater electoral benefits from an alliance with the socialists, but its share of the national vote has continued to hover around 20 percent. Instead, the socialists now have hopes of winning a presidential election, and no prospect is less appealing to the communists than a socialist president who would be able to draw away still more of their support. For this reason, the path of moderation and collaboration holds least attraction for the French party. Also, in the past the French party has been closely tied to Moscow, and this longstanding tie is difficult to break.

If Eurocommunism causes unease in the West, it is suspect also in Moscow. To the Soviets the assertion of independence can become an unwelcome challenge. The doctrines of Eurocommunism could help to undercut Russian control over its satellites, as well as the entire Moscow-inspired system of repression practiced in those regimes. If the Western parties succeed in defying Moscow's authority, the parties of Eastern Europe may be encouraged to do the same. Nonetheless, the Kremlin can tolerate a good deal of ideological deviation and even criticism from other communist parties, so long as the vital interests of the Soviet Union are not at stake. So far nothing the French party—nor, for that matter, the Italian and Spanish parties—has done threatens those interests.

The acid test of Eurocommunism must lie in what the communist parties of Western Europe do, rather than what they say. It is too soon to tell how they would act if they came to national power, although in Italy the occasion may soon be at hand. But even now there is one thing the Western parties have not done, despite their expressed belief in democracy and political competition: They have not given up the disciplined hierarchical structure of their own party organization. Since Lenin, this structure has been fashioned for conspiracy and centralized control rather than political pluralism and internal opposition. It would be persuasive evidence that Eurocommunism does indeed mark a historic new departure if the communist parties of Western Europe were ready to abandon the distinctive organizational structure which Lenin prescribed for them as the vanguard of the proletariat in an international revolutionary movement.

For Further Reading

ALLWORTH, EDWARD, ed., *Soviet Nationality Problems*. New York: Columbia University Press, 1971.

AMALRIK, ANDREI, *Will the Soviet Union Survive Until 1984?* New York: Harper & Row, Publishers, Inc., 1970.

ARMSTRONG, JOHN A., *Ideology, Politics and Government in the Soviet Union* (3rd ed.). New York: Praeger Publishers, Inc., 1974.

CHALIDZE, VALERY, *To Defend These Rights: Human Rights and the Soviet Union*. New York: Random House, Inc., 1974.

CLARK, MARTIN, *Antonio Gramsci and the Revolution that Failed*. New Haven: Yale University Press, 1977.

DEBRAY, REGIS, *Revolution in the Revolution?* New York: Grove Press, Inc., 1967.

DJILAS, MILOVAN, *The Unperfect Society: Beyond the New Class*. New York: Harcourt Brace Jovanovich, Inc., 1969.

DUBEY, VINOD, *Yugoslavia: Development with Decentralization*. Baltimore: The Johns Hopkins University Press, 1975.

EBENSTEIN, WILLIAM, "Revolutionary Communism," in *Great Political Thinkers* (4th ed.), Chap. 23. New York: Holt, Rinehart and Winston, 1969.

GRAHAM, LOREN R., *Science and Philosophy in the Soviet Union*. New York: Alfred A. Knopf, Inc., 1972.

GRAMSCI, ANTONIO, *The Modern Prince and Other Writings*. New York: International Publishers, 1972.

HAMMOND, PAUL T., ed., *The Anatomy of Communist Takeovers*. New Haven: Yale University Press, 1975.

KOREY, WILLIAM, *The Soviet Cage: Anti-Semitism in Russia*. New York: The Viking Press, 1973.

LEYS, SIMON, *Chinese Shadows*. New York: The Viking Press, 1977.

LUXEMBURG, ROSA, *Selected Political Writings*. New York: Monthly Review Press, 1971.

MANDEL, WILLIAM, *Soviet Women*. Garden City, N.Y.: Anchor Books, 1975.

MEDVEDEV, ROY, *On Socialist Democracy*. New York: Alfred A. Knopf, Inc., 1975.

MORTON, HENRY W., and RUDOLPH L. TOKES, eds., *Soviet Politics and Society in the 1970s.* New York: The Free Press, 1974.

PARKIN, FRANK, *Class Inequality and Political Order: Social Stratification in Capitalist and Communist Societies.* New York: Praeger Publishers, Inc., 1971.

PERKINS, DWIGHT H., ed., *China's Modern Economy in Historical Perspective.* Stanford: Stanford University Press, 1975.

RUBENSTEIN, ALVIN Z., ed., *Soviet and Chinese Influence in the Third World.* New York: Praeger Publishers, Inc., 1975.

RUSH, MYRON, *How Communist States Change Their Rulers.* Ithaca: Cornell University Press, 1974.

SCAMMELL, MICHAEL, ed., *Russia's Other Writers: Selections from Samizdat Literature.* New York: Praeger Publishers, Inc., 1971.

SCHRAM, STUART R., *The Political Thought of Mao Tse-tung* (Rev. ed.). New York: Praeger Publishers, Inc., 1969.

SHAFFER, HARRY G., ed., *Soviet Agriculture.* New York: Praeger Publishers, Inc., 1977.

SKILLING, H. GORDON, and FRANKLYN GRIFFITHS, eds., *Interest Groups in Soviet Politics.* Princeton: Princeton University Press, 1971.

SMITH, HEDRICK, *The Russians.* New York: Quadrangle Books, 1976.

SOLZHENITSYN, ALEKSANDR I., *The Gulag Archipelago.* New York: Harper & Row, Publishers, Inc., 1973.

TOWNSEND, JAMES R., *Politics in China.* Boston: Little, Brown & Company, 1974.

ZUKIN, SHARON, *Beyond Marx and Tito: Theory and Practice of Yugoslav Socialism.* New York: Cambridge University Press, 1975.

2
Fascism

Background of Fascism

Communism was the first major twentieth-century revolutionary, totalitarian revolt against the liberal way of life; *fascism* was the second. Stripped to its essentials, fascism is the totalitarian organization of government and society by a single-party dictatorship, intensely nationalist, racist, militarist, and imperialist. In Europe, Italy was the first to go fascist in 1922, and Germany followed in 1933. In Asia, Japan became fascist in the 1930s, gradually evolving totalitarian institutions out of its own native heritage. In the western hemisphere, a semiconstitutional government of a landed oligarchy was destroyed in Argentina in 1943 in a revolt of dissatisfied officers, and a fascist dictatorship was subsequently built up under the leadership of Colonel (later General) Perón, lasting until its overthrow in 1955.

Clearly, then, whereas communism is typically linked with poor

111

and underdeveloped nations (Russia in Europe, China in Asia), fascism is the form of totalitarianism that typically grows in comparatively wealthier and technologically more advanced nations (Germany in Europe, Japan in Asia). In the Americas, Guatemala, one of the poorest and most backward of nations, for years encouraged the growth of communism until the procommunist regime of President Arbenz was overthrown in June 1954 with American military aid. Cuba, less poor than Guatemala, is a more recent example of communism in the Americas. Significantly, Castro fought his rebellion under the banner of democracy, not of communism, and publicly turned to Marxism-Leninism only after his victory. Fascism, on the other hand, saw its most intense development in Argentina, the wealthiest of the 20 Latin American republics.

Whereas communism is very largely the product of predemocratic and preindustrial societies, fascism is *postdemocratic* and *postindustrial:* Fascism is unlikely to seize power in countries with no democratic experience at all. In such societies, dictatorship may be based on the army, the bureaucracy, or the personal prestige of the dictator, but it will lack the element of mass enthusiasm and *mass support* (not necessarily majority support) characteristic of fascism. Moreover, although no fascist system is apt to arise in a country without some democratic experience (as in Germany or Japan), there is not much likelihood of fascist success in countries that have experienced democracy over a long period.

Paradoxically, experience has proved that, in general, the more violent and terroristic fascist movements are, the more popular support they tend to have. Thus fascism in Germany was both the most brutal and the most popular political movement; in Italy fascism was less brutal and popular. Such fascist dictatorships based on mass support are not to be confused with traditional dictatorships such as existed in Europe in several countries during the 1930s, particularly in the Balkans and Eastern Europe.

In Latin America also there are numerous dictatorships, but they are not fascist (with the exception of Argentina from 1943 to 1955), for usually they typically rest on the personal magic or force of one man, typically a general. Relying as he must on the goodwill of his army, the Latin American dictator has no need for—and rarely enjoys—the mass support that characterizes fascism. Popular political movements hardly enter the picture.

Another condition essential to the growth of fascism is some degree of industrial development. There are at least two principal points of contact between fascism and relatively advanced industrialization. First, fascist terror and propaganda require a good deal of technological organization and know-how. Second, as a system of *permanent mobili- zation for war,* fascism cannot hope to succeed without considerable industrial skills and resources.

It may be argued that the connection between fascism and modern industry goes even deeper. Every industrial society brings about social and economic tensions. Such tensions can be dealt with in one of two ways: the liberal way or the coercive way. A liberal society recognizes the variety of economic interests and their necessary conflict (such as between labor and management, agriculture and industry, skilled and unskilled workers) and seeks to reconcile such conflicts by the experi- mental method of peaceful, gradual adjustment. A fascist state either denies that there are divergent social interests (abhorring as it does the notion of variety, especially in the form of departures from state- imposed uniformity) or, if it half-heartedly concedes the existence of divergent social interests, resolves such differences by force.

The difference between communism and fascism on this point may be briefly (and with some oversimplification) formulated in this way: Communism is the coercive way of *industrializing an underdeveloped society;* fascism is the coercive method of *solving conflicts within an industrially more advanced society.*

In its social background, fascism has appealed to two groups particu- larly: first, a numerically small group of *industrialists* and *landowners* who are willing to finance fascist movements in the hope of getting rid of free labor unions. Industrialists are not, as a class, any more fascist- minded than other social groups; in countries with strong liberal and democratic traditions, for example, industrialists have neither more nor less faith than other people in the democratic process. But where democracy has been weak, as it was in Germany, Italy, and Japan, it took only a few wealthy industrialists and landowners to supply fascist movements with ample funds.

Where the pressure of public opinion is strongly democratic and liberal, individual industrialists who are inclined toward fascism find that the supporting of fascist groups is bad business; but where demo- cratic traditions are weak, leaders of big business, like Thyssen and Krupp in Germany or the Mitsui trust in Japan, find it possible to side openly with the cause of fascism.

The second main source of fascist support—and numerically by far the most important—comes from the lower middle classes, mostly in the salaried group. Many persons in this class dread the prospect of joining (or rejoining) the proletariat and look to fascism for the salvation of their status and prestige. The salaried employee feels jealous of big business, into whose higher echelons he would like to rise, and fearful of labor, into whose proletarian world he would hate to descend. Fascism very cleverly utilizes these jealousies and fears of the salariat by propagandizing simultaneously against big business and big labor. Although such propaganda is neither logically nor politically consistent, its very inconsistency both reflects and appeals to the confusion of the salaried class, uncertain as that class is where to turn politically.

In the United States, anxiety over preserving one's threatened status has been one of the main psychological forces exploited by the radical right (John Birch Society, Minute Men) and by fascist groups. This status anxiety has been centered, above all, on the rising power of organized labor, which is perceived as a threat to the existing status quo. In addition, American fascist and semifascist propaganda has focused on white fears of the rising status of blacks. As in other countries, racial hostility is stronger in psychologically more insecure lower-middle-class groups than in the better-educated and more affluent middle and upper classes.

Paradoxically, organized labor frequently contributes to this uncertainty and demoralization of the salariat without meaning to do so. For psychological reasons, white-color workers are generally unwilling to organize into unions. As a result, the incomes of blue-collar workers, particularly those organized in unions, have tended to improve much faster than the incomes of salaried employees. As the gap between the economic status of workers and that of salaried persons widens, the latter become more and more resentful of losing what they consider their rightful place in society and may turn to fascism, which promises to keep unions under control. The leaders of organized labor may point out that the weak economic position of salaried persons is their own fault and that such persons are in error in refusing to organize in order to bring pressure upon their employers—an argument that, though valid logically, has never been psychologically persuasive. In times of prosperity the divergence between labor and the salaried class may not be too upsetting politically, but in times of crisis and depression the smallest class antagonisms may turn into political dynamite.

Another important social group that has shown itself particularly vulnerable to fascist propaganda is the military. Even in a strong and well-established democracy, professional military men tend to overestimate the virtues of discipline and unity; where democracy is weak, this professional bias of the military becomes a political menace. Thus, in the early stages of nazism in Germany, the military class of that nation either openly supported Hitler or maintained an attitude of benevolent neutrality. The top military leaders of Germany knew that a high proportion of Nazi bosses were criminals and unscrupulous psychopaths, yet they supported the Nazi movement as a step toward the militarization of the German people. In Italy too, fascism in its early stages received considerable support from army circles, and in Japan fascism developed with the active and enthusiastic support of the army, which had every reason to be the main pillar of a regime committed to imperialist expansion. In Argentina, semiconstitutional government was overthrown in 1943 in a revolt of the "younger officers" under Perón, who set up his own brand of fascism—*peronismo,* named after him.

Yet it should be pointed out that the military often play a leading part in getting rid of fascist and other kinds of dictatorial government. Perón himself learned this lesson in 1955, and the same thing has happened to several other Latin American dictators since the end of World War II. Once fascism is established, people often look to the army as one of the last remaining bulwarks of decency and legality. Therefore, fascism indulges in periodic purges of the armed forces, because fascist leaders realize that the army is one of the few institutions left that enjoy genuine popular respect.

Although fascism is not a direct or necessary result of economic depression, as Marxist-communist theory suggests, there is a relation between the two. In times of depression, fear and frustration undermine faith in the democratic process, and where faith in rational methods weakens, fascism is the potential gainer. The small businessman blames big business for his troubles; big business blames the unreasonableness of the labor unions; labor feels that the only way out is to soak the rich; the farmers feel that they are not getting enough for farm products and that the prices they pay for manufactured goods are too high; and—worst of all—there is a large mass of unemployed people.

What democratic nations have failed to understand sufficiently is that the worst feature of unemployment is not economic suffering (which can be mitigated by adequate relief), but the feeling of being useless, unwanted, outside the productive ranks of society. It is among these spiritually homeless that fascism makes serious inroads during a depression: By putting an unemployed person into a uniform, a fascist movement makes him feel that he "belongs," and by telling him that he is a member of a superior race or nation, such a movement restores some of his self-respect.

The sense of not belonging is, in a way, characteristic of life in modern industrial society in general. Industrialization and urbanization have debunked and frequently destroyed traditional values usually without providing adequate substitute values in their place. The disorientation and confusion resulting from these effects of industrialization provide the social and psychological background of fascism and its attempt to restore the old, preindustrial way of life in a modern nation.

Thus the Marxist interpretation of fascism in terms of class (identifying fascism with capitalism in decay) is not borne out by the facts.

Fascism cuts across all social groups; wealthy industrialists and land-owners support it for one reason, the lower middle classes for another, and some blue-collar workers for still another. Finally, there are the many nationalists and chauvinists in every country who prove themselves vulnerable to promises of conquest and empire. In terms of explicit programs, fascist movements must make the most contradictory promises in order to satisfy all their adherents; such contradictions are a main weakness of fascism. Yet in terms of implicit psychological background, fascism looks within all social groups for the great common denominators: *frustration, resentment,* and *insecurity.* These psychological attitudes can easily be turned into hatred and aggression, against both internal and external "enemies."

Because these social and psychological attitudes are not the monopoly of any one social class, fascism manages to appeal to large masses of people in some countries. When Adolf Hitler joined the Nazi party in 1919, he was Member No. 7. Yet within fourteen years nazism became the greatest mass movement in German history, including in its ranks members of all groups of German society, from hobos to members of the imperial family and the royal houses of the German states. By 1932, the Nazi vote had mounted to 14 million, and in March 1933, 17 million Germans (almost half the total vote) voted for Nazi candidates; several more millions voted for nationalist and militarist parties that were Nazi in all but name. It is obvious that 17 million voters cannot consist exclusively of wealthy bankers and industrialists and that only a party with national, rather than class, appeal can obtain such large votes. In no other country has fascism ever been as widely popular as in Germany, but there has been no fascist regime anywhere without considerable public support.

PSYCHOLOGICAL ROOTS OF TOTALITARIANISM

The clue to understanding fascist tendencies in countries like Germany and Japan, lies in broad social forces and traditions. In those countries, the authoritarian tradition has been predominant for centuries, whereas the philosophy of democracy is a frail newcomer. As a result, a German or Japanese with fascist tendencies is no outcast and may be considered perfectly well adjusted to his society. Even when his society explicitly condemns fascism, much in the implicit habits and customs of German and Japanese life tends toward the authoritarian way of life, and from authoritarianism to fascism is only a step. In democratic societies, on the other hand, the appeal of fascism can be more fruitfully judged from the angle of individual psychology.

Traditional analysis of political dictatorship has been centered on the motivations of dictatorial leaders, driven by lust for power and sadistic cravings for domination. The followers and subjects of a dictatorship are viewed exclusively as "victims" who just happen to fall into the misfortune of oppressive rule. Every insurance company knows that some persons are more accident-prone than others, and every policeman knows that some persons are more likely to attract criminals than others.

Similarly, it is not too farfetched to suggest that some people and some nations are more "dictatorship-prone" than others. Plato's psychological insight led him to suggest in his *Republic* that constitutions grow not "from stone to stone," but "from those characters of the men in the cities which preponderate and draw the rest of the city after them." The very existence of an authoritarian mass movement like fascism depends on the desire of many persons to submit and obey.

Rational democrats may not understand why anyone would prefer to obey rather than take the responsibility of making decisions for himself; they take it for granted that citizens should make their own decisions rather than have their actions dictated by others. But this democratic attitude overlooks the comforts of irresponsibility to many persons. Children love the feeling of being sheltered and secure behind the benevolent power and authority of their parents. The mark of a mature adult is the willingness and capacity to stand on one's own feet, to take responsibility and to be independent of others. Yet relatively few persons ever attain this sort of maturity; the process of growing up is painful, and many individuals fear a cold competitive world where they must struggle for themselves without the care and omnipotence of parental love and security. In human beings there is a latent tendency toward dependence based on the parent-child relationship, although some people manage to achieve a more self-reliant adulthood than others. The totalitarian system, whether communist or fascist, appeals to people who constantly seek out the parent-child relationship, who grasp for security through dependence.

What are some of the traits that characterize an authoritarian personality, particularly the personality attracted to the fascist type of authoritarianism? A tendency to conform compulsively to orthodox ideals and practices; emotional rigidity and limited imagination; excessive concern with problems of status and strength; strong loyalty to one's own group coupled with vehement dislike of outsiders; and stress on discipline and obedience rather than freedom and spontaneity in human relations (education, sex, family, religion, industry, government). The "herd-minded" (or ethnocentric) element in the fascist personality is perhaps the single most important one, although no one element in itself conclusively defines a personality as authoritarian.

The key role of the family in the formation of basic attitudes seems to be brought out by all clinical and theoretical studies; but the family is not, after all, an isolated and independent agent. Rather, it reflects the predominant goals and values of the society, and constitutes to the child the cultural and psychological representative of society at large.

No person is ever completely authoritarian or completely democratic, just as no human being is ever an utter devil or a perfect angel. In each case it is a question of quantity and degree, though differences of quantity eventually become differences of quality. Although there has been no major fascist mass movement in the United States so far, it is a matter of record that some Americans looked upon German and Italian fascism in the 1930s as the "wave of the future" (as it was called in a book of that title) and that others sympathized with Argentine fascism in the 1940s and 1950s.

Dependence and submission in a totalitarian society—fascist or communist—give a person the security for which he or she hungers but deny individual self-expression and self-assertion, the needs for which are as deeply embedded in human nature as is the desire for security. Thus denied, these drives turn into repressed hostility and aggression, for the expression of which fascism provides two channels: one for the ruling class, and one for the ruled. Within the apparatus of a dictatorial party and government, there is a typical pattern: crouching before the superior above, pressing down on the subordinate below. Only the leader need not crouch before anyone—he only presses down. Below the top leader—"Big Brother," as Orwell called him in *1984,* the classic fictional portrait of totalitarianism—each member of the party and government hierarchy must kowtow to someone above him, although in return he may tread on those below him.

Persons outside the ruling class, however, have no one to command; they can only obey. How can they express their hostility and aggressiveness? Since the vast majority of people in a totalitarian state form the group of those who can only take orders but not issue them, this is a serious problem for every dictatorship. Although the dictator claims officially that he is universally beloved, he knows that there is much repressed hatred and hostility directed (or capable of being directed) toward him and his regime.

The solution of totalitarian dictatorships is to direct this latent hostility of the people against *real or imaginary enemies.* For the communist, the enemy may be the bourgeoisie, the Trotskyites, Titoites, or

Wall Street. Hitler first chose the Jews as the target of German aggression, and six million Jews perished in the gas chambers as a result. Later, new enemies took the place of the Jews: Britain, the United States, Churchill, Roosevelt, Bolshevism, the churches. When the end was close, Hitler and his cohorts unleashed their vengeance on the Germans themselves by refusing to negotiate a surrender; if they had to go down, the German people had to be destroyed with them. In a more recent fascist regime, Peronist Argentina, American imperialism and international finance were the chief targets of fascist hate propaganda.

To those who cannot be masters of their own lives, fascism promises mastery over others; and if fascism cannot deliver the triumphs it promises, the hatred of the people may turn against their leaders, as it did against Mussolini, who was tried before a committee of partisans in northern Italy in April 1945, executed, and then publicly hung from a lamp post in Milan. Having taught his people violence and hatred, he reaped himself what he had sown.

The psychological interpretation of totalitarianism—fascist or communist—is of particular value where the prevailing cultural pattern is not authoritarian, that is, where it takes some personal deviance to break with the democratic pattern of the environment. Thus, in societies like Britain or the United States, the psychological analysis of people who have embraced communism or fascism is of great value because from such an analysis emerges a definite pattern of personality factors that is typical of many American fascists or communists.

It would be futile to explain the strength of fascism in Germany or Japan, or of communism in contemporary China or Italy, by means of personal psychology however. It could be argued that an American or an Englishman who embraces communism or fascism is not well adjusted, comes from a broken home, or has had an unhappy childhood, but the same can hardly be said of 17 million Germans who voted for Hitler in 1933 or of the many millions of Frenchmen and Italians who have persistently voted communist since the end of World War II. Where totalitarianism assumes the proportions of a mass movement, the main avenue of analysis must be that of the great social, economic, and cultural forces and traditions of a nation.

Whereas the cure for an American fascist or communist may be found on the psychoanalyst's couch, the cure for millions of Italians who vote communist is more take-home pay every Saturday and a more decent life all around. Similarly, the origins of fascist totalitarianism in Germany, Japan, and Argentina lie deeper in the collective lives of those nations than can be revealed from a study of individual personalities.

Fascist Theory and Practice

Although fascism, like communism, is a movement that exists everywhere, it has no such authoritative statement of principles as communism has; moreover, no one country, at present, is directing a fascist world conspiracy. During the Nazi regime (1933–1945), Germany was the most powerful fascist state in existence, and world fascism was very largely directed, financed, and inspired by German brains and money. Since the defeat of the fascist Axis powers (Germany, Japan, and Italy) in World War II there has been no major fascist state; Argentina never possessed anything like the worldwide influence that Nazi Germany had until 1945.

The absence of a universally recognized, authoritative statement of fascist principles is not total. Hitler has left in *Mein Kampf* (1925–1927) a trustworthy guide to his thought, and Mussolini's *Doctrine of Fascism* (1932), a moderate statement of fascist principles, expresses the Italian brand of fascism. The latter has served as a model for most other fascist movements in the world because it is much broader in outlook; nazism, a specifically German brand of fascism, has proved less suitable for export.

Although there is no fascist manifesto with undisputed authority among fascists, it is not too difficult to state the basic elements of the fascist outlook:

1. Distrust of reason
2. Denial of basic human equality
3. Code of behavior based on lies and violence
4. Government by an elite group
5. Totalitarianism
6. Racism and imperialism
7. Opposition to international law and order

1. *Distrust of reason* is perhaps the most significant trait of fascism. The rational tradition of the West stems from ancient Greece and is a basic component of the West's characteristic culture and outlook. Fascism rejects this tradition of Western civilization and is frankly *antirationalist*, distrusting reason in human affairs and stressing instead the irrational, the sentimental, and the uncontrollable elements in man. Psychologically, fascism is *fanatical* rather than reflective, *dogmatic* rather than openminded; as a result each fascist regime has its taboo

issues such as race, or the empire, or the leader, the nature of which demands that it be accepted on faith alone and never critically discussed. During the fascist regime in Italy (1922–1945), Mussolini's picture was shown in every classroom in the country over the caption, "Mussolini is always right."

The communist states have the taboo issue of Marxism-Leninism, a set of final truths that must not be questioned. In addition, there are the more passing taboo subjects as defined by the top party leaders in the Soviet Union, China, Yugoslavia, and other communist states.

As a matter of basic principle, democracy recognizes no taboo issue: There is no subject that cannot be questioned or challenged, not even the validity of democracy itself. In practice, of course, democracies do not always live up to that ideal. Thus, it was argued by some in the 1950s that in the United States the question of the validity of democracy was on its way to becoming a taboo issue, especially in light of the Supreme Court's 1951 decision upholding the constitutionality of the Smith Act of 1940 under which the advocacy of the duty, desirability, necessity, or propriety of revolution is a criminal offense.

The individual, too, may have taboo issues, dark corners in his heart or mind that must not be pulled out and subjected to rational examination. The mentally healthy individual has few or (ideally) no taboo issues because she is able to face reality as it is and does not insist on living in a dream world in defiance of reality. Psychologically, the existence of taboo issues in the individual or in a group, party, or nation is due to a sense of insecurity or guilt or both.

Under conditions of stress and strain, an individual as well as a group may take refuge in the temporary shelter of a taboo and postpone facing reality, even if it is impossible to shut it out forever. Since totalitarian regimes operate in a permanent state of high tension and crisis, the taboo is part and parcel of their normal environment. Democracies succumb to the temptation of the taboo and its false security only in periods of exceptional strain; it is significant that the Supreme Court's decision on the Smith Act took place in 1951, at the height of the Korean War. In the 1960s, a more tolerant and reflective mood prevailed, and the Supreme Court progressively eliminated restrictions on the constitutionality of revolutionary propaganda and organizations.

2. The *denial of basic human equality* is a common denominator of fascist movements and states. True enough, democratic societies do not always live up to the ideal of human equality, but at least they accept equality as the long-term goal of public policy. By contrast, fascist societies not only accept the fact of human inequality but go further and affirm inequality as an ideal.

The concept of human equality goes back to the three roots of

Western civilization. The Jewish idea of one God led to the idea of one mankind, since all men, as children of God, are brothers among themselves. The Christian notion of the inalienability and indestructibility of the human soul led to the ideal of the basic *moral* equality of all men. The Greek-Stoic concept of reason posited the oneness of mankind on the basis of reason as the most truly human bond that all men have in common.

Fascism rejects this Jewish-Christian-Greek concept of equality and opposes to it the concept of inequality, which can be spelled out most simply in the contrast of superiority and inferiority. Thus, in the fascist code, men are superior to women, soldiers to civilians, party members to nonparty members, one's own nation to others, the strong to the weak, and (perhaps most important in the fascist outlook) the victors in war to the vanquished. The chief criteria of equality in the Western tradition are man's mind and soul, whereas the fascist affirmation of inequality is based ultimately on strength.

3. The fascist code of behavior stresses *violence and lies* in all human relations, within and between nations. In democratic type governments, politics is the mechanism through which social conflicts of interest are adjusted peacefully. By contrast, the fascist view is that politics is characterized by the friend-enemy relation. Politics begins and ends, in this fascist way of thinking, with the possibility of an enemy —and his *total annihilation.* The democratic antithesis is the *opponent,* and in democratic nations the opponent of today is considered the potential government of tomorrow. (The party out of power in the British Parliament is officially called "Her Majesty's Loyal Opposition," and the leader of the Opposition receives a special salary to do his job well.) The fascist knows only enemies, not opponents, and since enemies represent evil incarnate, total annihilation is the only solution. This doctrine applies to domestic as well as to foreign enemies; thus, the Nazis first set up concentration camps and gas chambers for German citizens and later used them for non-Germans.

Contrary to common belief, concentration camps and slave labor camps, as under Hitler and Stalin, are not incidental phenomena in totalitarian systems but are at their very core. It is by means of concentration and slave labor camps that totalitarian regimes seek to destroy the legal and moral person in man and to deprive him of the last residue of individuality. The technique of brainwashing deliberately seeks to warp a person's mind to the point where he will publicly confess to crimes he did not commit and perhaps could not have committed. After a period of brainwashing, the victim no longer has a mind of his own; he merely plays back, like a recording tape, what is expected of him.

By institutionalizing organized mass murder in concentration and slave labor camps, totalitarian regimes demonstrate to the entire population what is in store for anyone in disfavor with those in power, and at the same time they provide the shock troops of the regime with a peacetime outlet for savagery and fanaticism. Immediate death is often considered too humane a penalty by such regimes; moreover, the slow death of concentration or slave labor camps has greater demonstration value than the clean, old-fashioned method of the execution squad or the gallows.

4. *Government by an elite group* is a principle that fascists everywhere frankly oppose to the "democratic fallacy" that people are capable of governing themselves. The concept that only a small minority of the population, qualified by birth, education, or social standing, is capable of understanding what is best for the whole community, and of putting it into practice, is not an invention of twentieth-century fascism. Plato, one of the first Western political philosophers, strongly believed that only one class, the "philosopher-kings," are fit to rule society. The contrary belief, that the people as a whole are capable of self-rule, is of relatively recent origin and has worked successfully only in limited areas of the globe.

Although the fascist idea of government by a self-appointed elite is undemocratic (a fascist government usually shoots its way into power), such a government does not always lack popular approval. Strange as it may seem to the democrat, people frequently have approved of autocratic governments throughout history. Approval alone, however, is not evidence of democracy. What makes a government democratic is that it always depends on popular consent given frequently in free elections. In fascist regimes, even when the government enjoys popular approval, it is carried on independently of popular consent, without free elections, a free press, or a freely functioning opposition.

The fascist *leadership principle* expresses the extreme form of the elite concept. It reflects the irrational emphasis of fascist politics; the leader is said to be infallible, endowed with mystical gifts and insights. In a conflict between popular opinion and the fascist leader, the will of the leader prevails; he represents the public interest, the way all people would think if they knew what was best for the whole community (Rousseau's "General Will"), whereas the people express only individual whims and desires not necessarily in harmony with public good (Rousseau's "Will of All").

The emphasis on leadership is not compatible, in the long run, with the fascist enforcement of orthodoxy and conformity. Hitler, Mussolini, and Perón grew up in nonfascist societies with considerable free competition. So far it has been impossible to appraise the leadership qualities of a generation born and bred under fascism. The German, Italian, and Argentine brands of fascism did not last long enough to supply conclusive evidence on the matter.

5. *Totalitarianism* in all human relations characterizes fascism as a way of life rather than as a mere system of government. Many dictatorships, particularly in Latin America, apply the authoritarian principle only in government. If the people do not make any trouble politically and do not interfere with the rule of the dictator and his henchmen, they can lead their own lives pretty freely. Education, religion, business, and agriculture are not touched very much by these political dictatorships. By contrast, fascism is totalitarian; it employs authority and violence in *all* kinds of social relations, whether political or not.

With regard to women, the largest discriminated-against minority of the world, fascism is antifeminist. Women, said the Nazis, should stay in their place and their concern should be the famous three Ks-*Kinder, Küche, Kirche.* Since women are considered incapable of bearing arms, they are automatically second-class citizens according to the fascist view, and they are excluded from leadership positions in government or party. They have the right to vote, but since this right in fascist countries means only the right to be enthusiastic about the leader and his party, it is not much of a practical asset. Within the family the father

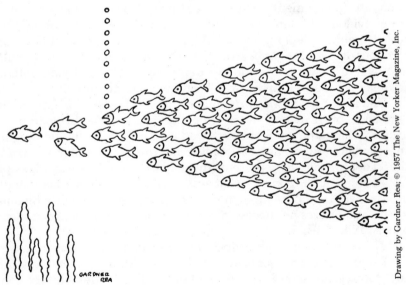

"God knows what we'd do if anything should ever happen to him!"

is the leader, and his wife and children get a strong taste of domestic authoritarian government, which has more effect on their everyday lives than the operations of a remote political government in the capital. In the extreme case of Nazi Germany, the contempt for women was finally demonstrated in the official ridicule of the institution of marriage as a false Jewish-Christian prejudice, and German women were encouraged to produce children for the fatherland outside of wedlock.

Fascist countries also preferred to employ male teachers in schools. From the fascist viewpoint, the purpose of schools is to teach discipline and obedience, specifically to prepare boys for military service and girls for domestic activities. In a program of such importance, fascist educators feel women teachers should play subordinate roles.

Thus it can be seen that fascist totalitarianism, unlike the traditional dictatorships of Latin America, is totalitarian in its objective to control all phases of human life, political or not, from the cradle to the grave. It may begin this control even before the cradle by pushing definite population policies, and has been known to reach into the grave, so to speak, to decide whether a dead person should have a burial at all and, if so, in what form.

Fascism is also totalitarian in its means. It will use any form of coercion, from verbal threats to mass murder, to obtain its goals. By contrast, the traditional authoritarian dictatorship was, and is, more restrained in its means and resorts to murder only on a limited scale. Thus, when a Latin American leader is ousted, he is usually permitted by his opponents to assemble his family and peacefully depart to a foreign country.

6. *Racism and imperialism* express the two basic fascist characteristics of inequality and violence as applied to the society of nations. Fascist doctrine holds that within the nation, the elite is superior to the mass and may impose its will upon the latter by force. Similarly, between nations, the *elite nation* is superior to others and is entitled to rule them. German fascism went furthest in its racist and imperialist policies. A straight line led from the theories of German-Nordic "race" superiority to the murder of millions of people. The German objective of world domination included the elimination of some nations through genocide and the enslavement of the rest. After the expected defeat of Britain and the Soviet Union, the United States was next on the list. The Japanese race theories found their practical imperialist expression in the concept of "co-prosperity," under which Japan would prosper by exploiting Asia and the Pacific.

Italian fascism was for a long time (from 1922 to 1938) remarkably free of exaggerated race theories; early Italian propaganda concentrated on the idea of reviving the old Roman Empire. In 1938, however, Mussolini announced that the Italians were a pure and superior race, and he became more closely tied to Hitler's Germany.

Racism and imperialism are not an exclusive monopoly of fascism, however. During World War II, the Soviet Union annexed Estonia, Latvia, and Lithuania. After the war, it held onto portions of Germany, Czechoslovakia, Poland, Finland, and Romania. Russian domination of the multinational Soviet Union has been increasingly stressed, differing only in degree from the Great Russian superiority concept held in tsarist Russia. More recently, China has used the propaganda argument of race and color in her struggle with the Soviet Union for supremacy in the communist world and for leading the developing "third world" countries—mostly inhabited by nonwhites—toward communist revolution.

In the democracies, too, there is a tradition of racism; in the United States, for example, racial discrimination has seriously corroded the vitality of democratic ideals. Called (by the Swedish social scientist Gunnar Myrdal) "the American dilemma," the race issue may ultimately decide the fate of democracy in the United States. Britain, with a much smaller proportion of nonwhites in its population (2 percent, compared with 12 percent in the United States), was also beset by racial tensions in the 1960s and early 1970s. While the issue of race is less burning in Britain than in the United States, it has brought to the fore latent prejudices and popular sentiments that sharply contradict the British liberal tradition of the last hundred years. Communists have exploited American and British racialism in their propaganda communications to the largely nonwhite developing nations and have been effective in this because there is enough substance to validate much of that propaganda.

7. *Opposition to international law and order,* or war, is the logical outcome of fascist beliefs in inequality, violence, elitism, racism, and imperialism. Whereas nonfascists (except nonresisting pacifists) accept war as a tragic fact, as something that should be abolished, fascists raise war to the ideal, because, as Mussolini put it, "war alone brings up to their highest tension all human energies and puts the stamp of nobility upon the peoples who have the courage to meet it."

Any type of international organization assumes some form of government by consent, which is directly contradictory to fascist *government by force.* Also, equality of states before the law of nations is a basic principle of international order. The fascist concept of an elite leads, as we have seen, to the leadership of one nation over the society of nations as it does to the leadership of one man within a nation's government. Fascist states limit or decline from participation in international organizations in which they are expected to abide by majority decisions and in which policy setting is carried on by methods of discussion rather than by force.

The fascist regimes of Italy and Germany had no use for the League of Nations; Germany withdrew in 1933 and Italy in 1937. In the United Nations, Peronist Argentina consistently played a lone-wolf role. In the Organization of American States, she did all she could to prevent effective cooperation between the American republics—a policy later copied by Cuba under Castro.

In West Germany, neo-Nazi groups merged into the National Democratic Party (NDP) in 1964. In addition to taking a hard line on communism and law and order, the NDP has since stressed a strong nationalist position on issues affecting Germany's relations with other nations. Thus, the NDP favors German withdrawal from all supranational bodies, such as the Common Market, NATO, and special agencies of the United Nations, since the NDP states there must be no outside interference with German sovereignty. The NDP also takes a belligerent stand regarding the German territories ceded to Poland and the Soviet Union after World War II, and favors the use of German armed forces for strictly nationalist objectives.

FASCIST ECONOMICS: THE CORPORATE STATE

The corporate state applies fascist principles of organization and control to the economy. The fascist economy is subdivided into *state-controlled* associations of capital and labor, and each association has a monopoly in its trade or occupation. Thus, the one-party state is the ultimate arbiter of conflicts between capital and labor.

The philosophy of the corporate state rests on two assumptions. First, the individual should not be politically articulate as a citizen (except for the small ruling elite) but only as a worker, entrepreneur, farmer, doctor, or lawyer; general political problems are assumed to be too complicated for the masses, who are expected to understand only those issues that bear directly on their vocational or professional work. Second, members of the ruling elite are supposed to understand broad problems that affect the whole society, therefore they alone are qualified to govern.

The democratic concept rejects this corporate approach to economic and political organization for several reasons. First, it is not always easy to separate economic from political aspects. Tariffs seem to be a purely economic issue, yet they directly affect political and diplomatic relations with other states. Immigration seems at first sight to be an economic problem, yet involved in it are delicate psychological and diplomatic issues. Economic aid to other nations, as the United States has learned since the end of World War II, has profound military and political aspects as well as economic effects.

Second, democratic theory holds that only the one who wears the shoe knows where it pinches; the mystic knowledge or insight of a ruling elite is no substitute for the experience of the ruled—or, as Aristotle put it, the guest is a better judge of the meal than the cook. Fascists insist that the cook not only ought to be the final judge of the product but should impose that judgment on the guests, by force if necessary.

Finally, democratic theory rejects the fascist assumption that members of one particular class are superior in judgment to the rest of the people and are therefore the nation's natural rulers. Democratic theory rejects the assumption of fascist doctrine that only an elite group has insight into the public good. From the democratic viewpoint, only God has a perfect understanding of Truth with a capital *T,* but everyone is capable, at least partially, of seeing truth with a small *t.*

What the one-party state with secret police and concentration camps is to the political side of fascism, corporatism is to its social and economic sides. Just as in the political sphere fascism replaces the pivotal concept of individual liberty with unlimited state authority, so in the economic sphere it rejects the free welfare economy—be it capitalist, socialist, or middle-of-the-road. The objective of the corporate state is to guarantee the power of the state rather than the welfare of the individual. More specifically, the ultimate objective of corporate organization of the economy is the preparation of a *permanent war economy,* because aggressive imperialism is the ultimate aim of fascist foreign policy.

The Italian fascist regime set up a corporate state that was to show the Italians and the world that fascism was not mere reaction against liberal capitalism and socialism, but a new creative principle of social and economic organization. The economy was divided into syndicates, or associations, of workers, employers, and the professions. Only one syndicate was recognized in each branch of business or industry, and although membership in a syndicate was not obligatory, the payment of dues was. Syndicate officials were either fascist politicians or persons of reliable loyalty to the fascist regime. In effect, these associations of workers and employers were instruments of state policy, with no will or life of their own. Since each syndicate had a monopoly of organization in its field, state control was made that much easier.

To make this method of control more nearly complete, the fascist government established *corporations* which were administrative agencies in a given industry designed to unite and control the syndicates of workers and employers in that industry. According to law, the syndicates were autonomous; in fact, however, they were run by the state. The corporation, supreme instrument of fascist economic organization, made no pretense of autonomy, being but an administrative agency of the state in no way different from the other tools of fascist government.

Despite the name, the fascist corporation is not to be confused with the business corporations of other countries. They have nothing whatever in common. The Italian fascist unit was a government agency, whereas the typical business corporation is a company of limited liability, owned by private citizens, and engaged in business.

Italy's much-advertised corporate state did not represent any new principle of social and economic organization, but merely signified that economic relations, like all other aspects of society in the totalitarian system of fascism, could not be left to the free interplay of competition. In Mussolini's own words, the essential bases of the corporate state were a *single party, a totalitarian government,* and an atmosphere of *strong ideal tension.* The Fascist party provided the first two essentials of the corporate state; the strong ideal tension was induced by ceaseless propaganda of expansionist imperialism.

The first real test for the corporate state in Italy came with that country's entry into World War II in June 1940. Fascist Italy revealed itself to be wholly unequal to the task of fighting a major war, not only from the military and political viewpoint, but from the standpoint of economic efficiency as well. For 20 years the corporate state had sacrificed the welfare and happiness of a poor people to the dream of a powerful empire and the megalomania of a would-be conqueror of continents. Yet when the first real test of battle came, Italian fascism failed on the economic front even more conclusively than on the military front. The economic legacy of the corporate state was not wealth and empire, but the loss of the colonies, poverty, and destitution.

After the execution of Mussolini in the spring of 1945, the Italian people destroyed whatever vestiges were left of the corporate state and embarked upon a new chapter of economic rehabilitation based on a mixture of economic liberalism and political democracy. Much of the economic ruin of Italy was ultimately paid for by the American taxpayer, as the United States poured billions of dollars into Italy after World War II to help her stand on her own feet again. Since 1950, the Italian economy has been one of the fastest growing economies in the world and has provided standards of living undreamed of during the fascist era. During the 1960s Italy doubled its gross national product.

In the western hemisphere, Colonel Perón, speaking for the fascist regime in Argentina just after its successful coup of June 1943, declared his admiration for the fundamental conceptions of the corporate state at the very moment when Italian fascism, the model and inspiration for Argentine fascism, had reduced Italy to ashes and ruins. To Argentina under Perón, as to other nations, the corporate state brought inflation and meatless days—in a country that had been the largest exporter of meat in the world. Above all, corporatism in Argentina (called *justicialismo*) meant the end of free labor unions and their replacement by government-sponsored puppet organizations. The employers, too, were put under the control of the government. Finally, the Peronist regime followed the corporate systems of other fascist states by dedicating the economy to the hasty development of heavy industry and the manufacture of armaments. Thus, *justicialismo*, which set out to defend justice against both capitalism and socialism, became the servant of a militaristic dictator and his political machine, until both were overthrown in 1955.

IS FASCISM STILL A THREAT?

Is fascism still a threat in the contemporary world, particularly to the democracies? In 1958, after France had lost the war in Algeria and a military *coup* took place there a real danger arose of a military dictatorship being imposed on France itself. Only the prestige of General de Gaulle, who came out in favor of republican government, saved France from the threat of fascism or civil war. More recently, some elements of the New Left in the United States have argued that this nation has become fascist or is on the road to fascism. While no democratic government is completely secure from the possibility of fascism, the United States at present is neither fascist nor moving in that direction. Thus Corliss Lamont, chairman of the National Emergency Civil Liberties Committee and life-long defender of left-wing causes, wrote that he did "not see in the offing any constellation of forces that could put fascism across here. With all the factors in American life that violate or threaten democratic principles, they still do not add up to a clear and present danger of fascism."

This appraisal may be correct, but to say that fascism is not now a clear and present danger in the United States (or in other political democracies) is not to say that it may not become a serious possibility. To the extent that an *anti-intellectual tendency* exists in the United States or other democratic systems, it undermines faith in rational processes; such a tendency need not lead straight to fascism, yet it lays the groundwork for the mentality without which there can be no effective fascist movement. Intellectuals may, and do, contribute to this corrosion of faith in reason by identifying with doctrines of violence on the extreme right or left. Intellectuals who abandon their commitment to

"Yes, son, this is what happens to a country when the eggheads take over."

rational processes and advocate violence as a legitimate means of social change will find that such advocacy is more likely to lead to a rightist reaction than to anarchy or a successful leftist revolution.

In 1970, as acts of terrorism, bombings, and arson by Weathermen and other revolutionary groups spread throughout the United States, Senator Margaret Chase Smith said: "Extremism bent upon polarization of our people is increasingly forcing upon the American people the narrow choice between anarchy and repression. And make no mistake about it, if that narrow choice has to be made, the American people, even with reluctance and misgiving, will choose repression" (June 1, 1970). Condemned by the Communist Party of the United States and other Old Left groups, terrorism abated, and with it the threat of an extreme rightist or fascist reaction.

Racism is another important source—some think the most important source—feeding the fascist potential in the United States, as in other democracies. For example, democracy no longer exists in the Republic of South Africa; while South Africa still has a multiparty system and a mild (and harrassed) opposition press, it has moved steadily in the direction of the fascist police state. It practices imprisonment without trial, confinement of "dangerous" persons to specific localities, forced residence of millions of blacks in assigned reservations, and censorship of books, movies, and radio according to racist concepts. The racism that started out in South Africa against blacks and Indians later turned into chauvinism against English-speaking whites, nearly one-half of the white population.

South African racial policy has been based on the concept of *apartheid,* or separation. Under this policy, nonwhites are forced to live in separate areas and are kept apart from whites socially, culturally, and politically. In the United States the danger of separation of whites and nonwhites has become very real. The *Report of the National Advisory Commission on Civil Disorders* (1968) stated as its basic conclusion: "Our nation is moving toward two societies, one black, one white—separate and unequal." Should this trend continue, the threat of fascism or a fascist-type government will be very serious, since such separation and inequality could not be maintained by traditional processes of constitutional government. As South Africa officially justifies its racist policies as measures against communism, racist-fascist forces in the United States will also feed on anticommunism, as they have done in the past. Black separatists—still a minority in the black community—are convinced that a trend toward separation is inevitable in the United States, and many have demanded the establishment of a separate black nation carved out of the territory of certain southern states. *Apartheid* in the United States would be no more reconcilable with democracy than it is in South Africa.

Possibly the most dangerous softening up of democratic resistance to fascism is the destruction of democratic habits and institutions, not by outside attacks, but within democracy itself. If there is any fascist threat to democracy today—and there is—it no longer comes from Berlin, Rome, or Tokyo. It derives its strength from the inertia and apathy of the citizens of a democracy, because without such civic indifference there can be no support for demagogues who seek to aggrandize themselves at the expense of the whole body politic.

The danger in a democracy like the United States is not outright fascism on the German or Italian pattern, but the unnoticed corroding of democratic institutions by profascist attitudes. Huey Long, who as governor of Louisiana in the early 1930s set up the nearest thing to a fascist dictatorship in the United States, once jokingly said that if fascism ever came to the United States, it would be under the slogan of 100 percent Americanism.

Long was right. The open, self-confessed fascist will not get a sympathetic hearing in the United States because the verbal symbols of fascism are identified too profoundly with evil in the American mind. By publicly declaring himself to be what he is, the fascist cannot work under the mantle of respectability. A politician with fascist leanings who denies that he is a fascist and who emphasizes his patriotism can do much more harm than the admitted fascist within the institutional framework of public life.

Spain: The Aftermath of Franco

The fascist regimes of Germany, Italy, and Japan were destroyed through military defeat in World War II. One major fascist regime escaped this fate: Franco's Spain. By shrewdly avoiding formal intervention on the side of his fellow dictators, Franco spared Spain the agony of invasion by the Allies and prolonged his own rule for 30 years more. Unlike Hitler, burned in a Berlin bunker, and Mussolini, hung from a lamppost by Italian partisans, Franco died peacefully in bed mourned by masses of his followers.

THE SPANISH CIVIL WAR

Francisco Franco came to power in a Civil War that lasted three years, took 600,000 lives, and became for the late 1930s an emotional cause comparable to the Vietnam War in the 1960s. The Civil War began in 1936 when Franco and several other nationalist generals rebelled against the government of the Spanish Republic, which had been in existence since 1931. The generals were actively aided from the outset by two other anti-Republican forces: a varied group of monarchists, who wanted to overthrow the Republic in order to restore the Spanish monarchy; and the Falangists, a group of self-conscious fascists who hoped to create in Spain the kind of system that already existed in Italy and Germany. In the course of the Civil War, General Franco emerged as the leader of the Nationalist (anti-Republican) forces and adopted the fascist ideology of the Falange as the rallying creed of his new regime.

The occasion for the revolt in Spain was the growing inability of the Republican government to maintain order in face of mounting and often violent unrest among important segments of Spanish society. One source of conflict was regionalism: the demand of several provinces, notably Catalonia in the northeast and the Basque provinces in the north-central sections of the country, for greater autonomy from the central government in Madrid. Although these once-independent provinces of Spain had been united centuries before under a national monarchy, provincial loyalties remained strong and were the basis for periodic separatist movements. When the new Republic was established in 1931 the separatists gained a sympathetic hearing. Following a popular plebiscite, the government enacted the Statute of Catalan Autonomy, which gave Catalonia significant powers of self-government and reinstituted the Generalitat—ancient Catalan council. This encouraged the Basques and other people to demand similar autonomy. But popular as these measures were among the separatists, from the standpoint of Spanish nationalists they heralded the disintegration of central authority, and so were bitterly opposed.

A second source of conflict was the issue of clericalism, another longstanding division in Spain. The Catholic Church had been a staunch supporter of the Spanish monarchy, and the attitude of organized Catholic groups toward the Republic was mixed. The most conservative churchmen denounced the Republic, and some priests later took up arms in the Nationalist cause; more moderate Catholics initially supported the Republic, and participated in the elected government. This support was undermined, however, by strongly anticlerical clauses in the Constitution of the Republic directed against ordinary priests, who were being paid from the public treasury; influential religious orders, especially the Jesuits; and parochial schools, which dominated the educational system. These constitutional clauses reflected the intense anticlericalism of the Republican forces. Among the anarchists, the most extreme of the Republicans, anticlericalism was literally a burning issue, for they sacked and razed numerous churches and monasteries.

A third source of conflict was economic: basic unresolved issues in both the agricultural and industrial sectors. In the 1930s Spain was still predominantly an agricultural country, but lay stagnant and undeveloped in the hands of landowners who behaved like feudal barons rather than modern landlords. The laborers or tenants who worked this land lived in grim poverty and insecurity. To begin the long overdue process of reform, the Republican government passed an Agrarian Law which distributed unworked estates to individual peasants or peasant cooperatives. This hardly endeared the Republic to the landowners and their agents. At the same time, in the recently developed industrial areas of Spain, conflict was aroused by two special circumstances: the effects of a world-wide depression and the growing strength of the anarchist movement. Elsewhere in Western Europe the claims of anarchism, espoused by the theoretician and agitator Michael Bakunin, lost out to the socialism of Karl Marx. But in Spain, more remote from the power centers of socialism, anarchism struck deep roots among peasants and workers alike. In the heart of industrial Spain—the city of Barcelona—anarchism became the prevailing doctrine in the trade unions and working-class political organizations.

Unlike both socialists and communists, whose aim is to win political power by gaining control of the institutions of government—in one case democratically, in the other case by revolution—the Spanish anarchists aimed at direct appropriation of farms and factories by the workers who labored there. The goal was not to seize the State but to dismantle the government and replace it with associations of workers who would own and control the resources, tools, and organizations of production and distribution. As Bakunin summarized the anarchist program: "Full restitution to the workers: all the capital, the factories and all the instruments of work and raw materials to go to the associations, and the land to those who cultivate it with their own hands." In addition, the anarchists used distinctive tactics in carrying on their revolutionary struggle: periodic political strikes leading to paralyzing general strikes, and sporadic acts of violent destruction. About strikes, Bakunin wrote: "The dominant news in the labor movement of Europe can be summed up in one word: *strikes*. When strikes begin to grow in scope and intensity, spreading from one place to another, it means that events are ripening for a general strike, which will regenerate society." Bakunin also celebrated the workers' "passion for destruction:" "A rebellion on the part of the people, which by nature is spontaneous, chaotic, and ruthless, always presupposes a vast destruction of property. The working masses are ever ready for such sacrifices: When the exigencies of defense or victory demand it, they will not stop at the destruction of their own villages, and cities, and inasmuch as property in most cases does not belong to the people, they very often evince a positive passion for destruction."

The anarchists posed a continuing threat not only to the capitalists and landowners who were the immediate objects of their strikes and violence but also to the political leaders of the Republic. Whatever steps the government might take to deal with pressing economic and social issues were subject to disruption through the extreme actions of the anarchists. In fact, however, the government had little real chance to solve the country's deep-seated economic ills, for throughout its life the Republic felt the chilling effects of world-wide economic depression. In the eight years from 1929 to 1936 the production of minerals and manufactures fell precipitously, and the value of the peseta, the Spanish dollar, was cut almost in half. Even without the anarchists the economic situation was deteriorating yearly. Like the Weimar Republic in Germany, the Spanish Republic could not have begun at a worse time.

Bitterly divided over basic issues of separatism, clericalism, and socialism, the political groups of both left and right became increasingly polarized, as the authority of the Republic declined. By the election of 1936—the last legislative election of the Spanish Republic—the opposing forces had coalesced into two major blocs: the Popular Front that

supported the Republic; and the National Front, made up of its enemies. Although the Popular Front emerged as the single strongest
group in the electorate (the registered voters) and the Cortez (the
Spanish parliament), the Republic's days were numbered. Arrayed
against it were Monarchists, the Catholic Party, Fascists of the Falange,
and conservative elements in the army. Although divided among themselves on a number of important issues, including the kind of regime to
replace the Republic, these groups were able to coordinate their actions
with growing effectiveness as the crisis deepened. On the other side,
the Popular Front comprised an uneasy coalition of moderate liberals,
democratic socialists (themselves divided into competing factions),
communists, Trotskyites, and anarchists. They drew together in defense
of the Republic but agreed on little else. Even in the throes of the
ensuing Civil War, communists and anarchists carried on their bloody
fratricidal struggles as much intent on murdering their opponents
within the Republican ranks as in fighting the common enemy.

As dissatisfaction with the Republic continued to grow, militants on
both sides began to arm and train for combat. Conspiracies flourished,
coups were attempted, and assassinations became commonplace. The
country was slipping into chaos. In this situation several generals, including Francisco Franco, a hero of the recent wars in Morocco against
the Riffs under the legendary Abd-el-Krim, intervened to restore order.
This was hardly unusual in Spanish politics: The army had a long history
of political intervention. Within the preceding century the army had
imposed a liberal constitution, supported a succession of military coups,
deposed one monarch and restored another, and established a military
dictatorship. On July 17, 1936, the generals acted again as they saw it,
to secure the unity and greatness of the Spanish nation. The Civil War
that followed took three bloody and devastating years, and plunged
Spain into a political and spiritual abyss from which she is only now
emerging.

From the very beginning the Civil War was not confined to the
Spanish alone but involved the governments, soldiers, and ordinary
citizens of the major powers. The Spanish Civil War became one of the
melancholy preludes that prepared the way for World War II; others
took place in the Rhineland, Czechoslovakia, and Poland. Both sides in
Spain's Civil War appealed for help to the outside world, and the responses foreshadowed the greater tragedy soon to follow. The Western
democracies—France, Britain, and the United States—to whom the
Republicans appealed for help, adopted a policy of nonintervention,
including an embargo on all shipments of arms; the dictatorial governments of Italy, Germany, and Portugal, to whom the Nationalists appealed for help, paid lip service to nonintervention but eventually

supplied arms, material, and several divisions of troops to aid the Nationalist cause; the Soviet Union encouraged the Republicans with strong words and sent limited aid to stave off disaster at least temporarily. In view of the vital assistance provided to the Nationalists by Italy and Germany, the democracies' policy of nonintervention and embargo in effect condemned the Republic to defeat, while the showdown with fascism was postponed only briefly. What would have happened if the democracies had abandoned nonintervention and instead supplied the Republic with needed aid, as President Roosevelt later conceded they should have done? This is one of those intriguing but unanswerable historical "ifs." As it was, the Spanish Civil War provided Hitler with an ideal opportunity to try out the weapons and strategies that would be used on a much grander scale a few years later.

Whatever the policies of their governments, ordinary citizens in the Western democracies reacted to the plight of the Republic with intense emotion and some heroic action. The Civil War became a test of political convictions. Volunteers, including many writers and journalists, flocked to Spain to join the fight against fascism. Major works of art and literature were created out of the experience: Picasso's searing mural *Guernica* memorializes the destruction of the historic Basque town by German planes, the first of the all-out airraids that would be launched again over Rotterdam, Coventry, London, Dresden, and Tokyo; George Orwell's vivid memoir *Homage to Catalonia* captures the heroism and futility, idealism and myopia, within the Republican ranks; W. H. Auden's evocative poem *Spain 1937* conveys the urgent sense of momentous stakes which his generation saw in the Civil War; and Ernest Hemingway's moving novel *For Whom the Bell Tolls* epitomizes the experiences of foreign volunteers who went to Spain to fight, including Americans of the Lincoln Brigade.

FRANCO'S NEW STATE

Allegedly coined by the fiery Communist leader "La Pasionaria," their watchword was *Non Pasaron*—They Shall Not Pass. But after three years of protracted campaigns and indecisive battles the Republicans, depleted in arms, food, and hope, at last succumbed.

Franco, self-proclaimed "El Caudillo," or Leader, proceeded to consolidate his power and exacted bloody retribution from his enemies. His *New State* or National Revolution bore striking similarities to Mussolini's *Fascismo* and Hitler's *National Socialism*. Like his fellow dictators, Franco affirmed the totalitarian nature of his regime. He declared that "Spain will be organized from a broad totalitarian approach by means of all national institutions guaranteeing its totality, unity, and continuity."

In keeping with this conception, all political opposition was outlawed and suppressed, the economy was organized into corporatist
structures subordinated to Franco's political objectives, and trade
unions were replaced by a *Syndical Organization,* led by active Falangists, to which all workers were forced to belong. One way or another,
Franco handled the basic issues that had bedeviled the Republic—
separatism, clericalism, and socialism. Catalonia was occupied as a conquered territory and ruled under a policy of subjugation designed to
destroy not only its political expressions of separatism but its cultural
roots as well. The Church regained its position of privilege and influence, and Franco won warm approval from the Catholic hierarchy in
Rome as well as in Spain. Agricultural and industrial workers were
forcibly integrated into syndicates in which they could raise no independent voice of protest, and their standard of living fell sharply. In
every city and town, heavily armed troops patrolled the central streets
—the visible strong arm of an oppressive police state. Franco was prov-
ing to be a worthy associate of his German and Italian benefactors.

Yet from the outset there was a fundamental difference between
Franco and his fellow dictators. Whereas Mussolini and Hitler rose to
power as leaders of revolutionary political parties dedicated to fascist
ideology, Franco came to power as a victorious general whose primary
base of support was the Spanish army, not the fascist party of the
Falange. The founder and principal ideologue or theorist of the
Falange, Jose Antonio Primo de Rivera, son of a former military dictator
of Spain, had promulgated a doctrine that echoed the nationalist, elitist,
statist, and expansionist principles of Italian fascism. But Primo de Rivera, a popular personality and an astute politician, who might have
challenged Franco for leadership of the Nationalist forces eventually,
was arrested and executed by the Republicans. No other Falangist of
comparable stature ever emerged. Franco made effective use of the
Falange—both its ideology, which provided a doctrine for his National
Revolution, and its militant members, who provided loyal managers for
his New State. During the first decade of the regime, from 1939 to about
1950, its distinctive Falangist character was especially evident. But
unlike his Italian and German counterparts, Franco was first and foremost a conservative general rather than a revolutionary fascist, and as
political circumstances changed he gradually restricted the role of the
Falange while relying increasingly upon the traditional bulwarks of
Spanish conservatism—the army, the Church, the landowners, and at
the end the monarchists.

A major political circumstance that directly affected the character
of Franco's regime was the defeat of the Axis powers in World War II.
Reminded of the debt he owed from the Civil War and urged to join

the international fascist cause, Franco sent his Blue Division to fight beside Hitler's army in Russia. Yet he avoided a formal declaration of war against the Allies, which the more militant Falangists advocated and the Axis would have welcomed. No doubt Franco's military sense that Spain was simply too weak to fight another war overcame whatever ideological fervor he felt for the fascist cause. In any event by 1942, with the Allied invasion of North Africa, it was clear to Franco that he had nothing to gain from joining the Axis side; the fascist dictators would face their Armageddon alone, without Spain. This policy of neutrality saved Franco's regime but confirmed Spain's unenviable position as a country isolated politically and backward economically.

Apologists for Franco's regime have argued that repressive methods were necessary in order to resolve the bitter conflicts of the Republican period so that the vital task of modernizing the Spanish economy could get underway. In this view Franco is presented as the progressive innovator of Spanish economic development. But the record during the first decade of his rule does not support this interpretation. Despite Franco's announced intention to foster economic development, the 1940s were not a period of growth but rather of stagnation and recurring economic crisis. Whether measured by real income, volume of output, or rate of capital accumulation, the achievements of the regime were negative or meager. By 1950 per capita income had yet to regain its prewar level. The fact is that Franco's fascist corporatism was not conducive to growth. Only after 1951, with the introduction of capitalist-style competitive markets, did significant progress occur. For a dozen years Franco did not so much facilitate as impede the modernization of Spain.

Conditions of life began to change in the 1950s. Caught up in the Cold War with the Soviet Union, the United States saw Spain as a likely place for military bases, and the prevailing political and economic neglect came to an end. The Pact of Madrid, formally ending Spanish isolation, was signed in 1953. Benefiting both from large-scale American loans and investments as well as Franco's newly liberalized economic program, Spain started on the road toward economic development and political change.

Economic progress was rapid and marked; political change was slower and less certain. In the 1950s industrialization proceeded at a steady pace despite serious difficulties with high inflation and balance of payments deficits. The experience confirmed the confidence of Spanish leaders in liberal economic policies. During the 1960s and into the 1970s Spain benefited from the general European prosperity; tourism became a major industry, contributing nearly $2.5 billion to the economy by the early 1970s, and thousands of Spanish workers streamed over the border to factories abroad, sending home millions of dollars more in remittances to their families. But the sustained growth during this period was due primarily to sound domestic policies: a Stabilization Plan, which dealt with inflation, and three subsequent Five-Year Development Plans. Inevitably, the economic progress had its effects on politics.

The economic growth of the 1950s bore political fruit in the 1960s, with an outburst of strikes and mass protests. Actually, despite Franco's brutal repression, murmurs of dissent and opposition had never been stilled completely. There were hundreds of thousands of Republican refugees in exile in the 1940s and 1950s who kept alive the hope of liberation wherever they settled. And even within Spain pockets of resistance remained. Basque separatists kept up their dogged campaign for autonomy; Spanish communists conducted a rudimentary armed struggle of their own (against the wishes of Moscow), thereby maintaining a continuous independent organization throughout the Franco years and into the post-Franco era; and remnants of Republican forces formed guerrilla bands to engage in sporadic attacks of sabotage and harassment. During the 1950s new signs of opposition appeared, rooted not in memories of the Republic but in immediate dissatisfactions. By the early 1960s conditions were ripe for major expressions of protest. In two months of 1962 a wave of strikes spread across the country, which clearly revealed the strength and determination of restive workers; in 1965 more than 6000 students held a mass meeting of protest in Madrid, a dramatic demonstration of increasing pressure for liberalization. Winds of change were felt also in the Church. A growing liberal faction, composed mainly of younger clergy, sided with the workers and dissidents and demanded the severing of official ties between the Catholic church and the Spanish state. Some accommodation by the government was obviously required.

However visible these signs of opposition had become, there was never a real possibility of overthrowing the dictatorship. The regime itself was enjoying new-found strength. On the international scene, Franco had been transformed from a political pariah, whose downfall would have been generally welcomed, into a valued ally in the Cold War, the recipient of substantial American aid. At home, prosperity led to increased support for the regime among middle- and upper-class groups who were the main beneficiaries of the economic upturn. Even the recurring strikes, though troublesome to Franco's government, were not directed toward political reform but toward economic objectives such as higher wages and control of inflation. Among Franco's genuine opponents—former members of the Republican Popular Front —the old dissensions of a generation earlier broke out once again.

Anarchists, socialists, and communists resumed their ideological polemics and jockeying for leadership. Unity on the left was once more lacking. In these circumstances Franco felt confident enough to permit political concessions: A few independent political groups were allowed to organize; some political prisoners were released from jail; censorship was partially relaxed; police brutality was muted. But these were tactical adjustments, not basic reforms. During its final years the regime vacillated between liberalization and repression.

With Franco securely in power, attention focused increasingly on the issue of succession: Who, and what kind of regime, would replace the aging Caudillo? Franco used the issue with his customary shrewdness, giving encouragement to as many groups as possible while discouraging as few as possible. Finally, in 1969 a decree was issued naming as successor Prince Juan Carlos, son of the deposed King Alfonso. Revival of a monarchy was thus assured, but the nature of the monarchy—how liberal or conservative it would be—remained to be settled. Clues to Franco's intentions came in 1973, with the appointment of a conservative cabinet headed by Carrero Blanco to oversee the transition. This cabinet was short-lived: Within six months Carrero Blanco was assassinated by a Basque extremist, a member of the separatist ETA movement. A repressive reaction seemed likely; instead a middle-of-the-road government was formed, headed by Arias Navarro and supported by moderate elements in the army, pledged to further liberalization. Hope for a genuine transformation of the regime after the death of Franco began to grow. On November 20, 1975, Franco died, and Juan Carlos became King of Spain.

TOWARD SPANISH DEMOCRACY

The accession of Juan Carlos marked the beginning of a new era for Spain. But it was a beginning clouded in uncertainty. There were questions about Juan Carlos himself. He was Franco's hand-picked successor, educated inside Spain under Franco's guidance, and he had the support of traditional right-wing groups. During his years of schooling and waiting, Juan Carlos had made few public statements to reveal his own political beliefs. Yet his role in the transition would be crucial. Amid the rancorous divisions between extremists of the left and right this King would have to serve as a focus for national unity and a source of consensual policies. He was in a difficult situation. He might favor the right-wing groups that had been the mainstay of Franco and now supported his monarchy, or he could move toward genuine democracy, including representation for the radical groups of the left. Whatever he did was bound to antagonize some influential elements. Once he began to act, would he continue to command the loyalty of political groups all across the political spectrum? No one knew for certain.

There was uncertainty also about the political role of the left. Both dissension and extremism on the left had played a major part in the undoing of the Spanish Republic. Even in the face of political collapse and military defeat the bitter divisions among anarchists, communists, and socialists did not subside. Revolutionary violence, whether of the anarchist or communist variety, was also deeply ingrained. Would the introduction of democracy bring a revival once again of these fierce animosities and extreme tactics? If so, the fate of the new monarchy was no more promising that the fate of the old Republic. The attitude of the communists was especially critical. As the largest radical grouping on the left, if they resumed their former intransigent ways the left would again be disrupted and peaceful liberalization would hardly be likely. The actions of the Communist party in nearby Portugal, including their support of an abortive coup against the moderate transitional government that followed the death of Salazar, did not bode well. If the Spanish communists took the same path the result would surely be repression from the right.

The attitude of right-wing groups was yet another question. Until the end, Franco had enjoyed widespread popular support—more than 400,000 people filed past his body to pay their last respects—and the response of these Francoists to greater democratization was by no means certain. More particularly, the response of influential organized groups on the right was in doubt: the military forces, industrialists, members of the *Movimiento* (Franco's political party), conservative elements in the Church, and veterans of the nationalist struggle against the Republic. Would these groups accept the democratization demanded by the left, or would they again oppose the liberal practices against which many of them had fought in the Civil War? Juan Carlos was clearly in a difficult political situation.

In his inaugural speech, King Juan Carlos touched upon the broad issues facing his new regime and gave general indications of his own intentions. He acknowledged the popular demand for "profound improvements," the legitimacy of regional claims, and the importance of "social and economic rights." He noted that "A free and modern society requires the participation of all in the centers of decision, in the media, in the different levels of education, and in the control of the national wealth." But if these statements indicated general sympathy with the cause of democratization, the King nonetheless moved slowly and cautiously, too cautiously for many of his critics. The Carlists, longtime rivals for the Spanish throne, denounced the regime as a "fascist monarchy"; the communists called for a plebiscite on the issue of the monarchy itself.

Within six months Juan Carlos felt ready to move more decisively toward democratization. In July of 1976 he appointed a new prime minister, Adolfo Suarez, a former official of the National Movement who had since expressed clear liberal views, and a now-trusted political adviser of the King. With the King's support Suarez began to dismantle the Francoist political structure. Amnesties were granted to political prisoners; public meetings were legalized; political parties were allowed to organize; independent trade unions were permitted, as well as the right to strike; the National Movement was abolished; and a comprehensive Political Bill was enacted to reintroduce basic political rights in anticipation of a general election to be held within the year. Political competition, stifled for so long under Franco's harsh repression, burst into life with remarkable vigor. New parties and coalitions of parties sprang up on all sides: Democratic Co-ordination on the left; Popular Alliance on the right; Union of the Democratic Center, drawing support from a wide range of liberal groups, in the center. A month before the election the Communist party was legalized and its leader, Santiago Carillo, an outspoken advocate of Eurocommunism, promptly acknowledged the legitimacy of the monarchy as well as his intention to work for political reconciliation within a democratic regime. Longtime political exiles returned to Spain, including the fabled "La Pasionaria," president of the Communist party since the days of the Republic. It was an emotional time of celebration and hope, tinged with apprehension about what the future might hold for the fragile institutions of Spanish democracy.

On July 15, 1977, for the first time in 40 years, the people of Spain went to the polls in a free election to choose their representatives for the Cortez. Of the eligible voters, 80 percent turned out to vote. Candidates were nominated by 156 different parties grouped in 10 national and 12 regional coalitions. The results vindicated the moderate approach of King Juan Carlos and his prime minister, Adolfo Suarez. Of the 350 seats in the lower house of the Cortez, 165 were won by the Union of the Democratic Center (UCD), headed by Suarez; the Socialist Workers Party (PSOE) was second, with 118 seats; the communists (PCE) third, with 20 seats; and the Popular Alliance (AP) fourth, with 16 seats. Suarez was reappointed as prime minister and soon revealed the outlines of his proposed policies. They dealt with a wide range of political, economic, and international issues.

One of the most pressing issues was the old question of separatism. Political parties representing the regionalist claims of Catalonians and Basques had won a total of 19 seats in the new legislature, unmistakable proof of the strength of regional sentiment. The government had already restored the traditional institutions of Basque and Catalan self-rule—the Basque *General Juntas* and the Catalan *Generalitat.* It now promised a new constitution to institutionalize decentralization and regional self-government. The government also decided to apply for membership in the European Community, a step of major political and symbolic importance. In the past, both communists and rightists had opposed formal affiliation with the liberal states of Western Europe; moreover, to the rest of Western Europe, Franco had always been an unsavory neighbor. To enter the European community was therefore a reflection both of the changed attitudes of domestic political groups as well as the changed character of the regime. Spain was rejoining the democratic community.

The most difficult immediate issues were economic. The prosperity of the 1950s and 1960s gave way in the 1970s to a disturbing situation. Spain was in part feeling the effects of economic slowdown throughout the Western world. Formation of the Organization of Petroleum Exporting Countries (OPEC) and a drastic increase in 1973 in the world price of oil was an historic turning point for the world economy. Through this single consortium action the inexpensive fuel that had fired the industrial growth of the twentieth century suddenly vanished. The financial consequences swayed the Western economies and were felt even stronger in the developing countries: reduced investment, higher inflation, lower consumption, increased unemployment. In Spain high inflation cut directly into the tourist industry, which had become so significant to the Spanish; it also produced widespread unrest among workers who saw their real income shrinking month by month. To meet the deteriorating conditions the government introduced an austerity program, including devaluation of the peseta, progressive income taxes, wage and price controls, and other necessary but unpleasant measures.

These policies of Juan Carlos and the newly-elected government could hardly satisfy everyone, and throughout this transition period ominous echoes arose of the old extremist practices that had plagued the Republic: political strikes, kidnappings, rioting, and assassinations. Fears for the viability of Spanish democracy were voiced again: Perhaps the bases for a stable democracy simply did not exist in Spanish society and culture.

But conditions in 1979 were profoundly different from those of 1931. A skillful and popular monarch had become chief of state, drawing support from across the entire political spectrum. The King formalized his position as a constitutional monarch, and the arrangement was willingly accepted by groups on the left as well as the right. The Communist party, the leading force on the left, had seemingly undergone a major transformation. Instead of the Soviet-dominated extremist party of Republican days they now proclaimed their independence and nonviolence. Following the doctrines of Eurocommunism they envisioned "a Spanish road to socialism characterized by democracy and a multiparty system." On the right, Franco's National Movement had been disbanded and its dissolution had provoked protests but no popular uprising. The Church had also undergone a change. From at best a jaundiced observer of Spanish democracy, and at worst its enemy, the Church had become its advocate. Officiating at the inauguration of King Juan Carlos, the Cardinal Archbiship of Madrid spoke of respect for human rights, protection of civil liberties, and popular participation in government. The Church, he asserted, demands that the government "protect and promote the exercise of adequate freedom for all and the necessary common participation in all common problems and in decisions of government." Equally important, he called for separation and mutual autonomy of Church and State.

However, the most significant internal difference between 1931 and 1979 relates to the altered nature of Spanish society itself. Economically and socially backward in the 1930s, with anachronistic attitudes among its elite groups, Spain in the 1950s had entered the modern world. By the 1970s a generation had grown up amid the realities of industrialization, international interdependence, and political liberalization. For these people the future development of Spain lay in a continuation of economic growth and political moderation, not in the stagnation and extremism of the past. Awareness of this fundamental reality by increasing numbers of Spaniards, both on the left and the right, is perhaps the most important and encouraging difference between the old Republic and the new democracy.

The modern Spanish democratic monarchy finds itself in a radically different international setting. The Republic faced the twin menaces of world-wide depression and rampant fascism. While the condition of the international economy in the late 1970s is hardly cause for celebration, neither is there a severe depression; as for fascism, Franco himself was the last European vestige of its former triumphs. As a world-wide revolutionary movement fascism is dormant, at least for the time being. So the renewed Spanish experiment in democracy gets underway free from the international crises which helped undo its predecessor. For these reasons its prospects for the future are hopeful.

For Further Reading

ARENDT, HANNAH, *Origins of Totalitarianism.* New York: Harcourt Brace Jovanovich, 1966.

BRACHER, KARL DIETRICH, *The German Dictatorship: The Origins, Structure, and Effects of National Socialism.* New York: Praeger Publishers, Inc., 1970.

DIGGINS, JOHN A., *Mussolini and Fascism: The View from America.* Princeton: Princeton University Press, 1972.

EBENSTEIN, WILLIAM, *Fascism at Work.* New York: A M S Press, 1973.

———, *Fascist Italy.* New York: American Book Company, 1939; Russell & Russell, 1973.

———, "National Socialism," in *International Encyclopedia of the Social Sciences,* XI:45–50. New York: Macmillan Publishing Co., Inc. and The Free Press, 1968.

———, *The German Record.* New York: Holt, Rinehart and Winston, 1945.

———, *The Nazi State.* New York: Holt, Rinehart and Winston, 1943.

FROMM, ERICH, *Escape from Freedom.* New York: Holt, Rinehart and Winston, 1941.

GALLO, MAX, *Spain Under Franco.* New York: E. P. Dutton & Co., Inc., 1974.

———, *Mussolini's Italy.* New York: Macmillan Publishing Co., Inc., 1973.

GREGOR, A. JAMES, *The Fascist Persuasion in Radical Politics.* Princeton: Princeton University Press, 1974.

HAMILTON, ALASTAIR, *The Appeal of Fascism: A Study of Intellectuals and Fascism, 1919–1945.* New York: Macmillan Publishing Co., Inc., 1971.

HAYES, PAUL M., *Fascism.* New York: The Free Press, 1973.

LAQUEUR, WALTER, *Fascism: A Reader's Guide.* Berkeley: University of California Press, 1976.

NATHAN, PETER, *The Psychology of Fascism.* London: Faber & Faber, 1943.

SHIRER, WILLIAM L., *The Rise and Fall of the Third Reich.* New York: Crest Books, 1962.

WOOLF, S. J., ed., *European Fascism.* New York: Vintage Books, 1969.

3

Capitalism

Evolution of Capitalism

Capitalism developed historically as part of the movement of *individualism*. In religion, that movement produced the Reformation; in learning, the growth of the physical sciences; in human relations, the social sciences; in politics, democratic government; and in economics, the capitalist system. The concept of capitalist civilization is therefore a legitimate one; it suggests that capitalism is more than a particular type of economy, that it is a whole social system. It developed in eighteenth-century Britain and was transplanted later to northwestern Europe and North America. A few basic traits have characterized it from the beginning.

147

Individual ownership

In the capitalist system, ownership of the means of production (land, factories, machinery, natural resources) is held by individuals, not by the state. This does not exclude public ownership of natural monopolies or basic public services (public utilities, post office), but such cases are considered the exception rather than the rule. Government may also own land. In the United States, the federal government owns one-third of all land, mostly in Alaska and the West.

The bias of the capitalist civilization in favor of private ownership of the means of production is based on two considerations. First, ownership of productive property means power over the lives of other people; from the libertarian viewpoint, it is preferable that such power be diffused among many property owners rather than held by one owner, the state. Moreover, the economic power of private property owners can be curbed by the popularly elected government; were the state to own all productive property, economic and political power would coincide, and the outlook for personal economic liberty would be uncertain. Second, the classical capitalist assumption is that *technological progress* is more easily attained when each person minds his own business and has the personal incentive to do so.

Market economy

Another principle of the capitalist system is that of the market economy. In the precapitalist era, the economy was generally local and self-sufficient; each family produced just about what it needed, supplementing its simple needs with some barter or exchange operations in a primitive local market. Division of labor was barely known, and each family had to do many jobs that are now spread among hundreds of various crafts and specialties. Also, the type of occupation a person held and the price he could charge for his goods and services were largely predetermined for him by custom and usage. In contrast, the market economy of the capitalist system is based on specialization of labor. Each person supplies only a small part of his needs through his own skills and labors. The products or services are designed not for the producer's own household, but for the market. As to prices, supply and demand are the determining factors—to the extent that competition is not distorted by monopolies, oligopolies, or "price leadership" of dominant companies in a particular business or industry.

Under fascism and communism the government tries to plan the whole economy. But in doing so it encounters limitations of the span of control. No planning group can anticipate all the possible contingencies in an intricate economic system that encompasses millions of persons and requires economic decisions that run into the tens of millions daily. As we saw earlier, the Soviet leadership abandoned the concept of rigid control planning in the middle 1960s, and has since decentralized the process of economic decision making by giving the managers of individual plants more discretion in adapting to changes of their markets. In the capitalist market economy, each decision maker watches over a much smaller area; therefore the span of attention and control is more limited and more manageable.

The comparatively unregulated operation of supply and demand is the most fundamental principle of the free market economy. Neither communism nor fascism believes in this; in fascism, ownership of the means of production is formally in the hands of private individuals, but is not important, because fascism does away with the free or open market economy and substitutes the *command economy*. The state tells individuals where to work, what jobs to choose, what to produce, what prices to charge, and how to invest savings and profits. In communism, both private ownership of the means of production and the market economy are abolished. Thus the communist economy is a command economy, too, in which economic decisions are made by the state. In contrast, the market economy is one in which corporations or individuals may make their own economic decisions in the light of their interest, experience, and capability.

The tremendous political implications of the market economy have been recognized by socialist economists. One, W. Arthur Lewis, examines this question in a book written for the Fabian Society, *The Principles of Economic Planning* (1949). As a socialist, Lewis opposed the orthodox concepts of laissez faire, as do most nonsocialist economists.

The real issue, Lewis argued, is not between planning and no planning, but between planning by direction and planning by inducement. In the former, the government (as under fascism or communism) tries to get the right things done by direct control and regulation of output, wages, and prices. A government agent watches every step in the plan, and those workers or managers who fail to fulfill their quota may be punished as saboteurs, although neglect or incapacity rather than willful disregard may have been the cause of their failure.

In a democracy, the government stimulates certain economic activities indirectly by means of the budget, taxation, interest rates, and other policies of planning by inducement, thus avoiding the two main defects of planning by direction: bureaucratic centralization and economic inefficiency. Far from rejecting the free market as the normal mechanism of economic adjustment, Lewis held that "our aim should be to preserve free markets wherever possible." It is of no little interest that, in accepting the principle of the market economy, Lewis is driven to the conclusion that the nationalization of all industry is undesirable because of the usual reasons against monopoly: inefficiency, lack of initiative, and concentration of power.

Thus, the function of the free market as a mechanism of political liberty is increasingly being recognized by socialists as it becomes apparent that the question of ownership is less important than the question of whether economic decisions are made by independent business people on the one hand, or by the state on the other.

Thus the distinction between a command economy and a market economy reflects in the economic field the more basic political distinction between totalitarianism (fascism and communism) and liberalism (socialism and capitalism). The symbiotic relation between market economy and relative political liberalization can also be seen in the comparative study of either fascist or communist states. Fascist Italy had more of a market economy than Nazi Germany and was politically less coercive. Among communist states, it is significant that Yugoslavia, politically more liberal than any of the other communist states, has moved further in the direction of a market economy than have other communist economies.

The most important specific factor in a market economy is consumer sovereignty: The consumer not only has the freedom to choose between the goods offered for sale, but ultimately determines through such free choice what and how much is to be produced. In a market economy the government does not determine how many automobiles or television sets are to be produced—as is still the case after the economic reforms of the 1960s in the Soviet Union; rather, this determination is cumulative, made by the individual choices of millions of consumers. Even in a market economy, however, the government may adopt policies that bear on the level of production. In a period of an "overheated" economy, the government may increase the rate of interest, thus acting to discourage corporations and individuals from borrowing at high interest rates for the purpose of expanding business. In such a period the government may even go further and set up wage and price controls, as President Nixon did in his "New Economic Policy" in 1971. Such governmental intervention, often only temporary, is basically different from the government determining, as in a fascist or communist command economy, how much of a particular item is to be produced regardless of the preference of consumers.

Competition

Another essential characteristic of the market economy is competition. In the precapitalist economy, custom and usage dictated what goods and services were worth, and there were many persons who could not compete at all because they were excluded from some occupations or trades. In the modern economy, the alternative to competition is either the private monopoly or the legal monopoly of the state. In both cases, arbitrary determination of the prices of goods and services by a de facto authority (as in the case of private monopoly) or by a legal authority (as in that of the state) takes the place of the free interplay of buyers and sellers.

In industry, *research* has become one of the keenest areas of competition. Research today means cheaper and better products tomorrow, and the vitality of competition is seen in the fact that companies are spending an increasingly larger share of their budgets on research. In 1930, research expenditures in the United States amounted to $160 million; currently they exceed $30 billion. About two-thirds of this outlay comes from the federal government, most of the rest from private industry. By accelerating the rate of change in the economy, research promotes competition at an early stage, long before the product or service reaches the market. Research is also an important factor in the competition between whole economies. One of the disturbing features of the American economy during the 1970s has been a decline in the proportion of private and public investment in basic research, upon which technological leadership ultimately depends. The growing strength of Japan and West Germany in world trade, at the expense of the United States, is attributable in part to their high investment in research.

Profit

The *profit* principle is another basic characteristic of the capitalist system. There is a tremendous difference between capitalism and precapitalist systems: A capitalist economy provides more opportunity for profit than any previous economy because it guarantees three freedoms that were not commonly found in precapitalist systems—freedom of trade and occupation, freedom of property, and freedom of contract. In the Middle Ages, products were made by guilds and sold at prescribed prices. The profit system was thus doubly limited. Only a member of the guild could enter the process of production; furthermore, prices were established not by freedom of contract between buyer and seller, but by the authority of custom, the church, or the state.

When the capitalist system is described as a profit system, it is frequently forgotten that the other side of the transaction is equally important—capitalism is also a *loss* system. Although it is true that never have so many made so much profit as under capitalism, it is equally true that in no other system have so many lost so much as under capitalism. In American economic development, bankruptcies and failures were very heavy in the early stages of the mining, railroading, and automotive industries. In the computer industry, the Radio Corporation of America, a giant company, tried in vain to get a permanent place in the business. After making computers for two decades, RCA finally decided in 1971 to close down computer production—at an estimated loss of over $500 million.

In a typical year, about four out of ten corporations report net losses. Of ten business firms started in an average year, five close down within two years, and eight within ten years—lack of success being the main reason.

The theory of capitalism approximated reality most closely during its classical period, roughly from the middle of the eighteenth to the end of the nineteenth century. In the twentieth century, capitalism has had to face unexpected stresses and strains.

The separation of the ownership from the management and financial control of a business firm was made legally possible by the invention of the *corporate* form of business: Each shareholder in a corporation is liable only to the extent of the shares he owns, no more and no less. In the precapitalist economy, a partnership involved full personal responsibility of each partner for the operations of the business. Partnerships tended to be relatively small, and each partner had a sense of personal involvement, financial and moral, in the business. In a large modern corporation, where 50 million or 100 million shares are owned by a half a million or more shareholders, the link between the individual shareholder and the corporation of which he is part-owner is very tenuous. The corporation may be located thousands of miles away from most of the shareholders; in most corporations only a small fraction of shareholders, generally less than 1 percent, attend the annual meetings in which officers are elected and other important business is transacted.

Management draws up the list of officers to be elected, management presides over the elections, management explains why its proposed policy decisions should be adopted, management decides the salaries of management, management finally submits all its proposals to a vote: The vote is normally between 95 and 99 percent in favor of management. This is a comfortable majority, as compared with average majorities of 52 to 55 percent in political elections. "Like a stockholders' meeting" is a common phrase used to describe any perfunctorily run meeting. According to a recent study of 500 large corporations, the probability of a serious struggle for control in a large corporation occurs, on the average, once every 300 years!

The essence of the problem is simple. In government, democracy has established the principle that those who wield power must be accountable to the public. The people are the principal, the government their agent. Political power in a democracy must not be held for the benefit of the rulers; it is a trust, the purpose of which is to protect the interests of the people.

In the economic realm a situation prevails that runs counter to the basic concept of democracy: Corporation managers wield far-reaching power over stockholders and employees, and constantly make decisions that affect the public interest without any clearly defined responsibility to the public. In a capitalist democracy, political policies are determined by processes of consent that begin at the bottom and move up to the top, whereas in corporate business, economic policies are made at the top and passed down to the bottom. The character of modern industrial organization is hierarchical, founded on discipline and obedience. Recently the traditional pattern in industry has been considerably modified by union negotiations, by legislation, by public opinion, and by the development among some business people of a sense of responsibility toward their communities and society as a whole.

The more capitalism succeeds, the more it destroys its original institutional and ideological character by collectivizing the framework of business. The first collectivists in the capitalistic era were not its critics, but successful capitalistic entrepreneurs—men like Andrew Carnegie, John D. Rockefeller, and Henry Ford—who created vast industrial empires.

Like other empires, industrial empires tend to become bureaucratic and conformity-minded, to follow routine and precedent, and, above all, to transform personal initiative and enterprise into impersonal rules of administrative routine. Whereas the original individual capitalists were bold, daring, and adventurous, the present bureaucratic administrators of modern industrial empires tend to put security above everything else. While risk-taking was one of the characteristic traits of original capitalists, corporate business leaders today prefer the riskless investments of "safe bets."

The danger is that, as business becomes bigger, the free-enterprise system may gradually become a "safe-enterprise" system.

In many respects there is less difference between large-scale capitalist enterprise and large-scale socialized enterprise than between small-scale capitalist enterprise and large-scale capitalist enterprise. Such defenders of capitalism as Justice Brandeis and President Wilson were afraid that the "curse of bigness" might eventually destroy not only big private enterprise, but private enterprise itself. Again, this problem of bigness is not peculiar to the economic institutions of liberal capitalism; in politics, too, there is the threat of "big government" destroying the very elements that give life and vitality to democracy.

Who owns American business? About 60 percent of all corporate stock is owned by individuals, the rest by investment companies, insurance companies, foundations, and institutions. On the positive side, there has been a substantial growth in the number of persons owning stock; on the negative side, there is the fact that fewer than 0.1 percent of the citizens own 20 percent of all individually held stock. While this concentration of stock ownership has been declining slightly in recent years, it is still high enough to suggest that American capitalism has a long way to go before it can be called "people's capitalism."

To get some idea of the role of big business in the American economy, consider that in 1976 the 500 largest industrial corporations accounted for 80 percent of total U.S. industrial sales, for 75 percent of all profits in industry, and for 75 percent of employment in all industrial corporations. This trend toward bigness has grown in recent decades. In 1948, the 200 largest manufacturing corporations held 48 percent of the assets of all manufacturing corporations; in 1976, their assets went up to 60 percent. In some major nonindustrial sectors of the economy —such as banking, life insurance, and public utilities—concentration of ownership and control is even greater than in industry.

The phenomenon of concentration can be illustrated by a giant corporation like General Motors, the largest manufacturing company in the world. In an average year, General Motors produces half or more of all passenger cars in the United States and is also the largest manufacturer of buses and railroad locomotives. It employs about 2 percent of the entire labor force in manufacturing, and its after-tax profits amount to about 7 percent of all corporate after-tax profits in manufacturing. Its annual sales in the United States alone exceed the gross national product of more than 100 other countries.

Yet there are other sides to the picture. First, the small businessman has by no means disappeared from the American scene. Retail trade and services have provided the largest opportunities for small business. Often, expanding big business is accompanied by a simultaneous growth of many new small businesses. For example, as people buy more cars, there are new opportunities for small manufacturers of parts, for gas stations, garages, motels, restaurants, and for all the other services and trades connected with automobile travel.

Second, there is no hereditary aristocracy in big business. Of the hundred largest industrial corporations in 1909, about one-quarter were among the hundred largest in 1979. Of the ten largest corporations in 1909, only two were in the same category in 1960. Moreover, the competition is not only between individual firms in this top group; changing conditions of the economy entail keen competition between whole industry groups. Steel, coal mining, and textiles were much more important in 1909 than in 1979, when the petroleum, chemical, and electrical equipment industries rose sharply in their relative importance in the top hundred corporations. This change in the composition of the top group during seven decades illustrates that bigness is not to be identified with monopoly. Similarly, business executives are not a hereditary aristocracy. Currently, about 10 percent of big business executives are children of wealthy families. By contrast, around 1900, about half of big business executives were born into wealthy families.

Defenders of big business maintain that a big country and a big market need big business. Individual security, too, has a better chance in big business than in small enterprises, they argue, because the former can do a better job in long-term planning of production, stability of employment, and the provision of services like pension and sickness benefits. In labor-management relations, the greatest progress has been made in mass production industries like steel and automobiles in which big business predominates; by contrast, labor unions have made little progress in agriculture and retailing in which the small and middle-sized unit prevails.

In research, too, big business carries most of the work and responsibility. Occasionally, important inventions are still made in small laboratories; then it takes the resources and organization of larger corporations to translate the inventions into economic realities. More and more, however, industrial research is carried out by big corporations because it requires large financial resources and many years of effort.

Concerning the impact of big business on competition, it is argued that the two are not incompatible. Big business produces a new kind of competition—internal competition. Not only is there competition between General Motors and Ford, but within General Motors itself the Chevrolet competes with the Pontiac, the Oldsmobile with the Buick. Moreover, there is competition in passenger transportation among automobiles, buses, and airlines.

The problem of competition in the changing American economy is the subject of *The New Industrial State* (1971) by John Kenneth Galbraith. In classical economics, the author points out, competition was conceived in terms of many sellers, each with a small share of the market, and restraint of excessive private economic power was provided by competing firms on the same side of the market. Galbraith concedes that this classical model of competition has largely disappeared, since many markets have come to be dominated by a few firms and frequently there is tacit collusion among these firms on major policy decisions.

Yet Galbraith does not conclude from the widespread disappearance of traditional competition that there is no longer any restraint of private economic power left. New restraints have, in fact, taken the place of overt competition, and these restraints—termed by Galbraith "countervailing power"—are the products of concentration and bigness.

These new factors of restraint have appeared not on the same side of the market but on the opposite side, not with competitors but with customers and suppliers. The concentration of industrial enterprises not only has led to a relatively small number of sellers but also has brought about the predominant position of a few buyers. In the field of labor, too, strong unions have developed mainly when faced by strong corporations, as in the steel, automobile, and electrical industries. In contrast, there has been no equally powerful union in the retail business or in agriculture, the closest approximations in the United States to pure competition.

The weakness of the concept of countervailing power lies in the fact that, though the power of the large seller may be checked by that of the large buyer, the resulting benefit need not be passed on to the consumer. Monopoly benefits may be amicably split between the large buyer and the large seller, or between the large corporation and the large union, at the expense of the consumer.

THE RISE OF THE SERVICE ECONOMY

In the initial phases of industrial development, under capitalism or any other system, the industrial working class constantly increases at the expense of artisans, landless peasants, and other social groups whose members seek employment in the expanding factories and mines. In a later and more advanced phase of industrial development, however, the industrial working class begins to decline in proportion to the total population, though it still continues to increase in absolute numbers.

In the United States, the volume of industrial production and the number of persons employed in industry have increased tremendously since 1900, yet the proportion of the industrial working class in the total work force has consistently declined for two reasons.

First, within industry itself, there has been an increasing shift of employment from production ("blue-collar") workers to nonproduction ("white-collar" and service) workers. Between 1947 and 1976, employment in manufacturing rose more than 25 percent. Whereas the number of production workers increased by one-fourth, the number of nonproduction workers more than doubled during that period. And, although the number of blue-collar workers rose only moderately, output from 1947 to 1976 more than doubled. Technological progress, particularly automation, reduced the number of blue-collar workers needed to produce a given quantity of goods, such as steel, coal, or automobiles.

The second, more important, reason for the sharp increase in white-collar workers is the rapid growth of employment in enterprises that provide services rather than produce physical goods. Between 1950 and 1977, the total number of employed persons rose from 60 million to 89 million. About 80 percent of this increase of 29 million was due to the expansion of the number of white-collar workers, which rose from 22 million in 1950 to 45 million in 1977. The increase in the number of white-collar workers was due to big expansion in the services-producing sector of the economy (government, schools, wholesale and retail trade, health services, insurance, finance, real estate, communications media, entertainment). The fastest and most important growth area in the services has been in government, particularly at the state and local level. Between 1950 and 1977, federal employment rose from 2.1 million to 2.8 million, but employment at the state and local level rose from 4.3 million to 12.2 million.

As a result of the massive shift from producing goods to providing services in the American economy, there has been a corresponding shift in the profile of employment. In 1950, less than half of the labor force held white-collar or service jobs. In 1977, 64 percent were employed in such jobs: 50 percent as white-collar workers (professional and technical workers, managers, clerical workers, salesworkers), and 13 percent as service workers (hotel and restaurant workers, repair services, household workers). Whereas in 1950 blue-collar workers outnumbered white-collar workers, in 1977 the latter outnumbered the former by about three to two. The office has replaced the production line as the typical place of work in the United States, and service has replaced the physical good as the typical form of economic output.

The new type of postindustrial economy is called a *service economy,* to distinguish it from the industrial economy that preceded it. Marx foresaw the transition from the agrarian to the industrial economy on a worldwide scale, but in his writings there is no inkling of the service economy that followed the industrial economy.

The year 1956 was a milestone in economic history: For the first time in American history, or in that of any nation, the number of persons engaged in producing goods was smaller than the number of persons performing services. In recent years a similar change has occurred in other industrially advanced nations, such as Canada, Sweden, and Britain, where more people now produce services than goods. So far, no communist economy has become, or is close to becoming, a service economy, since communist economies are still either industrial (Soviet Union, East Germany), in an early stage of industrialization (Romania, Poland, Bulgaria), or predominantly agrarian (China, Mongolia).

Farmworkers and service workers are neither white-collar nor blue-collar workers. These two groups are not as important numerically as are blue-collar and white-collar workers, but do show the same overall trend from goods-producing to service-rendering employment as living standards rise. In 1953, service workers for the first time exceeded the number of farm workers in the United States, and their numbers are consistently rising in absolute and relative strength, whereas farmworkers have gone down in both absolute and relative strength. Between 1950 and 1977, the number of farmworkers declined from 7.4 million (over 12 percent of the work force) to 2.7 million (about 3 percent of the work force). During the same period, the number of service workers rose from 6.5 million to 12 million, or from 11 percent to 13 percent of the work force.

The growth of the number of white-collar workers (or "salariat") from 22 million in 1950 to 45 million in 1977 has important political implications, since the salaried person—in capitalist as well as in communist economies—tends to identify with the middle and upper classes rather than with the working class, even if his or her income is below that of the worker. Marx assumed that the transformation of the independent middle class of artisans and shopkeepers into a dependent salaried class would necessarily change the outlook of the old middle class from bourgeois to proletarian. Yet the new middle class of the salariat in the United States has generally refused to join the ranks of organized labor and typically votes Republican, whereas blue-collar workers typically vote Democratic. Moreover, within the ranks of the salariat, various segments have grown at an uneven pace. Between 1950 and 1977, the top category of professional and technical workers grew by about 150 percent, clerical workers by 112 percent, and salesworkers by only 50 percent. Thus, the white-collar group was increasingly upgraded in education and income—and also changed its political outlook, since professional personnel are not only better educated and financially better off than are clerical or salesworkers but also more moderate in political attitudes. This upgrading of the labor force has also occurred among blue-collar workers. Politically, these changes are significant, because more skilled workers generally look upon themselves as middle class, adopt middle-class life styles, and tend to be politically more conservative than unskilled workers. In the 1972 presidential election, the AFL-CIO leadership refused to give its traditional support for the Democratic candidate (Senator McGovern); some unions went even further by abandoning neutrality and urging the reelection of President Nixon.

The political problems posed by the rise of the salariat and the changes within the working class are not limited to industrial development under capitalism; they also appear under communism. In its early phase of industrialization, Russia witnessed a tremendous growth of her industrial proletariat, largely composed of unskilled and semiskilled workers. But as industrialization proceeded a new salariat began to develop, with a way of life of its own and with its own ideas, different from those of the working class.

Despite official denials, class lines have crystallized in the Soviet Union and other communist states. One important line of differentiation is between the white-collar and the blue-collar worker, a distinction based more on social status than on income. The influence of the white-collar group—"intelligentsia" in the Soviet Union—is constantly rising at the expense of the working class, as can be seen in the changing composition of Soviet political bodies, university students, and other key groups of social importance. Thus, a class struggle along orthodox Marxist lines is beginning to take shape in communist societies undergoing industrialization, and—as in capitalist countries—proletariat and salariat are not generally on the same side of the barricades.

Finally, the rise of the service economy has profoundly affected the stability of advanced capitalist economies. Marx held that a major cause of the disintegration of capitalism is the recurring cycle of boom and bust, resulting in periods of inflation and unemployment. Economic experience has shown that substantial periodic changes in demand and employment occur in the goods-producing sector rather than in the services-producing sector, since goods can be overproduced and then have to be stored, whereas services cannot be stored. Thus, there is generally a better balance between supply and demand in the production of services than of goods, which leads to greater stability of employment in services-producing enterprises (government, schools, hospitals, banks). Since many services are provided by governmental or private nonprofit agencies, there is traditionally greater security of employment in such bodies than in goods-producing enterprises, which are almost invariably run by private businesses. However, even in business corporations that engage in the manufacture of goods, white-collar employees typically enjoy more stable employment than do production workers.

Before World War II, the capitalist economies used to be racked by periodic slumps and depressions. Since the Great Depression of the

1930s there has been no major economic depression in the capitalist economies. Such stability has been partly due to welfare-state policies resulting in the maintenance of high levels of effective demand by means of governmental action. Of at least equal importance have been the structural changes of advanced capitalist economies from industrial to postindustrial service economies, changes that Marx did not foresee.

THE NEW PLURALISTIC ECONOMY

The controversy of socialism versus capitalism has been rendered obsolete by the profound structural changes effected in the economies of the most advanced Western nations. The public attention received by a constant political tug of war over specific economic issues conceals some long-term forces that are at work.

A primary change, for example, is the increased government responsibility for social and economic welfare, which is not the result of moral conversion or of partisan struggles between rugged individualists and do-gooders, but of the increasing output of goods and services. Some of the more democratic developing nations have set up elaborate schemes of welfare-state policies, but in many cases these schemes exist on paper only, since the nations are too poor to pay for the desired welfare. By contrast, where economic levels are high enough to permit welfare policies, as in most advanced Western nations and increasingly in some communist states, there is a realistic foundation for such schemes.

Another structural change of capitalism has been the relative growth of the not-for-profit sector. Traditional economic analysis and popular thinking still concentrate on the private, profit-seeking sector of the economy while neglecting the importance of government and private nonprofit institutions, which together constitute the not-for-profit sector of the economy. In fact, the not-for-profit sector of the U.S. economy is growing at a faster rate than the profit-seeking sector. In 1929, the not-for-profit sector accounted for 12.5 percent of the gross national product. In the late 1970s, the share rose to more than 30 percent. In 1929, employment in the not-for-profit sector was about 10 percent of the civilian labor force. In the 1970s employment in this sector stood at over 20 percent of the labor force. Government employed 7 percent of the labor force in 1929, as compared with 20 percent in the late 1970s.

However, the economic impact of the not-for-profit sector is even larger if one adds its indirect contribution to the economy. These indirect effects derive mainly from the goods and services it buys, such as defense contracts of the federal government or laboratory equipment bought by colleges and universities. In 1929, these indirect effects of the not-for-profit sector were responsible for about 5 percent of the civilian labor force. In the 1960s, the share rose to about 12 percent. Combining the more than 20 percent of direct employment in the not-for-profit sector with the 12 percent of indirect employment generated by it, we find the not-for-profit sector responsible for one-third of the U.S. civilian labor force.

What are the reasons behind the growth of the not-for-profit sector of the economy? In the expansion of government, defense (on the federal level) and education, health, and welfare (on all levels of government) have been the main areas of growth. Private nonprofit institutions have also enlarged their activities, mainly in education and health. Finally, the growth of the not-for-profit sector is due to an inherent tendency in advanced economies which has nothing to do with capitalism or socialism. As an industrial economy advances, more and more labor goes into the rendering of services rather than into the production of goods. Since the scope of the not-for-profit sector includes services such as education, community services, health services, social welfare rather than goods, its role in the economy is likely to grow as the shift from goods to services persists.

So far, there has been little tampering with the traditional concept of leaving the production of goods to private enterprise working for profit, and this pattern is likely to continue. Even socialist governments in Scandinavia or Britain have concentrated their socialization programs on services (health, pensions, education) rather than on industrial production. As an economically advanced nation progressively increases its wealth, there is more demand for public provision of services which are considered essential but which many people cannot afford to buy, such as old-age pensions, health insurance, education, urban renewal, or cheap transportation in metropolitan areas.

Increasing wealth also makes it possible for private nonprofit institutions to enlarge their activities. Pension funds of labor unions or endowments of private colleges and universities in the United States run into many billions, and these vast funds had to be produced first in the profit sector of the economy before they could be channeled into the not-for-profit sector.

The profit sector and the not-for-profit sector are not antagonists engaged in a deadly struggle for supremacy. In health and education we see an interesting mixture of private profit, private nonprofit, and government. Most physicians are self-employed and are part of the private profit sector of the economy. Most hospitals are private nonprofit institutions. The largest general health insurance program is carried on by Blue Cross–Blue Shield, private and nonprofit, although there are also private, profit-seeking insurance plans as well as government health insurance programs (such as federal Medicare for the aged and similar state programs since 1966). The federal government contributes to the building of hospital facilities and, since Medicare, pays for some of the medical costs of the aged.

In education, too, there is cooperation between the private profit, private nonprofit, and government sectors of the economy. Harvard University's endowment is worth over $1 billion. Most of this endowment comes from gifts by wealthy capitalists, by nonprofit foundations originally set up by wealthy capitalists, or by individuals who generally earn their living in the private sector. Of its annual budget of well over $100 million, about one-third comes from government sources, the rest from interest earned on endowment funds, from student fees, and from annual gifts. Harvard, a private nonprofit institution, thus receives its funds from all three sectors of the economy: private profit, private nonprofit, and government. Its graduates then return to all three sectors of the economy, the majority working for private business or in self-employing professions.

The traditional socialist charge against the profit motive in capitalism was coupled with the hope that the removal of profit would abolish poverty. Economic reality has worked differently. To the extent that the profit motive has given way to nonprofit service—whether it be private or public—the cause has been not poverty but rising wealth and rising expectations of the people.

Also, nonprofit enterprise is not synonymous with absolute equality or uniformity. There is still room for ambition and even for competition. Labor unions, foundations, and colleges are all nonprofit, but their top salaries often compare favorably with executive salaries in private business. Frequently, successful men in any one of the three sectors of the economy move on to the other two. Former government officials, civilian and military, are to be found in important positions in business corporations or nonprofit foundations, and a top executive of an automobile company may become secretary of defense or president of the World Bank. As the number of men and women who have had experience in private business, private nonprofit institutions, and government increases, the result is likely to be a lessening of ideological rigidity.

THE WELFARE STATE

The main principles of the welfare state are relatively simple: First, every member of the community is entitled to a minimum standard of living; second, the welfare state is committed to putting full employment at the top of social goals to be supported by public policy.

Particularly in the United States, adherents of the welfare state believe that full employment can be attained without recourse to large-scale nationalization. Taxation properly adjusted to periods of prosperity and depression; interest rates determined by governmental decision according to economic needs; fiscal policies designed to redistribute purchasing power in harmony with the best interest of the nation; investment incentives in times of contracting business; public works for direct unemployment relief; government credits to builders or buyers of homes—these are but a few of the measures the government can adopt to stabilize the economy without changing its foundations.

In the United States, the Great Depression of 1929–1939 undermined faith in the orthodox philosophy of laissez faire, according to which the disequilibrium of the market would eventually be restored to a new equilibrium without any interference from the outside. When the American economy reached the stage in which one out of every four employable persons was out of work, in which the farmer could not sell products at reasonable prices, in which more and more business enterprises went bankrupt or were unable to pay wages to their employees or earn profits for their shareholders, something had to be done. The New Deal, starting with the first term of President Franklin D. Roosevelt in 1933, was not so much a set of premeditated philosophical principles to be superimposed upon the American people as a series of emergency measures in response to urgent practical problems.

The Agricultural Adjustment Act (May 12, 1933) attempted to help the farmer by raising farm prices to a level that would enable farmers to buy industrial products for the same relative amount as in the years 1909–1914. In order to make such "parity" possible, farmers were to reduce production, in return for which they would receive higher prices (as a result of decreased supply) from the consumer and subsidies from the government. Traditionally opposed to government interference—in theory at least—the farmers have been content with that part of the welfare state which directly protects their interests.

The National Labor Relations Act (July 5, 1935), commonly known as the Wagner Act, established full statutory regulation of labor-management relations for the first time in the United States. In the preceding half-century, the employer in the United States was free to recognize or not recognize labor unions and to bargain or not bargain with them. Employers frequently discharged employees for union activities, and if unions became too strong, employers would use various means to break them, including company unions, private police, labor spies, lockouts, and professional strike breakers.

The main purpose of the Wagner Act was to encourage collective bargaining between labor and management, thus substituting peaceful discussion for violence. Although the law did not, and could not, compel both sides to agree, and strikes and lockouts still remained legal, the experience of collective bargaining quickly resulted in a dramatic decline of violence in labor disputes.

Dissatisfaction of management with some provisions of the Wagner Act led to its replacement in 1947 by the Labor-Management Relations Act, commonly known as the Taft-Hartley Act. Although spokesmen for labor voiced deep dissatisfaction with the Taft-Hartley Act, it left the basic principle of the Wagner Act—collective bargaining—substantially unchanged.

The Social Security Act (August 14, 1935) marked another milestone in the movement for social reform in the United States. In modern industry the individual is frequently at the mercy of large impersonal forces over which he has no control. The efforts of the family, private charity, and the local community have frequently proved insufficient to protect the individual against the hazards of old age, disability, or unemployment. The passage of the Social Security Act marked the recognition that government, on the local, state, and federal levels, is partly responsible for assuring its citizens of some protection against want and insecurity. Apart from its humanitarian motivation, Social Security also has important economic effects since such payments provide people with a minimum purchasing power which contributes to the stability of the economy.

In a historic breakthrough in 1965, Congress amended the Social Security Act to include health insurance for persons over 65, covering both hospitalization and doctors' bills. Under this insurance program, popularly known as Medicare, the federal government pays the major cost of illness. Although federal Medicare covers only persons over 65, the federal government makes grants to state health insurance programs for families with dependent children whose income and financial resources are insufficient for necessary medical services. Numerous states quickly made use of this federal provision and set up supplementary state programs, known as Medicaid. Whereas federal Medicare has an age limit but no means test, state Medicaid programs have a means test but no age limit, since each state prescribes the income level below which it provides health insurance. Far from weakening private initiative, public programs seem to stimulate it. For example, private pension funds have grown faster than public pension funds.

In education, too, 1965 was a turning point in the expansion of the welfare state. Under the Elementary and Secondary Education Act the federal government makes direct grants, amounting to several billions annually, to individual school districts with children from low-income families. The Higher Education Act also expanded the federal government's role. In addition to grants and loans to educational institutions for construction, training, and research, the federal government gives financial help to millions of college students. These programs include work-study aid, grants for "disadvantaged" students, direct federal loans, and federally guaranteed private loans, wherein the government guarantees repayment of the loan and pays the interest while the student is at school. After graduation, the student pays the interest and repays the loan in annual installments.

The major categories that receive social welfare benefits from federal funds include: retired workers, their dependents, and survivors; veterans and their dependents; recipients of public assistance, including persons receiving AFDC (Aid to Families with Dependent Children) aid; and retired federal employees and their survivors. These figures do not include millions of people helped by Medicaid, children receiving federally subsidized school lunches, people receiving food stamps, and more than 2 million college students receiving federal grants, loans, or insured private loans.

The growing commitment of the U.S. government to social welfare can be seen in the changes in the federal budget in recent years. The federal budget for 1971 was the first in 20 years in which more money was allocated for human resources (education, health, income security, and veterans benefits) than for defense. In the budget for 1978, expenditures for human resources were earmarked at 51 percent of total expenditures, as compared with 25 percent for defense. By contrast, in the federal budget for 1963—before any major involvement in Vietnam —29 percent of the budget was spent on human resources, and 47 percent on defense.

One of the main mechanisms of bringing about greater equality through redistribution is *taxation*. Yet taxation cannot produce wealth; it can merely transfer it from one group to another. The improved material well-being of the American people in the last generation is due primarily to increased production of goods and services. At the same time, a heightened sense of equity underlying the philosophy of the welfare state has brought about more equality in the distribution of incomes than used to prevail in the United States. Incomes have improved both absolutely (in terms of actual size) and relatively (in terms of the distribution among various groups of the population).

Looking at income distribution in the United States from a worldwide perspective, an authority in this field comes to the following conclusion: "Do the rich get a larger share of income in the United States than they do in other countries? According to the available evidence this is not the case. The United States has about the same income

From each according to ability to pay

distribution as Denmark, Sweden, and Great Britain and a much more equal distribution than most of the other countries for which data are shown" (Herman P. Miller, *Rich Man, Poor Man,* 1971, p. 23). Denmark, Sweden, and Great Britain have been governed throughout most or much of the last three decades by socialist labor parties. Yet their accomplishments in reducing income inequalities have only been about the same as in the United States, which has no major socialist labor party.

The evolution of the welfare state in the United States is part of a worldwide trend to make the economies more responsive to the needs of man. The growth of the not-for-profit sector in the American economy—as in other economies—also indicates that profit need not be the sole mechanism of economic progress or of social advance. The welfare state has neither resulted in perfect justice and liberty for all, nor has it led—as its opponents predicted in the 1930s that it would—to the repressive society of authoritarianism or totalitarianism.

In adapting to the economic changes brought on by the expansion of the not-for-profit sector and to the social changes effected by the welfare state, capitalism has undergone profound transformation. This new and constantly evolving system is neither capitalist nor socialist— if capitalism means laissez faire and socialism means public ownership of the means of production. It is generally called a "mixed economy," combining predominantly private initiative and property with public responsibility for social welfare. Just as the mixed economy of today shows basic changes in relation to the predominantly laissez-faire economy of a generation or two ago, the economy 20 years hence may show equally revolutionary changes.

Capitalism and Democracy

TWO CONCEPTIONS OF DEMOCRACY

The close link between capitalism and democracy can best be seen in the fact that both first developed in one country, Britain. Britain retained its world leadership as a political democracy and capitalist economy throughout most of the nineteenth century, passing on this role to the United States in the twentieth century. While there is considerable ambiguity and confusion about the meaning of capitalism, there is even more misunderstanding about the meaning of democracy. George Bernard Shaw once proposed that, in order to eradicate misunderstanding and confusion about the meaning of democracy, the leading scholars and thinkers of the world be convened and the issue be settled once and for all. Unfortunately, the root of the trouble lies deeper. Disagreements about the concept of democracy are not semantic, but reflect differences of a more fundamental nature.

When representatives of the United States, Britain, or France talk about democracy, they assign to it a meaning that is different from what Soviet or Chinese communists have in mind when they use the same term. Thus at the end of World War II, when the United States, Britain, France, and the Soviet Union occupied Germany, one of their chief objectives was the democratization of Germany. At first all four powers wholeheartedly agreed on the objective, but it soon became evident that the Soviet concept was entirely different from the Anglo-American-French understanding of democracy.

The Western powers took the view that bringing democracy to Germany meant free elections; a free press; freedom of political association; freedom of religion, thought, and speech; equality before the law; the right to oppose the government; the right to choose one's job; the right to form free trade unions; the right to move freely within one's country, go abroad temporarily, or emigrate permanently.

Above all, freedom from fear is basic in the Western concept of democracy. No society can be called free unless its citizens feel safe from unwarranted intrusion into their affairs by governmental authorities, particularly the secret police.

The communist conception of democratizing Germany was entirely different from the Western. It meant the destruction of capitalism and the setting up of a state-owned economy in Germany. When communists speak of democracy, they have in mind, not government *of* the people, nor government *by* the people, but, as a leading Soviet philosopher put it, "whether this or that policy is carried out in the interests of the people, in the interests of its overwhelming majority, or in the interests of its minority" (G. F. Aleksandrov, *The Pattern of Soviet Democracy,* 1948).

Which doctrine reveals whether government is carried out in the interests of the people? Marxist-Leninist doctrine. Who interprets the doctrine correctly? The Communist party. Who in the Communist party determines the party line? The Politburo, a group of a dozen men or so. Who in the Politburo determines its general policy? The top leader who controls the party, army, and police. If the leader loses control over any one of these key elements of power—as happened to Khrushchev in 1964—he is removed and becomes an "unperson."

Communists call the essentials of democracy—freedom of speech, press, and association, equality before the law, and all the other fundamental democratic rights and liberties—*formal* democracy, as compared with the *real* democracy of communism, in which the means of production are owned by the state. In this conception, traditional democratic freedoms assume a new meaning.

Freedom of the press? By all means, provided the newspapers function "in conformity with the interests of working people and the socialist system" (1977 Constitution of the Soviet Union). Freedom of speech? Completely and unqualifiedly, provided the speaker's words support the communist cause. When an American told an acquaintance in Moscow that he could criticize and lambaste the president of the United States near the White House in Washington, D.C., the Soviet citizen sardonically replied he could do the same: He, too, could go to the Kremlin in Moscow and publicly lambaste the president of the United States. In 1968, when a handful of Russians tried to express in Moscow their public disapproval of the Soviet occupation of Czechoslovakia, they were quickly arrested, tried, and sentenced to prison and labor camp sentences.

Two criteria determine, in communist thinking, whether a government deserves to be called democratic: first, the nature of the economic system it operates and, second, the kind of foreign policy it pursues.

The case of Germany illustrates the importance of the economic system. In the elections of West Germany in 1953, only 2.2 percent of the vote was for the Communist party. Outlawed in West Germany in 1956, the party remained legal in West Berlin. In the West Berlin city elections of 1958, the communists obtained 1.9 percent of the vote; and in the elections of 1971, 2.3 percent. In 1972, a newly reconstituted Communist party participated in West Germany's national elections, but obtained only 0.3 percent of the popular vote. Yet from the communist viewpoint, West Germany is a dictatorship because the interests of its population are not determined by the one party that knows what is best for the Germans—the Communist party. In particular, the communists say, as long as capitalism exists in Germany there can be no democracy there because capitalism is by their definition a dictatorship of the wealthy over the poor. From the communist viewpoint, West Germany today could be called a democracy only if the Communist party ruled Germany, because only the Communist party could rule in the interests of the German people.

By contrast, East Germany is a true democracy, in the Soviet view, because it has abolished capitalism and operates a state-owned and state-run economy. The facts that a communist one-party dictatorship rules East Germany in dependence on Soviet military force stationed in its territory, that this artificial regime keeps its population behind frontiers of barbed wire and concrete walls to prevent flight into West Germany, that political prisons and "correctional" labor camps have been set up—all these are irrelevant to the communist proof of democracy.

The second criterion which, in communist political thinking, determines whether a government is democratic is foreign policy. In the view of Chinese communists, for example, Albania is a true democracy, because it sides completely with China on foreign policy (and particularly so in the Chinese campaign against the Soviet leadership). For this very reason, Albania is—in Soviet eyes—not a democracy, but a "deviationist, power-mad oligarchy."

DEMOCRACY AS A WAY OF LIFE

Whereas the Marxist-communist concept of democracy is primarily focused on the economic issue of the ownership of the means of production, the Western concept of democracy as a way of life is much broader and contains several principal elements defining the relations of the individual to society and government. Although these elements do not always reflect the reality of democracy, they provide standards and criteria by which a specific democratic society can be evaluated and judged:

1. Rational empiricism
2. Emphasis on the individual
3. Instrumental theory of the state
4. Voluntarism
5. The law behind the law
6. Emphasis on means
7. Discussion and consent in human relations
8. Basic equality of all human beings

1. *Rational empiricism* is perhaps the most important single element in the free way of life. It is based on confidence in reason and in the applicability of reason not only to physical nature but also to human relations. Dogmatists *know* what the truth is; for communists the concept of class is the ultimate in truth, whereas to fascists race and nation are the last repositories of truth. Since the dogmatist is so sure that he knows, he need not inquire further; his aim is to strengthen what he knows already, and he brands whoever questions his knowledge guilty of intellectual subversion. The psychological and historical relation between dogmatism in philosophy and authoritarianism in politics is clear: Absolute certainty of knowledge leads to fanatic enthusiasm in sentiment, which in turn leads to intolerant repression in government.

In contrast, empiricism, first fully developed by John Locke (1632–1704), is based on the idea that all our knowledge derives from experience. In this conception, truth (with a small *t*) is tentative, changing, and subject to constant checking and verification.

Since the history of both physical science and social thought is full of truths that turned out to be wholly or partly untrue, the rational empiricist refuses to believe, as the dogmatist believes, that mankind ever has arrived, or ever will arrive, at final answers. One of the paradoxical puzzles of the enlargement of knowledge is that, as understanding and knowledge of a particular problem or field increase, the awareness of our ignorance increases at an even faster rate. Many a problem solved—in the physical as in the social sciences—creates more new problems than existed before the solution.

It takes a lot of knowledge and inquiry to know what one does not know. The man who was first aware of his ignorance was probably, in the evolution of human thought, the first scientist; for, aware of *what* he did *not* know, he set about finding an answer. Without Newton's "solution" of the problem of gravity, there would have been no new world of physical phenomena unlocked by Einstein. Without the "solution" of the problem of government by the democratic method in the modern world, there would have been no Tocqueville discovering in his *Democracy in America* (1835) the new world of political problems created by the democratic solution.

The rational empiricist therefore views truth, in the study of nature as much as of man, as an endless process and considers the knowledge or truth of today no more than a *probability,* to be changed if new facts are brought to light. Bertrand Russell writes in his *Philosophy and Politics* that the genuine liberal says not "This is true," but "I am inclined to think that under present circumstances this opinion is probably the best."

Science and democracy also share the emphasis on procedure, on *how,* not what, answers will emerge as the result of the quest for true knowledge. The main justification of freedom of expression in both science and democracy is broader than the mere satisfaction of individual persons' desires for self-expression and self-fulfillment, defensible as that criterion alone may be. In science, the whole scientific community depends on, and feels entitled to, the free gathering and communication of all possible data and ideas. Similarly, the political community of democracy depends on the unhindered expression of the widest range of facts and opinions before a decision is made.

Ideally, a legislative body in a democracy acts like a judge who

The English House of Commons: Mother of Parliaments

renders a decision after listening to all sides presenting arguments that may be material or immaterial, important or unimportant. In fact, the oldest legislative body—the British Parliament—began and functioned during the first few centuries of its existence as a High Court: And even now the upper house of Parliament—the House of Lords—serves as Britain's supreme court. To this day, all democratic legislatures follow the British parliamentary procedure originally developed in a framework of judicial proceedings.

What most distinguishes a democratic from an authoritarian or totalitarian legislature is therefore not the final product—what laws are made in either institution—but what procedures are followed. Above all, democratic procedure requires, as do the judicial and scientific procedures, that all sides of an issue be heard. From this basic procedural requirement stem the essential democratic liberties of speech, publication, assembly, and association.

It is probably no coincidence that rational empiricism and democracy have developed more or less simultaneously in England, France, and the United States. In British thought, John Locke, the founder of empiricism, is still the most persuasive exponent of philosophical liberalism. In the United States, empiricism has been the dominant school of thought, culminating in John Dewey (1859–1952), whose application of rational empiricism to philosophy and politics has been a lasting contribution to the American liberal heritage.

In the mass society of contemporary capitalist democracy, the liberal commitment to critical rationalism has been confronted with several serious threats. In the revolution of communications media, the picture, with its powerful appeal to emotion, increasingly replaces the printed word, with its appeal to reason and reflection. Advertising techniques in the capitalist market have been refined to the point where the sales appeal is to unconscious and subliminal drives rather than to consciously felt needs and desires. In politics, too, some have argued, the rational orientation toward issues has given way to the emotional appeals of leaders and would-be leaders, and as a result of television the leader, too, has been replaced to a considerable extent by the *image* of the leader, by what he *appears* to be to the irrational response of the voters rather than what he really is in the light of cold reflection and sober reasoning. Finally, the revolution in communications media has produced the problem of "sensory overload." The individual is constantly bombarded by sensations, enticements, threats, and packaged bits of information and misinformation that demand immediate response or satisfaction—and such instant reactions are basically incompatible with the slow and plodding methods of critical rationalism.

2. *Emphasis on the individual* sharply separates liberal democracy

from both authoritarian and totalitarian regimes. In the eyes of a liberal democrat, no social or political institution—be it a local Boy Scout group, a party precinct, or the state—has a purpose other than to serve the individual.

In the totalitarian doctrine, the state is the master, the individual the servant. Hegel, one of the intellectual ancestors of both fascism and communism, says in his *Philosophy of Law* (1821) that the individual finds his liberty in obeying the state, and the fullest realization of his liberty in dying for the state. Only when the individual dies for the state does he lose the last trace of any personal whimsicality and uniqueness and become completely a part of the state.

By contrast, Locke sees the indestructible essence of man in resisting, rather than in blindly obeying, the state. The liberal principles of life, liberty, and the pursuit of happiness are thus the exact opposite of the authoritarian concept of citizenship as duty, discipline, and death for the state.

Thomas Jefferson, one of the greatest liberal individualists of all time, remarked in a letter to Colonel William Stephen Smith, dated November 13, 1787, that "the tree of liberty must be refreshed from time to time with the blood of patriots and tyrants." The Declaration of Independence, too, states that life, liberty, and the pursuit of happiness are among the unalienable rights of man and that "whenever any form of government becomes destructive of these ends, it is the right of the people to alter or to abolish it, and to institute new government, laying its foundations on such principles, and organizing its powers in such form as to them shall seem most likely to effect their safety and happiness."

The historical roots of individualism are three: First, the Jewish concept of one God leads to the idea that all men, as children of God, are brothers to each other. Second, the Christian doctrine of the indestructibility of the human soul maintains that whatever social, economic, and political inequalities may exist, all men possess a spiritual equality and uniqueness that no earthly power can override. Third, in the stoic view, the one principle of action that governs all things is *to be at one with oneself*, to know oneself, and to act in conformity with one's rational principles and purposes. The true self of man, according to the stoics, is not flesh or bones, but the faculty that uses them, the *reason*, the part that more than anything else characterizes one as human.

At no time, of course, has this individualism been fully accepted, and the counterforces of collective solidarity always threaten it. At the present time, in particular, the threat of all-destructive thermonuclear warfare leads to a strengthening of anti-individualist attitudes, stressing the idea of "let's close ranks" rather than "let each person decide what is right or wrong and act accordingly."

Apart from the pressures of international tension and conflict, there have been forces that have threatened, and still threaten, traditional liberal individualism. Above all, there is the emergence of the *group* as the decisive factor in government and the economy. In politics, individuals can be effective only to the extent that they join a political party or pressure group. The framers of the Constitution did not mention political parties in it and were strongly suspicious of them as forces that would dissolve the unity of the nation and lessen the importance of the individual in the process. Yet today the study of democratic politics is dominated by the concept of the group as the decisive force in the political process.

In economics, too, the individual farmer, merchant, or worker of classical capitalism has been largely supplanted by the group. Today, a labor union may bargain on a nationwide basis for an entire industry, the farmer depends on farm blocs in and out of Congress, and the individual businessman has either been replaced by the large corporation or, if he still exists, depends on his trade association to pursue his economic interests. All this does not necessarily mean that individualism is dead, for in a pluralistic society the individual joins a group to defend his individual integrity against threats that issue from other powerful interest groups or from government.

3. The *instrumental theory of the state* views the state as a mechanism to be used for ends higher than itself. Both Plato and Aristotle, the founders of Western political theory, conceived of the state as an organic entity, with a life and purpose of its own, superior to the purposes of the individual. Plato and Aristotle thought of the state as the *highest moral good,* the source of moral values and spiritual enrichment for the individual.

From the Jewish-Christian viewpoint of religion, the instrumentalist theory of the state maintains that the highest values in man's life relate to God and that no earthly law can claim to supersede God's. The function of the state is to maintain peace and order, so that men can pursue their activities devoted to higher ends. From the rational-humanist viewpoint, the instrumentalist theory of the state affirms that the ability of the individual to use his reason in discovering what is right and wrong is the ultimate test of political authority and that the state therefore cannot turn evil into good or wrong into right solely because it possesses the means of physical coercion.

The liberal doctrine stresses society far more than the state; in the classical liberal doctrine *society is considered basically self-sufficient, and the state is to step in only when the voluntary efforts of society fail.*

The instrumental theory of the state thus relegates the state to a supplementary position. As long as individuals can get along without the state, the liberal bias is against the state, even if the state could do the same thing a little better. In the totalitarian state, the assumption is always in favor of the state. It organizes and controls not only the sensitive areas of the economy, education, and religion, but even chess players and Sunday afternoon hikers.

4. By contrast, the democratic theory sees in the principle of *voluntarism* the very lifeblood of a free society. Fellowship can be experienced most deeply in small, voluntary groups. Such groups were first formed in seventeenth-century England on a religious basis, and to this day the English-speaking world abounds with thousands of religious sects that are small in size and entirely voluntary in nature.

Later, the principle of voluntary association was applied in the field of politics (parties), education (private schools), and economics (labor unions and employees' associations). In charity, the Red Cross and local community chests testify that there is still a strong sentiment for retaining voluntary activity. Even in England, which has national health and social security programs covering every person from the cradle to the grave, there has been a reassertion of the importance of voluntary organization in social welfare, supplementing the governmental programs.

The bias of the principle of voluntarism is for the smaller community and against centralized government. For long, this originally liberal principle was adopted by conservatives and states' right advocates in defense of conservative policies. Yet recently the protest against centralism has also been taken up by others: by blacks who demand community control over schools and police in their areas in large cities and by white liberals who want to restore the importance of state and local governments through revenue sharing with the federal government.

5. The concept of *the law behind the law* flows directly from the *federal* view of state and society in classical liberalism. Society is conceived as an aggregate of diverse voluntary associations, and the state itself is looked upon as an essentially voluntary body because its authority is derived from the consent of the governed. Whenever authority is organized on a federal basis, there has to be a higher law defining the relationships of the parts among each other and of each part to the whole.

Classical liberalism, therefore, has always adhered to the idea that the relations between state and society, between government and individual, are ultimately defined by a law higher than that of the state. In fact, classical liberal thought in Britain and the United States assumes that the law is not the product of the state, but *precedes* it. The function of the state in relation to man's basic rights is to protect and define such rights, not to create them.

In the United States, in particular, the concept of the law behind the law has never been challenged as the foundation of American political thought and experience. The Declaration of Independence specifically recognizes it, and the Constitution also recognized that no legislative body can make laws without due process or laws that otherwise violate basic principles of reason. The very existence of the United States is, of course, due to the insistence that above the law then ruling —the law of imperial Britain—there was a higher law to which the revolutionary colonists pledged allegiance.

Opponents of democratic government have charged that this concept of a higher law, making government dependent upon the consent of the governed, opens the door to rebellion and anarchy. In his *Two Treatises of Government* (1690), John Locke answers this charge with three counterarguments. First, Locke concedes that the democratic theory of government admits of the possibility of rebellion, but he denies that it does so more than any other theory. When the people are made miserable, they will rebel under any form of government; let the governors be "sacred and divine, descended or authorized from heaven, give them out for whom or what you please, the same will happen." Second, Locke says, men do not rebel "upon every little mismanagement in public affairs," or "for light and transient causes," as the Declaration of Independence puts it. Third—and here Locke moves from the defensive to the offensive—government by consent coupled with the right of the people to rebel is "the best fence against rebellion."

Locke could only guess in 1690 whether his arguments would be proved by experience, because democracy was then still a thing of the future. Yet experience has proved him perspicacious. Although democratic systems of government, based on the Lockean-Jeffersonian principle of the people's right to rebel, have periodically experienced civil disorder, riots, and violence, they have proved themselves comparatively stable in the long run. By contrast, where the concept of the higher law has been rejected in the name of law and order, the political results have been blood purges, conspiracies, plots and counterplots, and violent swings from one extreme to another—the political record, specifically, of illiberal dictatorships.

6. The *emphasis on means* in democratic life is based on the realization that ends lead no existence apart from means but are continually shaped by them. The totalitarian makes a clear-cut distinction between means and ends. He is absolutely certain of what the ends are, and

possessing this certainty, he pays little attention to the nature of the means. Thus, communists believe in universal brotherhood and cooperation as their officially professed end, yet they fail to realize that the means employed in bringing about communism—secret police, "correctional" labor camps, thought control, denunciations, repression of dissent—increase misery rather than diminish it.

One of the main difficulties in separating means from ends is the fact that in most practical situations a means is simultaneously an end. Thus, education is for some an end in itself; for others, it is but a means to an end—to a degree, for example. Yet, a degree may again be only a means to the end of a happier, fuller life, or a better job. Again, a better job is not necessarily an end in itself; it is likely to be a means to some higher end, such as expressing a sense of craftsmanship or serving society.

The central position of means in free societies is entrenched in their historical experience. Magna Carta, habeas corpus, and jury trial, to mention a few roots of liberty in the English-speaking world, are originally all procedural devices—means; and the history of liberty may aptly be described as a history of procedure. In representative assemblies, too, it is not the legislative product that distinguishes a democratic body from a nondemocratic one, but the difference of procedure. In the one case, procedure aims at the fullest and fairest guarantee of the right of the minority to be heard; in the other, procedure aims at silencing minorities.

At present, the danger in democratic societies lies in the possible waning of this awareness that differences over means are the heart of the difference between democracy and totalitarianism. In opposing an antidemocratic system there is a natural tendency to imitate its means, and because the tendency is natural, special efforts must be made to guard against it. In defending democracy, some persons are willing to use means that are bound to destroy the very thing they seek to defend.

7. *Discussion and consent* are the means by which a democratic society typically settles divergent viewpoints and interests. It is the democratic view that, since no one possesses absolute truth, both sides to an argument may make a contribution to the best possible answer and that the only way to get that answer is to marshal all the available evidence.

In the theory of the democratic society, governments derive "their just powers from the consent of the governed" (Declaration of Independence). If the state becomes oppressive and unmindful of the rights of the people, then the democratic theory, as was pointed out earlier, upholds not only the right but the duty to revolt against such government. This right to rebel can be claimed only where the methods of discussion and consent are blocked by tyrannical despotism; where the channels of discussion are open, a democrat cannot claim the right of rebellion against the state.

The communist or New Left revolutionary who today claims the right to revolution as a general democratic privilege bends this concept for his own purposes. From the democratic viewpoint, the democrat has the moral right, and duty, to rebel against the totalitarian system, but the totalitarian possesses no such right against the democratic system.

Violence by revolutionary or terroristic groups is not the only form —although it is the most obvious one—of interfering with the democratic process based on rational dialogue between opposing political interests. Street politics—by means of demonstrations, marches, lie-ins, or sit-ins—can also undermine the concept of democratic government by discussion, even if no violence is intended and none occurs. Such expressions of political sentiment have a legitimate place in the democratic process if they supplement, rather than replace rational dialogue. When demonstration politics results in violence, either by the intent of the demonstrators or by the course of events, confrontation politics is the next level of such conflict escalation, making compromise and consent through discussion even more difficult.

8. The *basic equality of all human beings* is a point of democratic doctrine and policy that is frequently misunderstood. No democrat has ever said that all people are identical, only that in basic respects they are equal. The very uniqueness of each individual creates a kind of equality that is important in the democratic outlook. From the religious viewpoint of the Jewish-Christian tradition, all people are equal before God; God's challenge to every human being is the same, although individual responses to it vary enormously. From the rationalist-humanistic viewpoint, all people share, over and above differences of race, sex, religion, nationality, and class, one common trait: the ability to reason. In this sense, all people are citizens of the world rather than of a particular, distinctive group, and their basic equality derives from what they have in common rather than from what separates them.

According to democratic theory, the equality that men receive at birth is not in the nature of an outright gift or grant but is an *opportunity,* a challenge. The Jeffersonian phrase "pursuit of happiness" aptly expresses the thought not that we have the right to happiness, in the sense that the state or our family or friends owe us happiness, but that we each have the right to *pursue* happiness, unhindered by unreasonable obstacles.

However, equality does not mean, as Plato said it meant, "dispensing a kind of equality to equals and unequals alike." The contrary is true, of the ideal democracy at least. In practice it is not easy to ascertain when equals are still equal and when they become unequal. To take an illustration: The most common interpretation of democratic equality is "equality of opportunity." A grave difficulty arises immediately. If all people were endowed with the same talents and abilities, and were born into the same kinds of home, and received the same schooling, then giving each an equal opportunity would be a fair solution. Yet people differ in native talent and even more in background and education.

Legislative action cannot equalize the I.Q. of the population, for there will always be differences of ability, drive, and motivation, but laws can make equality of opportunity more real by trying to equalize conditions before the competition starts: Increased inheritance taxes lessen the impact of inherited wealth, progressive income taxes favor the lower-income groups, and free education (from nursery school to university) benefits the indigent more than the affluent. In other words, equality of opportunity, if it allows ability alone to operate, quickly establishes and perpetuates a meritocracy of inequality. *Need,* too, must be considered; it adds to the principle of efficiency that of equity.

DEMOCRACY AS A POLITICAL ORDER

The classical formulation of political democracy as government by the people is applicable only in a community that is small enough to let each individual be heard in public assembly and vote there on specific policies and laws. Such direct democracy has functioned in the small city-states of ancient Greece and in the small towns of Switzerland and New England. In larger communities—nations, states, provinces, and cities—there has to be a division of labor. Some persons have to make the important political decisions for the whole society, and specially trained administrators and civil servants have to perform the tasks of management and administration for society as a whole. It makes a great deal of difference how the political decision makers and administrators are to be selected. Are they to come from royal families or aristocratic classes, in which case birth is the main criterion of selection? Are they to come from a small oligarchy of self-appointed rulers who have acquired their position by the gun and perpetuate their power by the threat of the gun? There is another method: political democracy.

In a large society, in which direct self-government is not feasible, political democracy may be defined as a political order in which adult citizens freely choose representatives in regularly scheduled competitive elections. Whereas citizens in the direct democracy of small communities decide specific policies through their own votes in public assemblies, citizens in the indirect democracy of representative government of large communities express their preferences for a cluster of policies by voting for representatives who favor similar policies. In the large-scale political democracy of nation, state, or city, citizens participate in the political process in many ways other than through voting (involvement in party activities, campaign contributions, adherence to civic groups), but voting is the central act of influencing policy formation.

The elections of representatives, of the political leadership, is indispensable to political democracy, but not every political system is democratic just because it holds elections. In making choices, the citizen must be free: free from governmental coercion to vote in a particular way, and free to obtain all the pertinent information about the various candidates and parties. Freedom of choice implies freedom of speech, assembly, radio, television, and the press. A free choice also implies a competitive election—that is, there have to be at least two parties or candidates vying for the vote.

This concept of political democracy as a political order in which the citizens freely choose their government in competitive elections states only *how* public policies are arrived at, but says nothing about their content. Political democracies may pursue economic policies of laissez faire, state intervention, social welfare, or progressive nationalization of the means of production. In the field of education, political democracies may provide a college education for the majority of high school graduates or only for a small minority. In religion, political democracies may adopt a basic policy of strict separation of state and church, or a policy supporting all religions, or they may favor one particular church. In regulating family relations and sexual morality, political democracies may adopt restrictive or permissive policies regarding divorce, abortion, and pornography. In foreign policy, political democracies may be isolationist, internationalist, or imperialist.

Not only do differences and contradictions regarding specific policies exist between democratic systems of different nations, but the same democratic political order may enact specific policies today that totally contradict policies of yesteryear. The question of whether such policies are democratic can be answered with reference not to their content but only to the method by which they are made. Some persons find this limitation of political democracy to method and procedure unsatisfactory and seek to incorporate into its meaning such broad terms as "the good society," "liberty," "equality," "justice," and the like.

However, such broad terms do not lend themselves to empirical verification. There are as many conceptions of the good society as there are persons holding them. What seems to one person the good society may appear to another barely tolerable or outright repugnant. By contrast, the meaning of political democracy in procedural terms can be easily verified: A political system that allows only one party and little or no freedom of speech and the press, that holds infrequent or no elections, that coerces citizens to vote in a particular way, or that punishes political opposition as a crime is not a political democracy, regardless of the content of its policies.

Those who favor political democracy cannot do so on the illusionary ground that it is absolute perfection, utopia here and now, or that it will ever approach utopia. Given the undeniable shortcomings of political democracy at any time and place, the inherent limits and imperfections of political democracy can be accepted, however, on the pragmatic

The machinery of democracy

ground that the shortcomings of an undemocratic system in which the preferences of a minority prevail over those of the majority, are even more serious.

Yet the very criterion that limits political democracy most seriously —the fact that it is a set of methods and procedures governing *how* policies are to be arrived at rather than *what* policies are to be effected —is also the source of its greatest strength. Precisely because the rules of the democratic political order relate to no one specific social or economic issue, they potentially affect all. Experience has shown that the political procedures of democracy, if practiced over any length of time, lead to their application to social, economic, educational, and religious issues. In the eighteenth century, democracy pursued objectives that were essentially political in character, such as the broadening of the suffrage to all social classes and the elimination of restrictions on the basic political freedoms of speech, assembly, and the press. But from the middle of the nineteenth century on, the procedures of political democracy have been increasingly used to broaden the concept of democracy from the realm of government to that of society.

Finally, the nature of political democracy as a set of methods and procedures also enables it to adapt to many kinds of political and economic institutions. Democracy is compatible, as experience has shown, with republican and monarchical forms of government, with two-party and multiparty systems, with more or less capitalism, socialism, or the welfare state, with varying types of religious belief and nonbelief, and with divergent levels of educational attainments and economic well-being.

Background of Democracy

CONDITIONS OF POLITICAL DEMOCRACY

The first condition of democratic government is the maintenance of a political climate in which *political liberty* can thrive. In every society, those who uphold the orthodox views may freely express them. Political liberty begins at the point where *unorthodox* opinions may be freely presented, without legal, social, or economic penalties.

The political liberty of a society can best be measured by the margin of unorthodoxy tolerated in that society. This yardstick enables us to go beyond the crude classification of dictatorship and democracy, which is valid only on a general level. Examining first the totalitarian states by this criterion, we find the least margin of unorthodoxy in China under Mao, in the Soviet Union under Stalin, and in Nazi Germany under

Hitler; a much wider margin in the Soviet Union under Khrushchev or in Yugoslavia under "national communism," and the relatively largest margin of unorthodoxy in some traditional Asian, African, and Latin American dictatorships. By comparison with the ideological dictatorships of either the fascist or communist type, the nonideological military dictatorships such as were set up in Brazil, Nigeria, or Panama, tolerate a considerable degree of unorthodoxy so long as the authority of the military rulers is not challenged.

Measuring the margin of tolerated unorthodoxy in democratic societies, we find Britain, France, Scandinavia, the Netherlands, Australia, and New Zealand on the top of the list, while the United States trails behind. Needless to say, the positions are never fixed, and the range of unorthodoxy constantly changes; by general agreement there is less conformity of thought in the United States today than 15 or 20 years ago, and there may be more again at some future time.

A second condition indispensable to the successful working of political democracy is *common agreement on fundamentals.* The most important agreement—and one no written constitution can by itself guarantee—is the common desire to operate a democratic system. Where there is no written constitution, as in Great Britain, there is no protection of political minorities or individual nonconformists other than the decency and restraint of the majority. Legally, the British Parliament could outlaw the Opposition and introduce a totalitarian state overnight. But the government is not doing that because it is party to an unwritten agreement to abide by democratic principles.

By the same token, written constitutions are not necessarily a protection. Fascism developed in Italy, Germany, Japan, and Argentina despite written constitutions, and the existence of a democratic constitution in Czechoslovakia after World War II did not restrain the communists from destroying it.

In the United States, too, the written Constitution is, in itself, no last line of defense of political democracy. There have been times when the Congress, the executive, or the judiciary—or all three—have shown little respect for political liberties; there have been other times when the spirit as well as the letter of the Constitution have been faithfully respected. Throughout these ups and downs of American democracy, the Constitution has basically remained the same; the variable was the greater or lesser determination of the people to defend liberty at all cost.

The lesson of all this historical experience is simple: *The strength of a democracy is only as great as the will of the people to uphold it.*

Where agreement on fundamentals is lacking, political democracy suffers from stresses and strains that may well become fatal. An irreconcilable division on fundamentals between major parties may lead to civil war or dictatorship. Such a situation existed in the United States in 1860 when there was no agreement on the basic issue of slavery. In 1930, the German political system was a democracy as far as the paper constitution was concerned, but two-thirds of the electorate wanted to set up dictatorships of either the communist or fascist type, and the fascists won in 1933. Obviously, no constitution, however perfect on paper, can save a democracy if the antidemocrats outvote the democrats two to one. A democratic constitution *assumes*, but cannot in itself create, the will to maintian democratic institutions.

The Fourth Republic of France (1945–1958) provides another example. During its existence, the forces favoring or tolerating republican government based on an omnipotent parliament mustered just a little over one-half of the electorate. On the extreme left, the communists, dedicated to the principle of revolutionary dictatorship, were supported by one-fourth of the electorate. On the extreme right, supported by about one-fifth of the electorate, were groups that either sought to set up a new republican regime based on a strong executive or that aimed at doing away with democracy altogether. A government hampered by such disagreement on fundamentals could not work and did not work. The Fourth Republic ended in 1958, and the new Fifth Republic was centered on the personality of Charles de Gaulle.

Is agreement on economic policy a necessary condition of political democracy? A generation ago, this question was answered in the affirmative more often than today. Conservatives frequently expressed apprehension lest the new socialist principle of public ownership undermine the whole fabric of democratic institutions. In contrast, socialists frequently expressed the fear that conservatives would be unwilling to adhere loyally to democratic principles if socialist parties were given a chance to change the economic organization of society by constitutional means and that the propertied classes would put property above constitutional democracy.

Experience has shown that both sides have been wrong. In theory, the disagreement on basic economic policy between conservatives and socialists looked bigger than it has worked out in practice. The conservatives have abandoned much of their old economic laissez-faire position, and most socialists, having considerably modified their economic philosophy, are now satisfied with a program consisting of welfare-state legislation and the socialization of only a few basic industries.

The very nature of the democratic process makes the choice of extreme programs unlikely. Since elections are generally decided by the floating independent vote, which by definition is middle-of-the road, no extreme program has much of a chance of being accepted.

Government by more than one party expresses the democratic principle, borrowed from the law, that "the other side must also be heard" *(audiatur et altera pars)*. The democratic viewpoint holds that different people perceive different aspects of truth, mainly in the light of their lives and experiences, and that there will be at least two sides to any major question.

Marxists say that the two-party system is a product of capitalism; that the opposing interests of capitalists and workers must be represented in opposing parties; and that, since capitalism has been abolished in communist states, there is no need there for an opposition party to the Communist party.

This line of argument has serious flaws. In the first place, it wrongly assumes that property is the only line of political party. In Europe, party loyalties are frequently based on religious or ideological loyalties; in the United States the regional factor is often important. Also, the communist argument exaggerates the impact of property on party. Only about 60 percent of the British working class vote Labour, and in the United States the correlation between income and vote is equally indecisive. If income were the only decisive factor, electoral prediction would be much easier than professional pollsters have found it to be.

Even if capitalism were abolished in a democratic manner, there would still be need for more than one party. Assuming a classless society in which all productive property is owned publicly and in which incomes are relatively equal, there would still be questions of vital concern to the community, questions admitting more than one answer. For example, every state, whether fascist, communist, socialist, or capitalist, has to decide each year what portion of its national product is to be consumed and what portion is to be saved and invested. Other typical questions that every community has to face is how much to spend on social welfare and which groups should be favored—the claims of the old compete with those of the young; education may compete with health. The answer to such questions cannot be found in the form of economic organization.

After all, even when there was no capitalism in the modern sense, there was a multitude of parties. When suffrage was limited to the propertied classes, as it was in most countries until about 100 years ago, the existing parties were divided not on the basis of rich and poor, but along other lines—town versus country, secularism versus clericalism, states' rights versus centralism, free trade versus protection, republicanism versus monarchism, and slavery versus freedom, to name but a few.

Man has lived for about a quarter-million years on this planet yet has had some knowledge of democratic ideas and practice for only about 2500 years. Even today, democracy as a way of life exists only imperfectly in a relatively small portion of the world. As to political democracy, out of some 140 states that presently exist only about one in four practices its basic procedures and tolerates an organized opposition. Democracy can hardly be called "natural." On the contrary, the democratic way of life—including, in particular, its political aspects— is the most difficult of all; it does not emerge spontaneously or by accident, but is the result of deliberate thought, seeking to correct what is natural—all too natural—in human behavior. Because it is so difficult, democracy is nowhere more than a goal, a commitment only partly realized.

Just as the behavior of the child is more natural than that of the adult, the behavior of the authoritarian is more natural than that of the democratic personality. The process of growth and development from childhood to maturity is natural only in the biological and physiological sense, not in the social and cultural sense. Socially and culturally, the transformation of the child into the mature adult demands much forethought, planning, and hard work.

Politically, the authoritarian personality is fundamentally the grown-up who has never become mature, the ostensible adult who still accepts the dependency and security characteristic of childhood. By contrast, the democratic personality is ideally the emotionally and intellectually mature adult, the person able to shape his or her own life. Mature adults do not need security provided by an external authority; they possess security within themselves. The price of this emotional and intellectual independence is high, since to attain it people must face responsibilities and make decisions by themselves, without being able to blame anyone afterward if the decisions are wrong.

There is no growing up without making mistakes, and the overprotected child *can* make no mistakes. Similarly, in a dictatorship the system prevents individuals from experimenting and acting on their own, so that (in theory, at least) they always do the right thing. By contrast, the process of growing up, of moving away from supervision to personal responsibility, implies the possibility of choosing the wrong thing, of making mistakes; in this sense, democracy may be defined as *the right to make mistakes.*

Implied in this concept is not the desirability of erring for the sake of erring, but the recognition that freedom implies choice between alternatives, and that no one can grow to maturity, can become truly democratic, without learning to make choices and without occasionally making a wrong choice.

The 200-percent-American defenders of democracy who want to make it a crime for anyone ever to think or act wrongly are trying to have a democracy with authoritarian personalities, people who think and do only what authority has allowed them to think or do.

The attitude of the democratic personality toward the leader is markedly different from that of the authoritarian personality. The latter regards the leader of the nation with a mixture of loyalty and reverence resembling the emotions first felt toward parents, particularly toward the father. The traditional reference to a chief of state as the "father of the country" is a linguistic expression of a profound psychological tie; the adult in such a society has really never outgrown the father-child relationship.

By contrast, the democratic personality puts more emphasis on the group than on the leader. This feeling goes back to that of the rebellious child, who joins with siblings in a league of equals to destroy the authority of their father. "Liberty, equality, fraternity," the three ideals of the French Revolution, express the attitude of the democratic personality toward authority.

For this reason, democracies frequently act with deep suspicion whenever a great leader appears. Churchill was opposed in England before World War II because he was not average enough, and therefore potentially dangerous. Clemenceau was removed from French public life after World War I because he was too much of a leader. Many American voters who cast their ballots against Franklin D. Roosevelt were to some extent motivated by the fear that he was not Mr. Average American. If only for this reason alone—there are others, too, of course, such as the perennial shortage of great leaders—democratic electorates often put mediocrities into high offices. However, a democratic political system proves its maturity and stability if it can safely survive mediocrities as presidents and prime ministers.

It is for this reason, too, that impersonal factors like constitutions, charters, and legislatures play such an important part in democratic states; leaders come and go, but the institutions continue unimpaired. In contrast, the authoritarian personality thinks in terms of allegiance to a particular person. For example, in Spain and Latin America political loyalty revolves around the phenomenon of *personalismo:* the political attachment and allegiance to one particular person rather than to a party, program, or constitution. Even democratic parties in such countries usually are split into various factions, each led by one individual to whom that group owes allegiance. But this is true, of course, of antidemocratic movements: thus we speak of Hitlerism, Peronism, Stalinism, but not of Churchillism, Kennedyism, or Carterism.

The formation of the democratic personality is first determined in the family. In the early years of life, the home is school, church, and government all rolled into one. One of Germany's leading child psychologists, Kurt Lewin, came to the United States in 1932 and stayed here until his death in 1947. In his paper, "Some Social-Psychological Differences Between the United States and Germany" (reprinted in his *Resolving Social Conflicts,* 1948), he made the following observations:

> To one who comes from Germany, the degree of freedom and independence of children and adolescents in the United States is very impressive. Especially the lack of servility of the young child toward adults or of the student toward his professor is striking. The adults, too, treat the child on a much more equal footing, whereas in Germany it seems to be the natural right of the adult to rule and the duty of the child to obey. The natural relation of adult and child in the United States is not considered that of a superior *(Herr)* to a subordinate *(Untergebener)* but that of two individuals with the same right in principle. The parents seem to treat the children with more respect.

Even a society with a comparatively unauthoritarian family structure may have a wide range of differences based on religion, region, or social class. Thus, empirical research in the United States has found that "lower-status child-rearing practices foster compliance to authority; upper-status socialization places a much greater emphasis on self-expression and individual aspiration" (Fred I. Greenstein, *Children and Politics,* 1965, p. 155).

The school is, next to the home, perhaps the most important single source of a child's basic psychological attitudes. What children learn formally in school is much less important than what they pick up unconsciously from the way in which the school operates. Democratic educational theory requires that the teacher help the child learn *how* to think rather than *what* to think. Mechanisms for self-government of students in high schools and colleges can become an important experience in democratic awareness, provided such mechanisms are not controlled and operated from the front office of the administration. The existence of private schools in democracies is a further expression of freedom in education. In totalitarian societies, the state generally abolishes all private and parochial schools, since there is only one pattern that is defined as right and the state defines it and has the means to enforce it. In democratic societies, many important educational innovations have been given their first trial in small experimental schools; if successful, such advances then spread to the public school system.

The attitude toward women sharply differentiates the democratic from the authoritarian personality. The authoritarian generally desires to keep women "in their place"; his scale of values is oriented strongly toward masculine traits and preferences. Many legal codes officially recognize the superior position of the male by declaring him to be the head of the family and by subordinating his wife to him in matters of property and other basic issues. The movement for full equality for women reflects not only the creed of women who wish to assert their equality, but also the feeling of democratically inclined men who resent the treatment of women as inferiors just as they resent the treatment of any other human being as an inferior on the basis of race, or religion, or nationality.

The Civil Rights Act of 1964 prohibited discrimination in private employment on grounds of sex (as also on grounds of race, color, or religion). Despite this important progressive piece of legislation, women still have a long way to go before attaining genuine economic equality. As the accompanying table shows, women in the United States earn considerably less than men in all major occupational groups. Currently, the median weekly wage or salary for full-time working women is about 60 percent of the median weekly pay for men. In a number of European countries, women's wages as a proportion of those paid to men are higher: In West Germany, working women receive 70 percent of men's wages; in Italy, 74 percent; in France, 86 percent. Moreover, women not only receive less pay than men in the same occupations, but they have much less access to higher-paying occupations. In 1976, only

Median money income of employed persons in the United States, by sex, 1976

	Male	Female
Professional and technical workers (includes doctors, lawyers, scientists, draftsmen)	$16,939	$11,072
Nonfarm managers, officials, and proprietors (includes office managers, government officials, business owners)	$16,674	$ 9804
Clerical workers (includes bookkeepers, stenos, file clerks)	$12,843	$ 8128
Operatives (mostly factory workers)	$11,688	$ 6649
Salesworkers	$14,586	$ 6272
Service workers (except private household workers)	$10,030	$ 5674

Source: U.S. Bureau of the Census, *Statistical Abstract of the United States, 1977* (Washington, D.C.: Government Printing Office, 1977).

3 percent of all gainfully employed women in the United States earned $15,000 and more, as compared with 27 percent of all men.

The democratic personality is more tolerant and more cooperative than the authoritarian personality. But the question is often raised whether these human gains are not paid for by a loss of efficiency. Controlled experiments with children and adults have shown that the efficiency of a group can be raised by substituting a democratic group decision for a lecture, request, or command from the top. In industry, management is increasingly using democratic group discussions to raise efficiency. This is still a new field of experimentation, but there is certainly no evidence that the autocratically run group produces more efficient individuals.

The feeling of being wanted is one of the strongest driving forces of action and allegiance; nothing can produce that feeling better than the democratic process of consultation, discussion, and free exchange of ideas. With love, greater things can be accomplished than with hatred. This old religious truth is also borne out by psychology, politics, and history.

INDIVIDUAL FREEDOM AND NATIONAL SECURITY

The best introduction to the problem of individual liberty is still John Stuart Mill's essay *On Liberty* (1859). Mill wrote his essay at a comparatively civilized time, when there seemed to be little need for it. Yet he foresaw that illiberal forces would gain in influence, and he hoped that men would then turn to *On Liberty*. Though Mill modestly disclaimed originality other than that which "every thoughtful mind gives to its own mode of conceiving and expressing truths which are common property," the essay has grown in stature because many of Mill's predictions have come true, and much that he has to say is still valid.

As Alexis de Tocqueville had done in his *Democracy in America* (1835–1840), Mill attacked the idea that the evolution of government from tyranny to democracy necessarily solves the problem of individual liberty. Tyranny can be exercised by one, by a few, or by the majority, and the last is potentially the worst of all, since it commands the widest moral support, whereas oppression by one or a few is mainly physical. The power of public opinion in a democracy often exercises more restraint and repression against dissidents than a dictator exercises by physical means in a dictatorship. Protection against political tyranny is therefore not enough. It must be supplemented by protection against social tyranny, which leaves fewer means of escape, "penetrating much more deeply into the details of life, and enslaving the soul itself."

Mill saw that the natural tendency of man is not to be tolerant and open-minded, but to impose his views on others, and that lack of power is frequently the major cause of tolerating dissent. It makes little difference how numerous the dissenting minority is: "If all mankind minus one, were of one opinion, and only one person were of the contrary opinion, mankind would be no more justified in silencing that one person, than he, if he had the power, would be justified in silencing mankind."

Silencing an unorthodox opinion is not only wrong but harmful, because it robs others of an opportunity to get acquainted with ideas that may be true or partly true. "All silencing of discussion," Mill argued, "is an assumption of infallibility." Therefore Mill stated that, unless *absolute freedom of opinion*—scientific, moral, political, and theological—is guaranteed, a society is not completely free. History is full of opinions held by one age as the last truth, only to be considered false and absurd by subsequent ages.

Just as liberty is not complete unless it is absolute, so discussion must be completely unhampered, and free discussion must not be ruled out when "pushed to an extreme," because the arguments for a case are not good unless they are good for an extreme case. Mill did not accept the "pleasant falsehood" that truth inevitably triumphs over persecution; history "teems with instances of truth put down by persecution." In the history of religion in the West, for example, there are numerous sects and churches that have been successfully suppressed, and Mill therefore concluded that "persecution has always succeeded, save where the heretics were too strong a party to be effectually persecuted."

Moreover, the greatest harm of persecution is inflicted not on those who dissent from established beliefs, but on those who do not, because the mental development of the latter is stifled by the fear of expressing unorthodox or dissenting views. In an atmosphere of cowed uniformity there may be a few exceptional great thinkers but not an intellectually active people. "No one can be a great thinker who does not recognize that as a thinker it is his first duty to follow his intellect to whatever conclusions it may lead."

The purpose of individual liberty is personal self-development. It is the privilege of every person to interpret experience in his own way, and his moral faculties can only be brought into play when he is obliged to choose between alternatives. A person who merely follows custom and tradition makes no choice, nor does he who lets others make his decisions for him. Different persons should be permitted to lead different lives; the principle of liberty thus inevitably implies that of variety and diversity.

Mill reminded those who are willing to repress individual liberty for the sake of a strong state that the worth of a state is no more than the worth of its individual citizens. When the state "dwarfs" its citizens and reduces them to docile instruments, it will find that "with small men no great things can really be accomplished."

Mill is still the best guide to liberty based on reason. Yet *On Liberty* is more than a century old, and it cannot be expected to give clear-cut answers to the problems that baffle us today. In particular, Mill did not deal with the problem of revolutionary movements in a democracy.

Going into the fundamental question of how to deal with those who advocate basic change, Jefferson had this to say: "If there be any among us who would wish to dissolve this Union or to change its republican form, let them stand undisturbed as monuments of the safety with which error of opinion may be tolerated where reason is left free to combat it." Jefferson was willing to allow even antirepublican doctrines (or antidemocratic doctrines, as we would say today), not only on the basis of rational argument, but also because he had tremendous faith in a free America, "the strongest government on earth." It is possible that our periodic wavering with regard to the Jeffersonian doctrine coincides with something deeper: a loss of self-confidence in the strength of liberty and a fear by some that antidemocratic propaganda, if unchecked, might gain too many converts.

Cold War, Detente, and the Future of East-West Relations

The future of capitalism and democracy will be determined not only by developments within particular countries but also by events in the international arena. It could be argued that during the twentieth century the main enemies of both capitalism and democracy have been international crises: two world wars and a worldwide depression. The triumph of communism in Russia and China and of fascism in Italy and Germany were directly linked to the profound dislocations brought about by prolonged wars and economic collapse. And democratic regimes throughout Western Europe, from France to Scandinavia, succumbed to conquering German armies in World War II. Anyone concerned about the fate of either capitalism or democracy may well ask: What are the prospects for international peace and stability? At the forefront of an answer to this question are relations between the United States and the Soviet Union.

During more than 60 years since the Bolshevik Revolution of October 1917, Soviet-American relations have undergone several major shifts, including the change from Stalin's belief in the inevitability of East-West conflict and Truman's policy of containment to Khrushchev's doctrine of competitive coexistence and Nixon's policy of detente. The Revolution itself was strongly opposed by the United States for an obvious reason: In October of 1917 World War I was far from over, and the new Soviet government proposed a separate peace with Germany at a time when the Allied armies were still being pressed on the Western front. However justified it might appear to Lenin, the defection of Russia from the Allied cause was hardly acceptable to the Allies. But there was more involved.

Lenin's October revolt was directed against the liberal Provisional Government headed by Alexander Kerensky, which had come to power eight months earlier following the overthrow of the Tsar. The Provisional Government had at once been recognized and aided by the United States. Now Lenin's attack on this government, accompanied by his vigorous espousal of the doctrine of world revolution, was seen as a first step toward fomenting communist revolutions in other countries as well, and also as the prelude to a new period of Russian territorial expansion. From the beginning, therefore, the Bolsheviks were recognized as a threat to both the internal and international stability of the democratic nations.

To meet this threat a number of measures were tried. First, the United States refused to recognize the new Soviet government, hoping to isolate the regime politically, a policy which lasted until 1933. In addition, the Treaty of Versailles that ended World War I established a number of new independent states in Eastern Europe, which could serve as buffers between the Soviet Union and the West. Finally, President Wilson sent some 10,000 American troops to Russia on a double mission of resisting Japanese encroachments in Siberia while at the same time aiding the anticommunist armies in the civil war that raged in Russia for three years.

These measures were not successful. While the Japanese were stopped in Siberia the communists won the civil war, and the Soviet government was recognized by other Western countries despite U.S. opposition. Moreover, communist parties sprang up around the world, coordinated by the Moscow-directed Comintern. Despite the inauspicious beginnings, Soviet-American relations soon underwent a temporary thaw. Faced with the economic devastation that followed the civil war, Lenin initiated a "temporary retreat" from socialism. He invited foreign capital to help in the task of reconstruction. American businessmen responded; major American firms invested millions of dollars in the Soviet economy. But these efforts came to a halt in 1928 when Lenin's successor, Stalin, embarked in earnest on his program to create in Russia a self-sufficient totalitarian regime.

To justify the brutal policies through which he collectivized agriculture, spurred industrial development, and concentrated political power in his own hands, Stalin invoked the doctrine of "capitalist encirclement." According to this doctrine the capitalist countries of the world, fearful that the success of communism would undermine their own systems, were implacable enemies of the Soviet Union and would resort to any means, including subversion and aggression, to destroy the Soviet regime. Because of "capitalist encirclement" the Soviet state, instead of withering away, must become still stronger. The climax of Stalin's political paranoia came in the Moscow Trials of 1936–1938, which involved a massive purge of the Soviet political and military elites. These trials, during which old-time dedicated Bolsheviks were forced to confess their crimes as counterrevolutionary agents of capitalism, became an international *cause celebre.* Many Soviet sympathizers, who had seen in the Bolshevik Revolution the dawning of a new age for Russia and all mankind, were at last disabused of their illusions. Revolutionary idealism had again spawned a reign of terror. Stalin's actions strengthened President Roosevelt's conviction that collaboration with the Soviet Union in the international arena was impossible. Although Roosevelt had recognized the Soviet regime in 1933, despite strong domestic opposition, he made no further moves toward closer ties.

Relations with the Soviet Union suffered their most traumatic shock in August of 1939, when Russia concluded a nonaggression treaty with Nazi Germany. The Hitler-Stalin pact came at a time when Britain and France were actively seeking Soviet participation in an anti-Nazi alliance; Western diplomats were actually in Moscow carrying on negotiations. The pact blatantly repudiated all previous Soviet denunciations of Hitler and fascism, confirming Western beliefs about the Soviet Union as a cynical, ruthless, and faithless regime. More important, it assured the Nazis that their eastern front was secure. A few days later Hitler invaded Poland, and World War II had begun.

The Hitler-Stalin pact and the outbreak of war provoked a bitter anti-Soviet reaction. Communist parties in Western Europe were suppressed. Moreover, Stalin used the opportunity to attack neighboring Finland (December 1939). The vigorous resistance of the Finns aroused strong sympathy in the United States and led to further condemnations of Soviet treachery. Soviet-American relations were at their lowest point.

Suddenly, everything changed. In June 1941, exhilarated by an easy victory over France, Hitler turned upon his Russian ally. Like Napoleon and the Kaiser before him, Hitler launched his armies on the ill-fated road to Moscow. At once ideological differences between the democracies and the Soviets were submerged in a common struggle against the Nazi invaders. Massive American aid to Russia was arranged through the Lend-Lease program. Then, within months, the Japanese attack on Pearl Harbor and the German declaration of war brought the United States and the Soviet Union together as full-fledged allies.

The war produced an upsurge of popular sympathy for the Russian people, who endured fearful losses in their battles against the German onslaught. Taken by surprise, despite Western warnings that an attack was imminent, and feeling the effects of Stalin's recent purge of senior officers, the Russian armies were thrown back to the gates of Moscow. In this deteriorating situation Stalin called repeatedly upon Britain and the United States to open a second front in Western Europe in order to relieve the military pressure on Russia. But the Western Allies were not prepared to hazard a landing against the main German strongholds. Instead they invaded North Africa and Italy, the Nazi's "soft underbelly," delaying the second front until June 1944, by which time the Russians had already turned the military tide. This disagreement about military strategy was the first in a series of basic differences between the Soviets and the Western Allies that emerged during the war, surfaced ominously at wartime conferences, and erupted afterward into the Cold War.

THE COLD WAR

Soviet-American relations are often discussed in terms of the presence or absence of "trust," as if the actions upon which trust is based proceed independently of national ideologies and interests. Mistrust among the Allies arose even during their wartime collaboration—notably over Western motives in postponing the second front. Underlying this mutual suspicion were fundamental differences of interest and ideology which the wartime alliance could conceal but not resolve. During the war ideological issues were muted. Stalin's wartime speeches make no mention of communism but stress instead the patriotic defense of Mother Russia. Nationalism aroused far more intense loyalties among the Russian people than did communism, and Stalin put nationalism first. The aims of the Western democracies were formulated in the Atlantic Charter, signed by Prime Minister Churchill and President Roosevelt in 1941. Besides statements renouncing territorial ambitions, denouncing the use of force, and proclaiming "freedom from fear and want," the Charter contained two articles that expressed distinctively Western objectives. One was political—the right of all people to choose the form of government under which they will live; the other was economic—the right of equal access to world trade and raw materials. These articles embodied the characteristic liberal conceptions of political democracy and economic competition. The contradiction between these principles and postwar Soviet objectives would soon become apparent.

The conflict that developed into the Cold War and dominated East-West relations for more than 25 years arose not only from ideological differences but also from competing national interests. The distinction between ideologies and interests is not always clear. Political leaders no less than ordinary citizens view the world through a complex intellectual screen in which ideological beliefs and practical interests are often so closely intertwined that it is difficult to determine where one begins and the other ends. Yet the distinction is important, if only because it is easier to compromise about interests than ideologies. When conflicts are seen as differences not just of interest but of principle there is less chance of reaching an accommodation. The Cold War was viewed on both sides as a conflict of principle, but it also involved differences of interest.

A primary interest of the Soviet Union after World War II was to assure the military security of her western borders. Three times in a century and a quarter Russia had been invaded from the west, each time with an enormous toll of death and destruction. To prevent another such calamity became an overriding concern among Soviet leaders. This meant that Russia must control or maintain a sphere of influence in Eastern Europe. From the Russian standpoint the only acceptable governments in Eastern Europe were communist regimes firmly tied to the Soviet Union. This political interest in security was reinforced by an economic interest in rebuilding and expanding the devastated Soviet economy. One means for doing so was to exploit the economies of Eastern Europe, by physically transferring industrial plants to Russia and by imposing advantageous terms of trade.

Two obstacles to these basic Soviet interests soon emerged. One was nationalism—the unwillingness of Poles, Czechs, Hungarians, and other nationalities to submit to Russian domination. The most successful national resistance occurred in Yugoslavia, where Marshall Tito, though himself a staunch communist, asserted his independence from Russian control. Unlike other countries of Eastern Europe, Yugoslavia had been liberated from German occupation not by the Soviet Red Army but by a national army of guerrillas. Elsewhere the revival of political life took place under the shadow of Russian guns, and one government after another was forced into the hands of of pro-Soviet communists. But in Yugoslavia Marshall Tito could proclaim an independent national road to communism. At first relations with Russia remained amicable, but by the late 1940s Tito's resistance to Soviet demands provoked a strong reaction. Stalin vilified Tito and tried to depose him. The plot was discovered, and Tito continued in power as a thorn in the Russian side.

The other obstacle to Soviet control of Eastern Europe was the Anglo-American commitment, affirmed in the Atlantic Charter, to democratic self-government. The first showdown between Russian interests and Western principles came in Poland. Would the Soviets permit democratic elections in Poland, as President Truman insisted was required by the Yalta Agreement of 1945 (signed by Roosevelt, Churchill, and Stalin) and the subsequent Declaration of Liberated Europe? Whatever the terms of these official statements, Soviet troops were present on Polish soil, and Stalin was not about to surrender vital Russian interests in favor of "bourgeois" notions of democracy. In fact, the fate of Poland had been sealed in the wartime decisions that allowed Russian armies to liberate Eastern Europe while the Western forces halted their advance. Now the Russians made a token gesture toward broadening the pro-Soviet communist government they had already recognized unilaterally. President Truman denounced Soviet actions in Poland in strong terms; the chill in Soviet-American relations was well underway.

The freeze deepened through a series of Soviet and American actions and reactions, both at home and abroad, which began during the late 1940s and led to the bitter and dangerous Cold War confrontations of the 1950s and 1960s. From the day he came into office, following the death of Roosevelt, President Truman took a strong stand against communist expansion. He regarded the consolidation of Russian control in Eastern Europe as provocative, rather than defensive, and he was determined to resist any further extension of Soviet influence. If the security and prosperity of the Soviet Union depended on control of the governments and economies of Eastern-European satellites, the security and prosperity of the United States depended on the existence, especially in Western Europe, of regimes able to resist the threat of Russian encroachment and to function as active members of a free-world economy. The imposition in Western Europe of communist regimes tied politically and economically to the Soviet Union would leave the United States isolated and vulnerable in a world of hostile powers.

A comprehensive response to the communist challenge came in 1947, in the far-reaching Truman Doctrine. The immediate occasion was a civil war in Greece, instigated by communist guerrillas who were trying to dismember that nation. Economic and military aid had been supplied to the Greek government by Great Britain, but by 1947 the British recognized that they were no longer able to keep up their former international commitments, including assistance to Greece and Turkey. President Truman, strongly supported by his future Secretary of State, Dean Acheson, saw an opportunity to assert America's determination to resist communist expansion, by force if necessary. The United States intervened in Greece with arms, aid, advice, and personnel. A hard line of political and military containment—the heart of American policy in the Cold War—was being drawn around the Soviet Union and the communist world.

In 1947 another significant response to the communist challenge was unveiled by Secretary of State Marshall. Under the Marshall Plan the United States pledged $17 billion to help the countries of Western Europe—including West Germany—rebuild their economies. The economic reconstruction of Europe was an essential requirement for maintaining a strong and prosperous free world. Underlying the Marshall Plan was a realization that communism cannot be contained by military means alone; only in healthy societies with productive economies would resistance to communism be effective.

At its height the conduct of the Cold War was based from the American side on several major assumptions. First, it was assumed that there is no significant difference between the expansion of the Soviet Union and the success of national communist movements outside Russia. This meant that all communist regimes, regardless of their relations with Moscow, were considered equally antagonistic. In fact, important divisions had developed within the communist world. Although the adjacent countries in Eastern Europe remained satellites of the Soviet Union, this was hardly true of all communist regimes. Yugoslavia and China were anything but docile instruments of the Soviet Union; on the contrary, both were as jealous of their independence in foreign policy as they were zealous about implementing communism in domestic policy. Other communist governments were able to assert greater or lesser degrees of independence—including Romania, Albania, and North Vietnam. These divisions might have been recognized years earlier as a basis for improving political and economic relations with at least some communist regimes. But so long as the communist world was viewed as a single monolithic whole, disregarding national variations, there was no room for flexible responses geared to specific countries and circumstances.

Second, the confrontation between the free world and the communist world was seen in global terms, as a conflict extending to every corner of the earth, in which a gain for one side was necessarily a loss for the other. This meant that the United States must be prepared to intervene in any situation on any continent, wherever there was danger of a communist success. The suggestions of people like Walter Lippmann and later George Kennan that disengagement might be possible in certain areas, or that some remote regions were simply of no strategic value, went unheeded. It also meant that countries like India, which attempted to follow a policy of neutralism between the two blocs, were regarded as hostile. There was no middle ground between the two sides: A country was either for us or against us.

Third, the conflict was viewed primarily in military terms, as involving threats of aggression and territorial expansion. This led the United States to sponsor a series of collective security arrangements around the world, including military alliances with countries that were potentially unstable, like South Vietnam, or overtly authoritarian, like Franco's Spain. The most important military alliance was the North Atlantic Treaty Organization, in which the United States joined a collective security arrangement with the countries of Western Europe—initially Britain, France, Italy, and Benelux (Belgium, the Netherlands, Luxemburg). The success of NATO as a military shield behind which Western Europe could resist Soviet threats while regaining its economic strength encouraged the United States to initiate similar alliances in Southeast Asia. But Southeast Asia is very different from Western Europe. European governments enjoyed mass support in societies that were willing and able to rebuild themselves after the devastation of war into viable and thriving communities. With American aid they were ready to assume their responsibilities as genuine partners in collective self-defense. Moreover, the members of NATO were democratic regimes, committed to the same basic values as the United States. U.S. allies in other parts of the world were a different sort. Some were unstable, undemocratic, or both. The whirlwind from this policy was reaped in South Vietnam, ostensibly an equal partner of the United States in the Southeast Asia Treaty Organization but actually a client state with neither the political viability nor economic capacity to act effectively in resisting invasion and subversion.

Finally, the Cold War was assumed to be rooted ultimately in irreconcilable differences of principle and morality. At stake were basic beliefs and convictions; the Cold War was finally a struggle for the minds of men. Anticommunism became not simply a policy but a creed, a moral crusade demanding ideological fervor and uncompromising dedication. To the crusading anticommunist no one was above suspicion—not even George C. Marshall, General of the Army, Chief of Staff, Secretary of State, Secretary of Defense, and originator of the Marshall Plan that helped save Europe from economic collapse. In 1950 General Marshall was denounced by Senator Joseph McCarthy of Wisconsin for conspiring against the United States in the Korean War as part of "an infamy so black as to dwarf any previous venture in the history of man." In the paranoid atmosphere of McCarthyism on one side and Stalinism on the other any suggestion of possible Soviet-American accommodations was out of the question.

DETENTE

The Cold War dominated Soviet-American relations for more than a quarter of a century, from the late 1940s into the early 1970s. But in the 1970s a new theme emerged—detente. Detente refers to an easing of tensions between the United States and the Soviet Union, expressed most notably in a willingness of the two countries to reach agreements and act together in a number of areas of common interest. The main architects of detente on the American side were President Nixon and his Secretary of State, Henry Kissinger. There is some irony in the fact that as a congressman and senator Nixon had been an ardent advocate of the Cold War, but as President he could move toward detente without provoking accusations that he was "soft" on communism.

The roots of detente lay in profound changes within the international system which led both the United States and the Soviet Union to recognize that despite their ideological antagonism there are areas of common interest in which joint action would be mutually advantageous. Two of the most important of these common interests are arms control and nonproliferation of nuclear weapons.

A central feature of the Cold War was a nuclear arms race between the United States and the Soviet Union in which each country sought to neutralize and overcome any military advantage the other might have. An arms race is nothing new in international relations: In a world of competing independent states, military strength has always been and still remains an indispensable basis for achieving vital national objectives, including physical security. But in one critical respect the Soviet-American arms race was unique: The deployment by both sides of vast arsenals of nuclear weapons introduced for the first time in history the possibility of assured mutual destruction for both great powers. The underlying motive for every previous arms race was to gain a relative military advantage over one's opponent, but the devastation from nuclear weapons raises the specter of absolute destruction for victor and vanquished alike. Beyond a certain point the accumulation of additional weapons brings no relative advantage; once the threshold of assured mutual destruction has been passed there is no good reason to continue the enormous expense of developing and deploying new systems of nuclear weapons.

The awful danger of nuclear competition was brought home vividly to both sides in the Cuban missile crisis of October 1962. An attempt by the Soviets to place nuclear-armed missiles in Cuba was met by a strong response from President Kennedy. Russian ships carrying the missiles toward Cuba were intercepted by American naval units. For several days it was uncertain what Krushchev would do next or how the United States would react. The world seemed to sway precariously on the brink of nuclear war. At last the Russian ships turned back for home. The crisis was over, but it helped convince both Washington and Moscow that a balance of nuclear terror had in fact been reached. It was becoming evident that both superpowers shared an interest in regulating nuclear weapons.

The first fruits of this common interest in arms control were several agreements concluded during the 1960s which limited where nuclear weapons could be tested and deployed. These included the Limited Test Ban Treaty—a major priority on President Kennedy's agenda of foreign policies—the Outer Space Treaty, Antarctica Treaty, and Hot-Line agreement to speed communications between the White House and the Kremlin in case of a nuclear crisis. A still more significant step was taken in 1969, when negotiations began on the crucial issue of strategic arms limitations. The talks culminated in 1972, in a five-year interim agreement limiting the number of each country's offensive missiles and launchers (SALT 1).

By 1977, when SALT 1 expired, Soviet and American nuclear strength had reached the following levels:

	U.S.	U.S.S.R.
Land-based intercontinental ballistics missiles (ICBMs)	1054	1500
Submarine-based ballistics missiles	656	880
Missile-armed heavy bombers	400	140
Warheads in multiple independently targetable re-entry vehicles (MIRVs)	7500	3500

Armed with these weapons each nation had at its disposal a destructive force 1000 times greater than all the bombs dropped in World War II.

Yet both countries continued to strive for further advances in nuclear weaponry, and a SALT 2 agreement was delayed.

The Cuban missile crisis also dramatized another common danger: the threat from nuclear proliferation. A nation with nuclear weapons has undeniable military and diplomatic advantages in its foreign relations. The urge to develop these weapons is therefore a constant temptation. In more than three decades since the first atomic bomb was dropped on Hiroshima, membership in the exclusive "nuclear club" has grown from one to half-a-dozen, with other nations likely to gain entry in the near future. The risk from proliferation is obvious: the more nations that possess nuclear weapons the greater the chance that the weapons will be used, and the greater the chance of a nuclear holocaust. In the 1960s the two superpowers recognized their common interest in halting further proliferation; in 1968 they signed the nuclear Non-proliferation Treaty (NPT). Since then 30 other countries have also signed this agreement.

The Non-proliferation Treaty provides that nuclear powers will refuse to assist other nations in any way in producing nuclear weapons, while the nonnuclear countries will develop atomic energy only for peaceful purposes under supervision of the International Atomic Energy Agency. Aside from the fact that aspiring nuclear powers declined to sign the treaty, its provisions are easier to endorse than to enforce. The export of nuclear material and technology for peaceful purposes is entirely legal under the treaty, but once a country has acquired enough of this material it is virtually impossible to prevent diversions of the material for military use. The atomic energy program in India is an example: Despite repeated avowals to the contrary, nuclear material obtained from abroad was used simultaneously for both peaceful and military applications. Only the strictest safeguards, with effective inspection, can prevent further instances of this kind. But the nuclear powers have as yet shown little inclination to antagonize their allies and customers by imposing such safeguards.

Detente has taken other directions besides agreements on arms limitations and nuclear non-proliferation. The most publicized was a series of summit meetings between, first, President Nixon and then President Ford with Secretary Brezhnev, beginning in 1972 and culminating in the Vladivostok agreement of December 1974. At Vladivostok both countries pledged to expand their cooperation in many fields so that the process of improving relations "will become irreversible." Less than a year later (September 1975) a Conference on European Security was held in Helsinki, Finland. The Helsinki conference may have been the high point of Soviet-American detente.

The agreement reached at Helsinki covered several important

areas: security and political stability in Europe; cooperation in economics, science, technology, and the environment; and joint efforts in humanitarian, cultural, information, and other activities. One section of the Helsinki accord—on Respect for Human Rights—was to gain special significance after the election of President Carter in 1976. The signatories, including the Soviet Union, affirmed that "they will promote and encourage the effective exercise of civil, political, economic, social, cultural, and other rights and freedoms."

In line with the principles of Vladivostok and Helsinki, Soviet-American relations seemed to improve along a number of fronts. One was trade. In recent years of poor harvests the Russians purchased large quantities of American wheat, with options for more grain deals in the future. Negotiations also began for increased trade in a broad range of raw materials and manufactured products. In addition, joint space ventures were scheduled, as well as scientific and cultural exchanges. All these developments were heralded on both sides as indications of an historic new era in Soviet-American relations.

THE FUTURE OF DETENTE

The promise of detente is obvious. Any prospect of a nuclear war between the United States and the Soviet Union is mind-numbing: Modern society as we know it would come to an end. Such a war is not beyond possibility. Strategists in both countries long ago began "thinking about the unthinkable," planning how to carry on after a nuclear holocaust. In the United States underground command posts, invulnerable to atomic blasts, have been in place for years as centers from which leading officials could continue the struggle. How many people would actually live through a nuclear attack is a matter of speculation; so also is the fate of these survivors under a deadly cloud of radiation. (The survivors' fate has been considerably brighter since the introduction of a radiation-free "clean" nuclear bomb, but this "humane" weapon is still a long way from general use.) No one in his right mind can look forward to such a catastrophe, and any developments that lessen its likelihood must be welcomed. It is in this light that Soviet-American detente has seemed promising.

Promise of detente has been tempered by stubborn realities. Cooperative Soviet-American ventures have not dissolved conflicts of interest and ideological antagonism. At Vladivostok, Ford and Brezhnev pledged to work together in resolving outstanding international issues. Yet as specific issues have arisen, notably in Africa and the Middle East, this pledge has been ignored in the familiar struggle for political advantage.

In a war between Ethiopia and Somalia, which erupted in 1977, the United States and the Soviet Union again found themselves on opposite sides, supplying sophisticated weapons and other assistance to each of the belligerents. And American peace-seeking efforts in the Middle East were hindered by Soviet support for extremist elements who have opposed an Arab-Israeli settlement. As these instances show, expansion of Russian influence is as much a goal of Soviet policy now as before detente, and resisting this expansion is no less an American interest now than before.

Another source of serious friction has been the issue of human rights. At Vladivostok the two countries pledged to promote civil, political, and other basic rights. President Carter responded to this pledge by making violations of human rights a direct concern of American foreign policy—including violations by the Soviet Union. Carter's criticism of Soviet repression and his encouragement of dissidents inside Russia reemphasized the fundamental disparity between an open and closed society. Insofar as the United States and the Soviet Union are committed to different types of society, no promises of cooperation can resolve the radical incompatibility between them. This issue surfaced at the conference of European countries held in Belgrade (June 1977) as a successor to the Helsinki meeting. Only by avoiding the question of human rights could the work of the conference proceed.

The overall conclusion from developments since detente is that Soviet-American cooperation in specific limited areas, such as nuclear non-proliferation or scientific exchanges, does not lead to more general accommodations if basic political interests or ideological principles are at stake. In light of this reality, American expectations from detente have been overoptimistic. Although a number of steps were taken toward reducing the danger of a military confrontation, no basic reorientation of Soviet-American relations ever occurred. The continuing build-up of armaments by both countries, beyond merely defensive requirements, is the most tangible evidence of the limits of detente.

At the same time, the scope of detente goes beyond Soviet-American competition to a wider range of East-West relations. Initiatives for detente came originally from Western Europe, notably from West Germany during the chancellorship of Willy Brandt. These efforts, intended to achieve an "opening" to the East, have had a marked effect on relations among the countries of Europe. Trade, travel, and information all flow more easily between East and West. A more flexible attitude toward the satellite regimes has also been reflected in American foreign policy, symbolized by the return of the historic Crown of St. Stefan to the communist government of Hungary and President Carter's visit to Poland (1978).

The most momentous instance of detente was the recognition by the United States of the People's Republic of China after more than a decade of determined hostility. In view of the continued Sino-Soviet conflict, as well as Chinese efforts to spur their internal development, relations between China and the West, including the United States, are likely to improve further. These changes comprise a significant departure from Cold War principles, despite the limited improvement in Soviet-American relations. The easing of East-West tensions outside the sphere of Soviet-American actions is doubtless the main achievement of detente.

For Further Reading

ARENDT, HANNAH, *On Violence.* New York: Harcourt Brace Jovanovich, Inc., 1970.

ARNOLD, THURMAN, *The Folklore of Capitalism.* New Haven: Yale University Press, 1937.

BELL, DANIEL, *The Cultural Contraditions of Capitalism.* New York: Basic Books, Inc., Publishers, 1976.

————, and IRVING KRISTOL, eds., *Capitalism Today.* New York: Basic Books, Inc., Publishers, 1971.

BERLIN, ISAIAH, *Four Essays on Liberty.* New York: Oxford University Press, 1969.

CROZIER, MICHAEL J., and others, *The Crisis of Democracy.* New York: New York University Press, 1975.

DAHL, ROBERT A., *Polyarchy: Participation and Opposition.* New Haven: Yale University Press, 1971.

DOGAN, MATTAIX, ed., *The Mandarins of Western Europe: The Political Role of Top Civil Servants.* New York: John Wiley & Sons, Inc., 1975.

FRIEDMAN, MILTON, *Capitalism and Freedom.* Chicago: University of Chicago Press, Phoenix Books, 1963.

GALBRAITH, JOHN KENNETH, *Economics and the Public Purpose.* Boston: Houghton Mifflin Company, 1973.

GINZBERG, ELI, and others, *The Pluralistic Economy.* New York: McGraw-Hill Book Company, 1965.

HEILBRONER, ROBERT L., *Business Civilization in Decline.* New York: W. W. Norton & Co., Inc., 1976.

LAFEBER, WALTER, *America, Russia, and the Cold War 1945–1975* (3rd ed.). New York: John Wiley & Sons, Inc., 1976.

LINDBLOM, CHARLES E., *Politics and Markets.* New York: Basic Books, Inc., Publishers, 1977.

MCCONNELL, GRANT, *Private Power and American Democracy.* New York: Vintage Books, 1970.

REVEL, JEAN-FRANCOIS, *Without Marx or Jesus: The New American Revolution Has Begun.* New York: Doubleday & Co., Inc., 1971.

SCAMMON, RICHARD M., and BEN J. WATTENBERG, *The Real Majority.* New York: Coward, McCann & Geoghegan, Inc., 1970.

STEINER, GILBERT Y., *The State of Welfare.* Washington, D.C.: The Brookings Institution, 1971.

WESTIN, ALAN F., ed., *Information Technology in a Democracy.* Cambridge: Harvard University Press, 1971.

4

Socialism

Background of Socialism

It is not easy to determine when socialism first appears. To some, the ideal commonwealth in Plato's *Republic* is socialist, inasmuch as its ruling class has no property of its own and shares all things. Others have claimed that the Bible, particularly the Old Testament, constitutes the first socialist code, covering the protection of workers, women, and the weak. The early Christians rejected the concept of "mine and thine," and practiced socialism in their everyday lives; and in the Middle Ages numerous sects and movements, mostly religious, attacked wealth and commerce as wicked and incompatible with the Christian life. Such sects frequently withdrew into isolation, living an austere existence and sharing poverty in brotherly love as a protest against the greed prevalent in the world around them.

During the Renaissance and the Reformation, there was a revival of protest against inequality based on wealth. The new arguments increasingly combined the older faith with the newer rationalism, as evidenced in Thomas More's *Utopia* (1516). In the Puritan revolution in seventeenth-century England, there arose, side by side with the main movement of middle-class origin, a more radical group—called "Diggers" or "True Levelers"—that sought to attain communal ownership of land not in use. The movement was short-lived, but its radical protest against private landed property was not to be entirely forgotten.

To the extent that socialism contains within itself an element of protest against social inequality—and no movement can call itself socialist unless it expresses that kind of protest—it is as old as Western civilization itself. Both Greek and Jewish-Christian thought categorically reject the conception of wealth as the basis of the good life. Another feature of socialism—the protest against money as the chief tie between human beings—is also not confined to the socialist tradition: Many nonsocialists have voiced their disapproval of the "cash nexus." But if we look in history for something more specific and concrete than a vague protest against social injustice, we find that socialism as an effective, organized political movement is the product of the Industrial Revolution. Despite all illustrations from earlier times, socialism as a major political force originated as the result of modern industrial capitalism. In contrast to communism, which is likely to happen only in countries *before* they have undergone the full impact of Industrial Revolution, democratic socialism develops primarily in societies *after* they have experienced considerable industrialization.

Whenever industrialization has taken place in societies that lack deeply rooted liberal institutions, the political adjustment to the resulting tensions is likely to be either some form of authoritarianism (Spain, Portugal, Brazil) or totalitarianism (fascism in Germany and Japan, or communism in the Soviet Union and China). In each case, the extent of governmental initiative and control in the economic sector of society will reflect the range and pervasiveness of political power that a particular authoritarian or totalitarian state possesses and seeks to enhance.

In contrast, where industrialization has occurred in relatively liberal societies (as in northwestern Europe, North America, Australia, and New Zealand), the purpose of the economy is the welfare of the individual, and the adjustment to the inevitable tensions and conflicts of industrial capitalism assumes some form of democratic socialism or the welfare state.

The basic distinction between the authoritarian and the liberal society can cut away a lot of confusion. Thus, the question is frequently debated whether a fascist economy is socialistic (because of the comprehensive regulation of economic activity by the state) or capitalistic (because the means of production are left in private hands).

Such discussions are insoluble because they are based on a false premise: that the basic distinction in the world's economic systems is between socialism and capitalism. In actuality, the line of division runs differently: between *free-market or welfare economies,* which aim at individual welfare, and *coercive or command economies,* which aim at the collective power of the state. Both capitalism and socialism fall into the group that is dominated by the concept of welfare economics, whereas fascism and communism fall into the second group, the command economy.

Differences among the species within each major group are important, but they are not crucial. Capitalism and socialism disagree on the best method of bringing the maximum welfare to the people; the former stresses individual property and effort, while the latter puts its faith in collective productive property and effort.

Fascism and communism do not see eye to eye in every detail on how best to operate an economy in the service of the state. Differences between fascism and communism, however, are insignificant if it is recalled that the objective—the power of the state—is the same, and that the means—ranging from friendly pressure to "corrective" labor and concentration camps—are amazingly similar and frequently identical.

In some ways, of course, socialism opposes capitalism, but such opposition is the rebellion of child against father, not the total war of stranger against stranger. Just as the rebellious child uses arguments learned from the father, socialism employs a whole arsenal of capitalist values and attitudes, especially pragmatic utilitarianism, in the controversy with its progenitor.

Socialism inherits from capitalism one basic goal: *to preserve the unity of work and ownership.* In the seventeenth and eighteenth centuries, the early phase of modern capitalism, that unity was a reality. In the England of John Locke or the America of Thomas Jefferson, the average farm, store, or workshop was generally small enough to be owned and operated by one person or family. Work and ownership coincided. The chief threat to this unity came from the state, which sought to prescribe, to regulate—in short, to play the role of an omniscient busybody in economic matters. The individual entrepreneur, who knew how to run the business without any unsolicited advice from self-confident state officials, resented this attitude.

As the capitalist economy progressed, however, the individual (or single-family) form of ownership and work was gradually replaced, by an economic system in which large-scale enterprise swallowed up the original capitalist-owner-manager. As the size of industrial enterprise grew larger and larger, work became more and more socialized, more collective, whereas ownership remained private.

In seeking to restore the classical harmony between work and property, the socialist reformer faces two alternatives: (1) the division of large-scale enterprises into small units, so that work and ownership can coincide again in one person or family, or (2) collective ownership.

The former method is feasible in agriculture, where large landed estates can be physically broken up and divided among landless farm-workers, as was done in France during eighteenth-century revolution, in Mexico and Guatemala during this century, and—on a smaller scale —in Italy after World War II and in Chile under President Allende. Whether such a breakup of large landed estates is economically sound is highly debatable. In many cases the productivity of dwarf farms created by agrarian reform is lower than that of the original large farm units. A reform government, however, may be willing to pay the price of lower productivity for the greater social benefit of having an independent farm class. The technology of agriculture is simple enough so that large units can be broken up and small units operated with relative efficiency.

In industry, this solution is physically out of the question. An automobile or aircraft factory cannot be divided up into 10,000 portions, each owned and operated by one worker. The technological nature of modern industrial enterprise is such that there is no alternative to collective work and operation. Thus, in facing the task of reuniting work and ownership in industry, collective ownership seems to socialists the logical answer, just at the classical liberal deduced the right to individual ownership from the fact of individual work. In both systems —classical liberal capitalism and democratic socialism—there is the underlying assumption that the right to property ultimately rests on work, effort, and industry, rather than on formal law, custom, or birth.

John Locke, the founder of modern political and economic liberalism, based the right to property on human labor, and the value of property on the amount of labor "admixed" to nature's resources. The socialists have accepted the Lockean and capitalist rationale of labor. What has changed since Locke is simply the technological character of labor, not its ethical implications. If the logic of capitalism demands individual property for individual work, the logic of socialism demands collective ownership for collective work—provided collective work is the only possible form of managerial organization.

Where small property has survived as a technologically efficient unit, as in agriculture, the professions, the arts, and some areas of retailing, servicing, and manufacturing, socialists generally agree with capitalists that private ownership should be kept and strengthened. Thus, socialist governments have enjoyed long tenure in predominantly agrarian countries like Denmark and New Zealand because farmers in those countries have been sympathetic to the socialist program of maintaining their economic integrity and individualism by cheap credits, guaranteed parity prices, and other policies designed to protect the small farmer against the threat of domination by banks, insurance companies, and wholesalers.

ROBERT OWEN: CAPITALIST-SOCIALIST

The filial link between socialism and capitalism can be illustrated by the first modern socialist, who was a wealthy and successful capitalist. Robert Owen (1771–1858), generally regarded as the founder of British socialism, first used the term "socialism." A self-made capitalist, he had made a fortune by the age of 40. He was a man of sound, practical judgment, and he could easily meet one test of experience frequently described by conservatives as essential whenever a reformer comes forth with some new scheme: "Have you ever met a payroll in your life?" Owen had. In his *A New View of Society* (1813), he described himself as a "manufacturer for pecuniary profit."

His views were the result not of study in the British Museum (like Marx's), but of experience in his own industrial enterprises. Owen dedicated his book to the Prince Regent of the British Empire; he was no refugee from his own society, as were Marx and Lenin later, but a respectable, wealthy man. He considered drink an incentive to crime and a main source of misery, and his list of virtues and vices would have appealed to Benjamin Franklin.

Far from looking upon capitalist Britain as a dungeon of inhumanity, he described the British constitution as being "among the best devised and most enlightened that have hitherto been established." Refusing to believe that evil can be transformed into good in a day, he advocated "progressive repeal and modification" of unjust laws and conditions; strongly rejecting the alleged blessings of revolutionary change, he felt that "the British constitution, in its present outline, is admirably adapted to effect these changes, without the evils which always accompany a coerced or ill-prepared change."

Realizing that love and fellowship cannot be conceived in hatred and born in strife, Owen appealed to "every rational man, every true friend of humanity," and he hoped for cordial cooperation and unity of action between the government, Parliament, the church, and the people.

Owen's rationalism also emerges from the fact that *A New View of Society* discusses one subject more than any other: *education.* Owen believed that the evils of his society were due to circumstances rather than to the depravity of man, and he was convinced that, just as crime and degradation were the result of specific social and economic conditions, education in a new environment could produce human beings endowed with rationality and the habits of order, regularity, temperance, and industry.

In his own time, children of six and seven years of age were employed in factories for 12 hours a day and more, and Owen made the suggestion, bold and radical for the capitalist conscience of 1813, that a regular workday of 13 hours, from six in the morning to seven in the evening, should not be imposed upon children under 12; after that age "their education might be finished, and their bodies would be more competent to undergo the fatigue and exertions required of them." Human nature, Owen says, is "universally plastic," and if education is the key to make men more rational and cooperative, "the best governed state will be that which shall possess the best national system of education."

Owen in the true liberal-capitalist tradition looked to society rather than to the state for important change. A century before Keynes and Beveridge, Owen understood the crucial importance of full employment for the maintenance of a civilized society. Yet he opposed the dole (cash relief to the unemployed) on the ground that the "industrious, temperate, and comparatively virtuous" should not be compelled to support the "ignorant, idle, and comparatively vicious." Owen clearly saw the human aspects of unemployment; yet he did not want the state to dispense employment, but to provide an educational system good enough to equip every person with the skills wherewith to find employment in the open market.

A believer in the individualist principle of self-help, Owen started the cooperative movement and supported the incipient trade union organizations springing up throughout England and Scotland. For Owen, cooperativism was more than selling milk to housewives; he believed that producers' cooperatives rather than consumers' cooperatives would establish a new social order. He sank much of his fortune in producers' cooperatives in England and spent several years and the better part of his wealth in a cooperative venture in the United States. Although his best-known experiment, the settlement of New Harmony in Indiana, did not succeed, his ideas are today more important than ever.

The British experiment in nationalizing selected basic industries and services has raised the fundamental question whether the Owenite method of cooperativism outside the formal machinery of the national government is not preferable to nationalization as effected in Britain since 1945. In the British labor movement, too, the Owenite bias against the state is still strong; if the labor unions have never been overenthusiastic about nationalization schemes, it is because they dread the growth of the state machinery and the transformation of free labor union officials, responsible to their members, into semigovernment officials, responsible to the state.

SOCIALISM AND DEMOCRACY

The link between democracy and socialism is the most important single element in socialist thought and policy. The history of socialism quickly shows that successful socialist movements have grown up only in nations with strong democratic traditions, such as Great Britain, the Scandinavian countries, Belgium, the Netherlands, Switzerland, Australia, New Zealand, and Israel.

The reason for this parallelism is simple. Where democratic, constitutional government is generally accepted, socialists can concentrate on extensive economic and social reforms: to create more opportunity for the underprivileged classes; to end inequality based on birth rather than service; to open the horizons of education to all the people; to eliminate discriminatory practices based on sex, religion, race, or social class; to regulate and reorganize the economy for the benefit of the whole community; to maintain full employment; to provide adequate social security for the sick, unemployed, and aged; to replan the layout of towns and cities; to tear down the slums and build new houses; to provide medical facilities for everybody, regardless of income; and, finally, to rebuild society on the foundation of cooperation instead of competition, incentive, and profit.

All these goals of democratic socialism have one thing in common: *to make democracy more real by broadening the application of democratic principles from the political to the nonpolitical areas of society.*

Freedom of worship and freedom of political association, historically the first liberties to be won, are still the essential foundations of democracy. Where these foundations exist, therefore, socialists can concentrate on the "finer points" of democracy.

In contrast, socialist parties have fought an uphill and generally losing struggle in nations in which democracy is not a living thing, but an aspiration, a hope, an idea yet to be realized. For example, the Social Democratic party in Germany always worked under a heavy handicap. In the Second Reich (1870–1918), political autocracy was a reality, and parliamentary institutions were a cover for the virtual dictatorship of

Bismarck and then of Emperor William II. In the 1870s, Bismarck outlawed the Social Democrats as "enemies of the state," and the party leaders who escaped imprisonment fled to England, other free nations in Europe, or America.

During the Weimar Republic (1919–1933), the Social Democratic party was paralyzed again by the insecurity of democratic institutions; the main issue of the Weimar Republic was not a social reform in which the socialists could take a special interest, but something much bigger: the issue of democratic government itself. Whereas in nations with long-established democratic habits socialists could argue over issues within democracy, taking the existence of democracy for granted, German socialists constantly had to fight over the issue of democracy itself. As fascism grew in the Weimar Republic, the German socialists became more concerned with the defense of republican and democratic institutions than with problems of economic reform.

In Russia before 1917, the situation was even simpler. The tsarist regime made no pretense of democracy or self-government; social and economic reform by peaceful means was thus virtually impossible, and the door for revolutionary communism opened.

In France the Socialist party had become far stronger than the Communist party by 1936. During World War II, however, under the German occupation, the political environment of underground and illegal activity was much more congenial to the communists than to the socialists. Democratic socialists in a country like France function best when they can carry membership cards rather than high explosives. The type of person who joins such a party is stable, probably a family man, in any event a skilled worker or civil servant with a steady job. People of this kind do not readily engage in illegal, terrorist activities such as were necessary in France under German occupation in World War II.

The communists, on the other hand, have attracted a different type of person, more devoted to the cause, and used to illegality and semi-illegality even in so-called normal times. What the Third French Republic (1870–1940) could never accomplish, four years of German occupation managed to do; at the end of World War II, the communists emerged as the strongest single party of France, polling about twice as many votes as the Democratic Socialists. The communists remained the strongest party until the elections of November 18 and 25, 1962, in which, as in subsequent elections, the Gaullist party (Union for the New Republic) heavily defeated them.

In contrast, the socialist vote in the British general election of 1970 was 429 times larger than the communist vote. The evidence (not only from Great Britain, but also from other democratic countries with strong socialist movements) indicates that fullest civil liberty for all ideas and parties including revolutionary organizations, seems to be the best antidote against fascism and communism, and that repression is the natural soil for the growth of revolutionary movements.

If democratic nations today were ranked according to their respect for civil liberty, Great Britain, Norway, Denmark, Sweden, the Netherlands, Belgium, Australia, and New Zealand would be at the top of the list; all these countries are, or recently have been, governed by socialist adminstrations or by coalition cabinets with strong socialist participation.

The reasons for this parallelism are not complex. Democratic socialists are keenly aware that without the opportunities provided by liberal, constitutional government they could not get to first base. Once in control of the government, socialists still maintain the psychology of the opposition, because they know that the possession of political power does not automatically solve the problems of social and economic organization. In other words, before socialists take over the government, they are in opposition to the government *and* to the wealthy classes; after they gain control of the government, the oppositionist psychology, directed as it is against the economic status quo, necessarily persists.

Moreover, even in the purely governmental realm, socialists tend to preserve a certain degree of caution and suspicion after they get into office, because they realize that, though they can gain control of the legislature in an election, the other sources of political power—the civil service and the judiciary—may be hostile to them.

Another factor essential to this discussion is all too frequently neglected. Examining the remarkably high state of civil liberty in nations with strong socialist movements, one tends to overlook the high respect for civil liberty demonstrated by the opponents of socialism. If the conservative and propertied classes had shown less respect for the letter and spirit of constitutional government, the chances of socialist growth would have been slim. From the viewpoint of dollars and cents, the conservatives' genuine acquiescence in socialism meant that they valued democracy more highly than their pocketbooks and were willing to be heavily taxed even for programs they considered undesirable or unreasonable.

Thus both groups took a gamble: The socialists trusted their opponents not to destroy the processes of democratic government in order to protect their financial interests; the propertied classes trusted the socialists not to abuse electoral victories and to act reasonably and moderately when in office.

Where the propertied classes were unconvinced that it is more blessed to give than to receive and were unwilling to pay higher wages and higher taxes for the sake of social justice, the natural response to distrust was more distrust. It is in this kind of political atmosphere that democratic socialism has been pushed back in Italy and India, giving way to the more radical demands of communism.

SOCIALISM VERSUS COMMUNISM

Socialism and communism have stood for two irreconcilable ways of thought and life, as incompatible as constitutional liberalism and revolutionary totalitarianism. Although recent advocates of Eurocommunism try to downplay the profound antagonism between communism and socialism, their claims have yet to be tested in practice. On the basis of experience in many different countries and circumstances it is clear that communists seek to end capitalism by a single act of revolutionary upheaval and civil war. Once in power, communists are determined to stay there indefinitely. Socialists, on the other hand, adhere to strict constitutional procedures; they seek power by ballots, and once in office they are subject to being voted out in the next election.

Because of the communist goal of revolution, it is understandable that socialist parties look upon communists as troublemakers who must be kept out of unions or any other organized working-class activity. It is understandable why the communists work with such energy for the control of organized labor: They know that no amount of propaganda will convert the middle and wealthier classes to communism. In contrast, the socialists have learned from elementary electoral statistics that parliamentary majorities cannot be obtained by appealing to one class only; a considerable proportion of the working class (in England about 40 percent) does not vote Labour and if the Labour party is to obtain a majority, it must appeal to other groups. The communists think in terms of *class* and class antagonisms; the socialists think in terms of *parliamentary majorities*.

The socialist rejection of Marxist thought also applies to the term *proletariat*. As former Prime Minister Harold Wilson put it, "The idea of a proletariat is nonsense. I am more interested in people as individuals than in the mass. I am interested in the family, because most happiness is family happiness. I am interested in Saturdays and Sundays and Bank Holidays."

In the crucial issue of public ownership, the gap that separates socialists from communists is unbridgeable. Communists visualize the transition from capitalist enterprise to public ownership as sudden and complete. There is no payment for expropriated property, because communists consider that capitalist ownership of property is no better than theft. In contrast, socialists do not believe that the transition from capitalism to public ownership of the means of production can be either sudden or complete. Public ownership of the means of production is to be built up gradually, by installments; if one phase works, then the next will be tackled. Responsible socialists feel that they must prove pragmatically, through actual accomplishments, the usefulness and practicality of public ownership in particular industries or services.

Concerning compensation, socialists share the general democratic conviction that no citizen may be deprived of his property without due process and compensation. Important as public ownership of the basic industries is to their plans, socialists consider public ownership not an end but a means to an end, and a means that does not justify the violation of property rights.

There is another vital difference with regard to public ownership. Communists seek to transfer all means of production, distribution, and exchange to the state, preferring publicly owned property to private enterprise. By contrast, socialists consider whether a specific industry or service is to be transferred to public ownership and control. The socialists' decision to nationalize may be because the industry is a monopoly (such as a utility); because it is financially ailing (as the British coal industry was before its nationalization); or because it is of such vital importance to the national economy that it seems socially undesirable to leave its operation in private hands (the British iron and steel industry was nationalized on these grounds). The British Conservatives are in substantial agreement with Labor on the first two criteria; on the third the two parties are in partial disagreement.

Philosophically and politically, the difference between communists and socialists is deeply rooted. As we saw earlier, Lenin's theory of the professional revolutionary is based on the assumption that the Communist party has the job of leading the proletariat; and that within that minority the professional revolutionaries are to formulate policies and assume leadership. Thus, a minority within a minority is the ruling elite. This elite concept is rejected by socialists, who believe in democracy and majority rule for party and nation. Clement Attlee, British prime minister from 1945 to 1951 and leader of the Labour party from 1935 to 1955, writes in his book *The Labour Party in Perspective* (1937) that his party's strength depends, "not on the brilliance of individuals, but on the quality of the rank and file."

Socialists believe in peaceful persuasion to promote their program. Communists feel that all means of communication, education, and propaganda are biased in favor of the capitalist status quo and that freedom of the press amounts to little if one lacks necessary funds to start a newspaper. For this reason the communists were stunned when the British Labour party gained electoral victory in 1945 and again in 1950, 1964, 1966, and 1974.

According to orthodox Marxism-Leninism, such victories were impossible. Since the British press was overwhelmingly in favor of the

Conservative party, how could the voters, who presumably had been reading the proconservative papers daily for years, vote Labour? According to Lenin, workers under capitalism cannot be converted to socialist thinking until there has been a change in the economic structure of society. Only then, Lenin argues, will the workers be able to think along anticapitalist lines, because (as Marx said) the conditions of man's life determine his thinking.

To the communist, every capitalist system, whether democratic, authoritarian, or fascist, is a bourgeois dictatorship; specifically, democratic institutions in a capitalist system are considered a façade which does not make the capitalist system less dictatorial. Once capitalism—even liberal capitalism—is identified with dictatorship, the communist insistence on violence as the sole means of change is a logical conclusion.

Socialists, on the other hand, draw a fundamental distinction between two types of capitalist system, the political dictatorship and the liberal democracy. In a liberal democracy socialists believe in playing according to the rules of the game—provided, of course, the other side does the same.

Finally, socialists reject the communist thesis that the choice in a democracy is between complete capitalism and complete collectivism. Democratic parties do not concern themselves with bringing about the millennium at a certain date but seek to tackle issues that are comparatively manageable and to avoid definitive solutions that are irrevocable.

Socialists therefore envisage the transition from a predominantly capitalist economy to a predominantly socialist economy, not as a result of a sudden revolutionary coup that makes the return to private enterprise impossible, but as the result of gradual measures, none of which by itself irrevocably alters the nature of the whole economy.

Whereas the communists think in terms of three absolutes—capitalism, revolution, communist dictatorship—socialists think in terms of three *relative* concepts: a predominantly capitalist economy as the starting point, a period of gradual change, and finally a predominantly socialized economy.

Socialist Theory and Practice

ELEMENTS OF SOCIALIST THOUGHT AND POLICY

Socialism, like many other liberal movements and ideas, has no bible, probably because liberals generally cannot agree on one set of beliefs and doctrines. Moreover, socialism has developed in different countries in accordance with different national traditions, and there has never been any central authority to lay down a socialist party line.

Despite the absence of such authoritative statements of socialist doctrine, the outlines of socialist thought and policy can be culled from socialist writings, and from the policies of socialist parties. What emerges, however, is not a consistent body of ideas and policies. The main strength—and weakness—of socialism is that it has had no clear-cut body of doctrine and that it has fed on contradictory sources, sources that reflect the contradictions of the societies in which socialism has developed.

The complex, and frequently self-contradictory, elements of socialist thought and policy can best be illustrated from the British socialist movement. The elements that stand out in the British movement are:

1. Religion
2. Ethical and aesthetic idealism
3. Fabian empiricism
4. Liberalism

Religion

In *The Labour Party in Perspective,* Attlee wrote that

the first place in the influences that built up the Socialist movement must be given to religion. England in the nineteenth century was still a nation of Bible readers. To put the Bible into the hands of an English-man is to do a very dangerous thing. He will find there material which may send him out as a preacher of some religious, social, or economic doctrine. The large number of religious sects in this country, and the various tenets that many of them hold, illustrates this.

The Christian Socialist movement, headed by two clergymen, Frederick Maurice and Charles Kingsley, reached its peak in the middle of the nineteenth century and was an important source for the later development of working-class and socialist organizations. The Christian Socialists had as their guiding principle the concept that socialism must be Christianized, and Christianity socialized.

George Lansbury, Attlee's predecessor as the leader of the Labour party, wrote in *My England* (1934):

Socialism, which means love, cooperation, and brotherhood in every department of human affairs, is the only outward expression of a Christian's faith. I am firmly convinced that whether they know it or not, all who approve and accept competition and struggle against each other as the means whereby we gain our daily bread, do indeed betray and make of no effect the "will of God."

In 1942, the archbishop of Canterbury, William Temple, came very close to socialism in his *Christianity and the Social Order.* Temple held that every economic system is, for good or ill, an immense educative influence and that therefore the church must be concerned with it. The church is thus bound to ask "whether that influence is one tending to develop Christian character, and if the answer is partly or wholly negative the church must do its utmost to secure a change in the economic system so that it may find in that system an ally and not an enemy."

This practical concern of Christianity was particularly strong in England throughout the whole second half of the nineteenth century. A sense of moral seriousness and dedicated disinterestedness characterized this period, and religion, while conceding that grace and faith were essential to salvation, nevertheless emphasized conduct and *salvation by works.* Many socialist leaders of the older generation who (like Attlee and Sir Stafford Cripps) came from upper-class homes were steeped in an atmosphere in which religion was taken seriously.

Another religious influence of profound importance in Britain was the tradition of religious dissent, of *nonconformity.* In other European states, Protestantism had resulted in freedom of the church in relation to Rome, but not necessarily in freedom *within* the church in matters of doctrine and church government. To the nonconformist, Protestantism meant freedom of individual conscience and the freedom to organize voluntarily in associations of like-minded believers. This principle of voluntary association was later translated from religion into politics, where it became the life principle of the democratic society.

It was in the village chapels of the eighteenth and nineteenth centuries that many local leaders of working-class organizations learned to think for themselves, as well as to conduct public meetings and administer finances. Wherever nonconformity was strong, labor unions and cooperatives were strong; in fact, the trade unions have been aptly called the present-day descendants of the earlier nonconformist congregations. Nonconformity supplied more than a particular religious outlook: It was also the source, in the labor movement, of the idealism, the moral dedication, and the seriousness that have characterized the movement and its leaders.

The study of the internal organization of some nonconformist churches shows its similarity to the organization of trade unions: Both are loosely federated unions of voluntary bodies freely associating with each other. The Labour party today is also a federal union, made up of three main bodies—trade unions, cooperatives, and local constituency organizations—each of which is in turn made up of loosely federated organizations. Because the Labour party has a federal character, its internal structure resembles more the American federal system than the much simpler and more streamlined political system of Britain itself.

The complexity of the religious root of modern British socialism becomes apparent in the fact that nonreligious, rational humanism has also played a vital role in the evolution of socialist thought and action. Robert Owen was a rationalist; among more modern socialist leaders in Britain, Sidney and Beatrice Webb, Harold J. Laski, G. D. H. Cole, and Hugh Gaitskell, to mention but a few, have not been much inspired by formal religious beliefs. It remains, however, of some interest that the political leaders of the labor movement—men like George Lansbury, Clement Attlee, and Sir Stafford Cripps—have more often been profoundly religious, whereas the principal intellectual figures, the men who formulate ideas rather than policies, tend to represent the *rationalist* root of socialism. Harold Wilson, a professional economist, came from a background of strong religious nonconformity, and religion meant a good deal to him. Although reluctant to express his religious feelings in public, he often preached in nonconformist churches. His type of socialism has been called by a fellow Labourite "Methodism, not Marxism."

In the United States, too, religion has played an important part in the cooperative and communal settlements established in the eighteenth and nineteenth centuries as well as in more recent socialist activities of a political and propagandistic nature. In the twentieth century, democratic socialism in the United States has been symbolized above all by Norman Thomas, who was a minister of religion before he took up the cause of socialism as his life's mission.

In contrast, religion has played a much smaller part in continental European and Latin American socialism. In England religious dissent was the bridge between religious and political unorthodoxy; in the virtual absence of nonconformity outside the English-speaking world, however, dissent from the established social and political order has generally also included dissent from the established church or from religion itself.

Before World War I, Russian radical and socialist movements were notably free of any religious influence or inspiration. In his monumental study, *The Spirit of Russia* (1913), Thomas Garrigue Masaryk, a renowned philosopher and later the first president of Czechoslovakia, observed that "Christian socialism is practically unknown in Russia." Masaryk's analysis in 1913 was later confirmed by the victorious rise of

Leninist communism. In France and Germany there were small groups of religious socialists, but, on the whole, socialists tended to be anticlerical or at least indifferent toward religion since most churches in continental Europe openly supported the political and economic status quo. During World War II, the struggle of many priests and ministers against Nazi-fascist oppression brought about a closer understanding between churches and most socialist parties. Since then, the churches have become less committed to one particular set of social and economic theories, and the socialists have abandoned much of their earlier anticlericalism. Also, British socialism has proved to many socialists in other lands that socialism and religion do mix, provided the mixture is accomplished in the right spirit.

Ethical and aesthetic idealism

Ethical and aesthetic idealism is another source of British socialism, although its impact cannot be measured in votes and membership cards. Expressed by writers like John Ruskin and William Morris, ethical idealism was not a political or economic program, but a revolt against the squalor, drabness, and poverty of life under industrial capitalism. Developing first in England, capitalism probably produced more ugliness there than anywhere else, because English industrialists had no way of imagining how it would change clean air and water and the beauty of the English countryside, no way of foreseeing the rapid disfigurement of graceful old towns and villages by slums and factory centers.

Whereas Marx approached industrial capitalism in terms of cosmic laws—the development of world history according to inevitable social laws, philosophical materialism, the law of the falling profit rate, to name but a few—Morris kept his gaze closer to the ground. He saw around him ugly household goods and furnishings, and men and women who lacked joy and beauty in their daily lives. Once, when asked in a public meeting what he thought of Marx, Morris said, "I am asked if I believe in Marx's theory of value. To speak quite frankly, I do not know what Marx's theory of value is, and I'm damned if I want to know." What Morris cared about was human beings, not this or that "system." He felt intensely that the arts must be brought back into everyday life and that people's creative impulses should be given expression in their daily life and work.

The influence of Ruskin and Morris was more negative than positive. They showed what was wrong—physically and morally—with a civilization that was built on strife and squalor, but they did not formulate any specific program to improve the conditions to which they objected. Nevertheless, this aesthetic and ethical revolt was important in preparing the intellectual environment in which socialism could later find a sympathetic response.

Ruskin and Morris were read mainly by the more educated class, which absorbed from them—as well as from Charles Dickens, Thomas Carlyle, and other writers—a groping understanding of what industrial civilization does to man, not only as a worker, but as a human being. The aesthetic and ethical rebels of Victorian England undermined the self-confidence that then prevailed and fostered self-criticism; out of that doubt and self-criticism more positive socialist ideas could later be developed step by step.

Particularly in town and country planning the Labour party reflects directly and explicitly the message of Ruskin and Morris. The whole concept of community planning—which is more than tearing down slums and building neat little row houses of uniform size and style— owes much to the outlook of the early pioneers of socialist thought, for whom problems of industry merged with more general problems of creating a community in which each member would have access to the means of civilized enjoyment.

Fabian empiricism

Fabian empiricism is perhaps the most characteristically British aspect of the British labor movement. The Fabian Society, founded in 1884, was named after a Roman general, Quintus Fabius Maximus Cunctator—the "delayer." The early motto of the society was: "For the right moment you must wait, as Fabius did; but when the right moment comes you must strike hard, or your waiting will have been vain and fruitless."

The founders and early members of the Fabian society included George Bernard Shaw, Sidney and Beatrice Webb, H. G. Wells, and Graham Wallas. It was noteworthy that none of them came from the poorer classes and that there was a sizable proportion of writers in the group.

In Sidney Webb's historical survey of the basis of socialism, included in the *Fabian Essays* (1889), we find what is still the basic philosophy of Fabianism and, more generally, of British socialism. Webb looked upon socialism (11 years before the foundation of the Labour party) as an inevitable outcome of the full fruition of democracy, but he insisted that his "inevitability of gradualness" was sharply different from the Marxian inevitability of revolutionary, catastrophic change.

Webb emphasized that social organization can come only bit by bit and that important "organic changes" can take place, in England at least, only under four conditions: First, such changes must be democratic, acceptable to a popular majority, and "prepared for in the minds of all"; second, they must be gradual, causing no dislocation; third, they must not be regarded as immoral by the people; fourth, they must be constitutional and peaceful.

Marxians on the Continent and elsewhere aimed their propaganda at the proletariat. The middle and upper classes were to be liquidated, not converted to socialism. Because the propaganda was thus aimed exclusively at the proletariat, it tended to be highly emotional and sloganized, taking into consideration not only the educational level of the workers, but also the fact that they were expected to be half-converted before they were ever exposed to Marxist agitation.

The Fabian Society started from the assumption that there could be no progress toward a just social order in Britain unless the middle and upper classes could be shown the reasonableness and equity of the basic claims of socialist thought and policy. Since government in Britain was by persuasion and consent, and since the governing classes of Britain were largely recruited from the middle and upper classes, there could be no change of policy in Britain without the consent of those classes. It was fortunate for the Fabians that they spoke the same language—literally and metaphorically—as did the governing classes and knew how to permeate the latter in ways that would have been closed to formal propaganda from persons outside the same class.

The Fabian technique of permeation was based on the premise that you do not change a reasonable person through a single brilliant argument, lecture, or emotional appeal. It was Fabian policy to work on the minds and feelings of their hearers in a slow, gradual process rather than in one sudden act of conversion, and preferably on social, informal occasions rather than on formal, official ones.

An emotional appeal to a high British civil servant, telling him that according to the Marxian dialectic the capitalist system is doomed, and that such doom will be followed by the classless proletarian society, was likely to have less of a long-term effect than a casual reference at luncheon to a new government report, written by a fellow bureaucrat, on the incidence of disease and crime in slum areas. Similarly, serious discussion of a recent book by a reputable and scholarly economist on changes in the distribution of income among various social and economic groups was likely to have more effect on a conservative political leader than the shorter appeals of "Down with Capitalism" and "Long Live Proletarian Solidarity."

Permeation had also another side. The Fabians did not consider it their job to pass resolutions, make appeals to kings and Parliaments, or address themselves to the masses of the people. They were interested in convincing a small group of persons who had two qualifications: First, they had to be persons of continuous influence in public life, so that the long process of permeation, if successful, would pay off; second, such persons would have to be reasonable, by which the Fabians meant not partisan extremists. Since such persons could be found in all political parties, the Fabians cultivated conservatives as well as liberals.

This sort of Fabianism assumes a Fabianism in reverse, or else it would not stand a chance of success. For example, Fabians and other socialists in England religiously read *The Times,* not because they agree with its editorial viewpoint (generally conservative), but because it is "a good paper." In many other countries socialists consider the local version of *The Times* a source of bourgeois contamination from which they should steer clear.

The difference between the Fabian and Marxian-communist approaches can best be seen by contrasting the writings of the two groups. Marx was little interested in the minutiae of life; his magnum opus, *Das Kapital,* is an attempt to give meaning to history as a whole, and much of his thought was devoted to fundamentals of economics and philosophy. Lenin wrote volumes on such subjects as *Materialism and Empirio-Criticism.* In contrast, more than 95 percent of all Fabian publications have been pamphlets rather than heavy tomes, and pamphlets lend themselves more to small subjects like *Municipal Milk and Public Health* (Fabian Tract no. 122) than to the future of Western civilization. The Fabian Society is rarely to be found in high intellectual altitudes, sniffing the thin air surrounding the metaphysical peaks; it is more often found "nosing about in the drains," seeking to remedy some immediate and specific condition.

Early in the history of the Fabian Society, Fabian Tract no. 70 (written by George Bernard Shaw) made it plain that Fabianism was no rival to existing philosophies trying to explain the whole cosmos and that it had "no distinctive opinion on the Marriage Question, Religion, Art, abstract Economics, historic Evolution, Currency, or any other subject than its own special business of practical Democracy and Socialism." This sense of practicality and concreteness is indicated by typical titles of Fabian tracts and other pamphlets: *Liquor Licensing at Home and Abroad; Life in the Laundry; Public Control of Electrical Power and Transit; The Case for School Nurseries; The Endowment of Motherhood; The Reform of the House of Lords;* and *The British Cabinet: A Study of Its Personnel, 1909–1924.*

Two Fabian pamphlets, *Metropolitan Borough Councils: Their Constitution, Powers, and Duties* and *Borough Councils: Their Consti-*

tution, Powers, and Duties, were written by Clement R. Attlee in the spring of 1920, when Lenin was busy, not with the reform of borough councils, but with the destruction of states and empires.

The Fabian approach can perhaps best be shown in a simple illustration: If a slum clearance project is debated in terms of fundamental issues—such as socialism versus capitalism—agreement between advocates of the project and their opponents is unlikely. However, if the pertinent facts can be clearly brought out—the cost (in dollars and cents) of a slum area in terms of disease, crime protection, fire hazards, compared with the cost of building new houses with public assistance —the original gap has been considerably narrowed, and agreement will be likelier than it was when the argument centered on issues of apparently irreconcilable ultimate values.

The successes of Fabianism have probably stemmed chiefly from this concern with reducing questions of principle to questions of fact. Fabians gambled on the notion that facts do matter and that the impact of facts ultimately determines how people think and act.

In his autobiography, *Power and Influence* (1953), Lord Beveridge had an interesting sidelight on the Fabian faith in facts. One of the greatest contributions of Sidney and Beatrice Webb was the creation of the London School of Economics and Political Science in 1895 in order to provide an adequate opportunity for the study of economics and allied subjects. The Webbs themselves chose the first four directors of the London School. Of the four, Beveridge tells us, the first two became Conservative members of Parliament, the third had socialist sympathies, and the fourth (Beveridge himself) was a Liberal. Beveridge says the Webbs "believed that the impartial study of society would further the Socialism which was their practical aim, but they were prepared to take the risk of being wrong in that belief."

The Fabian technique of trying to reduce apparently irreconcilable differences of principle to negotiable disagreements over facts is no invention or novelty but is implicit in the very nature of the democratic society. We have peace in a free society to the extent that people are willing to keep to themselves conflicting fundamentals in religion, morals, and philosophy. Separation of state and church in the United States was effected and has been maintained not because Americans are indifferent to religion, but because the framers of the Constitution thought it wise to keep this fundamental issue out of politics and to concentrate on issues in which people of all religions can cooperate without injury to their religious belief.

Fabianism has frequently been described as reform without resentment, social reconstruction without class war, political empiricism without dogma or fanaticism. Despite its small size (its membership never exceeded a few thousand), the Fabian Society has had an enormous impact. In the 1945 election, which led to the first Labour government based on a substantial parliamentary majority, 229 of the 394 Labour members of Parliament were Fabians, and more than half of the government, including Attlee (prime minister from 1945 to 1951), was Fabian. Hugh Gaitskell, who succeeded Attlee as leader of the Labour party, was also a Fabian of long standing, as was Gaitskell's successor, Harold Wilson.

Liberalism

Liberalism has become an increasingly important source of socialism, particularly since Liberal parties have dwindled to insignificance in many countries. In England, the Liberal party has virtually disappeared and the Labour party seems to have inherited about one-third of the estate. Temperamentally, many Liberals do not find it easy to join a socialist movement; the passion for individual liberty and individual difference is still the most distinguishing trait of the Liberal.

Apart from the tendency toward red tape and regulation for the sake of regulation, there is also in socialism a tendency toward the state, the mass, and collectivity. Both tendencies are repugnant to the true Liberal, the man who occasionally still likes to be himself and not just a number in the National Register. Yet, during the last 40 years, more and more Liberals have joined the Labour party. Why?

In the first place, the weakness of the British Liberal party is due to the fact, not that it has failed, but that its success has made it unnecessary. Both the Conservative party and the Labour party are now thoroughly committed to Liberal principles of respect for individual freedom of worship, thought, speech, and association. Liberalism as a protest against clericalism is no longer a live issue in England (or in most other countries).

Free trade, another great ideal of nineteenth-century British Liberalism, no longer arouses passionate political interest. Both Conservatives and Labourites are committed to some form of tariff protection, and even the Liberals realize that free trade no longer has the importance it once had.

In the 1960s and early 1970s, the issue of free trade reappeared in the controversy over British membership in the Common Market. The division of public opinion was within as well as between, the two major political parties. Liberal ideology played a less important part than the estimates of economic benefits expected from British membership. In

1973 a Conservative government led Britain into the Common Market; in 1974 a referendum called by a newly-formed Labor government confirmed the action by a vote of two to one.

In the question of empire, too, the Liberal approach of the nineteenth century is no longer relevant, since nearly all of the empire is gone. The liquidation of the empire after World War II occurred under both Labour and Conservative governments.

The specific issues gone, many Liberals have joined the Labour party, or vote Labour, or think of themselves as vaguely socialist. Liberalism has generally been to the left of the Conservatives, and in a country with a two-party system, like Britain, if one wishes to stand to the left of Conservatism, the Labour party is now the only platform to stand on.

On issues of public ownership, the Liberal elements in the Labour party are opposed to doctrinaire policies of nationalizing for the sake of nationalizing—i.e., the Liberals in the Labour party are generally on its right wing, just as the Liberals in the Conservative party are on its left wing. The right-wing Labourite is so close to the left-wing Conservative in mentality, outlook, temperament, and policies that it takes a pencil of electronic sharpness to draw the line of demarcation between them.

Liberalism has contributed much that is lasting in British socialism. Because of the Liberal influence, socialist leaders are more moderate and less doctrinaire than they might otherwise have been, and they have a deeper respect for individual liberty. Liberalism has turned the Labour party into a national party rather than one based on class, and it has bequeathed to the Labour party the Liberal message that there can be reform without bitterness and hatred.

SOCIAL-ECONOMIC CHANGES AND REFORMS

The victory of the Allied Powers in World War I provided a strong stimulus for the growth of socialist parties throughout the world. The war had been fought in defense of democracy against the authoritarian militarism of Germany and her allies, and during the war promises were made to the peoples of the major democratic belligerents, particularly Britain and France, that military victory would be followed by the establishment of a new social order based on greater opportunity and equality.

In England, the Labour party reflected in its growth and development the protest against the old social order. Founded in 1900, the party polled only two seats in the Parliamentary elections of that year. By 1910, 40 Labourites sat in the House of Commons, and the party had ceased to be a negligible factor. In 1929, the Labour party became for the first time in its history the largest single party in Britain, obtaining in the general election 288 out of 615 seats in Parliament. The coming of the world depression in 1929 weakened Britain economically, and the minority Labour government, being unable to follow socialist policies to cure the depression and unwilling to adopt conservative remedies, resigned in the summer of 1931. As long as the shadow of Nazi-fascist aggression hung over Britain there was little chance for embarking upon a major experiment of social and economic reform.

Between 1935 and the end of the war in Europe there was no general election. In the first postwar general elections, held on July 5, 1945, the Labour party obtained 394 out of 640 seats, with the result that for the first time in British history a Labour government was formed with a clear majority in the House of Commons.

Between 1900 and 1918, the Labour party was not officially committed to socialism, although it included many individual socialists. In 1918, when the party adopted socialism in its program, its commitment to the nationalization of industry was just about complete. But the party changed its outlook drastically and urged nationalization *only* where it had been proved pragmatically that public ownership would do more for the welfare of the nation than private ownership. In the election of 1945, for example, the Labour party did *not* enter the campaign with a program of "socialism" in the abstract, but promised to nationalize specifically listed industries and services if elected to office.

In each case, it explained why nationalization was necessary. For gas and light, water, telephone and telegraph, and other utilities, the criterion of nationalization was the existence of a natural monopoly. Regardless of party, there was general agreement in Britain that the coal industry was so sick and inefficient that it could not be put on its feet except through nationalization. The iron and steel industries were declared to be so vital to the nation that their management could not safely be subject to the decisions of private persons. The nationalization of all inland transportation by rail, road, and air was proposed on the ground that wasteful competition could best be avoided by a coordinated scheme of transportation owned and managed by public authorities. The Bank of England was also proposed for nationalization on the ground that its purpose was so obviously public. Finally, the election program of 1945 also promised to set up a National Health Service, so that the best possible health and medical facilities might be available to every person without regard to ability to pay.

After the electoral triumph of 1945, the Labour party methodically carried out its program. With one exception, there was little argument over nationalization. Regarding the exception, iron and steel, the Con-

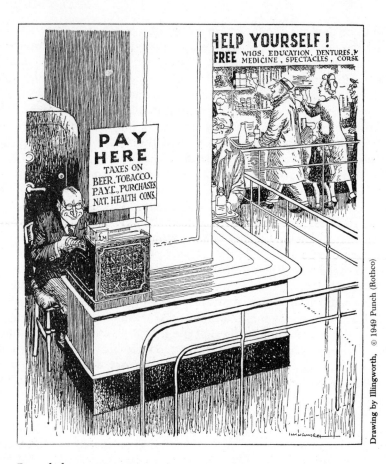

Round the corner

servatives argued that the industry was highly efficient and that the needs of the national welfare could be accommodated without nationalization.

The attitude of the British toward nationalization was generally one of indifference. The exception was, and is, the National Health Service, because of its direct effect on the everyday life of the individual citizen. Although no one was compelled to join the National Health Service, 97 percent of the population and 96 percent of the doctors are in it. At first the administrative and technical difficulties in setting up the necessary machinery caused considerable delay and confusion. As the program began to hit its stride, however, adverse criticism largely died down. Now the National Health Service has established itself as a part of

British life. The Conservative party, like the Labour party, is fully committed to the program. The medical profession, while not enthusiastic about it, has nevertheless publicly accepted it as essentially "sound." Public opinion polls have found that about 90 percent of those questioned are on the whole satisfied with the National Health Service. The British no longer discuss the basic issue of a national health insurance program, but the ways of improving its practical operation. One serious problem has arisen in recent years that was not anticipated when the program was set up. Low pay and inadequate career opportunities have induced many British physicians to emigrate, mostly to the United States, Canada, and Australia. In recent years, about 400 doctors have left Britain annually, or the equivalent of about one out of three medical school graduates. As a result, British hospitals have had to rely increasingly on immigrant physicians—mainly from India and Pakistan.

The Labour government elected in 1945 also set up a comprehensive cradle-to-grave scheme of social security. The system provides protection against sickness, unemployment, and old age, supplemented by maternity grants, widows' pensions, and family allowances. Social security as set up by the Labour government was no invention of the Labour party, but the culmination of several decades of social legislation enacted by Conservative and Liberal governments. A fully integrated system of social security was first proposed during World War II in the *Beveridge Report* (1942); in the middle of the war, both the Conservative and Labour parties pledged themselves, if elected to office after the war, to introduce a comprehensive system of social security.

A further policy of the Labour government in the years 1945–1951 aimed at greater social equality. The setting up of the basic institutions of the welfare state in itself contributed to greater social equality by bringing within the reach of large sections of the population many facilities and services that hitherto had not been available to them. Educational opportunities on the secondary and university levels, for example, were made available to children of lower-income families. In addition, several new colleges and universities were founded in an attempt to combine British educational features with the American goal of providing higher education for the many rather than for the select few.

In 1965, the Labour government tackled one of the keys to social equality—the secondary school. In Britain, as in most other countries, there are two main types of secondary school: an academic, for a small minority, that leads to college; and a vocational, for the mass of the people, that ends at age 15. The main disadvantage of such a system is that the decision about going to college must be made at age ten or

eleven on entering a specific type of secondary school; an additional
disadvantage is that the system segregates the members of different
social classes at an early age. For these reasons, the Labour government
started to adapt the British system of secondary education to the American pattern, in which most high schools combine academic with vocational education. Interestingly, Labour spokesmen for this reform often
refer to the American experience; as in so many other instances, what
socialists in other countries call the socialist ideal of equality is accepted
in the United States, in theory at least, as the noncontroversial American concept of equality of opportunity.

Taxation was the greatest leveler. Thus, in 1910 a person with an
income of £100,000 retained, after payment of taxes, about £94,000.
Currently, the net income after payment of taxes runs to about
£20,000. Estate (or inheritance) taxes took about 50 percent of larger
fortunes in 1938, but currently go up to 80 percent—one of the highest
rates in the world. As a result of high income and estate taxes there has
been a significant shift in the distribution of wealth. In 1911, the top 1
percent of the British population held 69 percent of the nation's wealth;
currently, the share of that 1 percent is about one-quarter. Similarly,
the share of the top 10 percent has dropped from 92 percent in 1911
to about one-half of the national wealth.

While the share of high incomes in terms of the national income has
declined in Britain, there has been a sharp increase of the middle-
income groups, particularly skilled workers. The trend toward more
social equality can also be seen in the fact that the proportion of the
national income paid in wages and salaries increased from 60 percent
in 1938 to the current figure of well over 70 percent, whereas the
income from dividends and interest declined considerably during the
same period. All these policies have by no means brought about equality, but they have gone a long way toward eliminating extremes of
inequality.

Dropping much of the traditional socialist belief in nationalization,
the Labour party has come close to the Conservative party, which in
turn no longer opposes the basic principles of the welfare state. Inasmuch as both parties seem to be united on kindred principles of social
policy, and because so much of the British economy depends upon
factors external to it (such as its ability to compete with other countries
in foreign markets), there is little room left for such differences in
principles as characterized the classic nineteenth-century struggles between the Whigs and the Tories.

In the 1960s and early 1970s, British politics thus gave the impression of ideological peace and near-uniformity. The Labour party, in
particular, is in search of a new program and set of principles that can

inspire the country, for the impulse of early socialism—nationalization plus social security—has been largely spent. The very acceptance of the welfare state by all political parties has thus become the main source of social stagnation.

On the Continent, the Scandinavian countries have had the most impressive record of social reforms, both in the interwar years and after World War II. From the early 1930s onward, the Scandinavian countries generally have been governed by socialist administrations based on parliamentary majorities, and as a result communism has been kept down to minor proportions in all three countries (Norway, Denmark, Sweden). The Scandinavian socialist movements have emphasized economic development and social security rather than nationalization, and their economic policies have been centered on fiscal measures (such as cheap money) and taxation rather than on public ownership. Full employment is a major point in Scandinavian (as in British) socialism.

One of the important lessons of the social and economic reform in Scandinavia in the last 30 years is the emphasis on socialization rather than nationalization. One of the most serious political weaknesses of the British Labour party's program of economic change has been the tendency to substitute state ownership and management for private ownership, thus increasing the tendency toward governmental centralization. In contrast, the Scandinavian reform programs have experimented with other types of social ownership in lieu of private ownership.

The most significant contribution of Scandinavia to social reform is the use of the cooperative movement rather than the state as the agent of social and economic reform. Whereas in Britain, as in most other countries, the cooperative movement has been largely confined to retail and wholesale trading in a selected group of articles, the Scandinavians have set up cooperatives for slum clearance, health insurance, and industrial production. This Scandinavian middle way seeks to avoid the evils of unbridled capitalism and, at the same time, the dangers of statism.

PROBLEMS OF NATIONALIZATION

Socialist theory and practice have undergone drastic changes on the issue of nationalization in the last 50 years. When the British Labour party adopted a socialist platform in 1918, it demanded (in clause IV of its revised constitution) "the common ownership of the means of production, distribution, and exchange." At that time, this formula expressed the prevailing socialist orthodoxy.

Today, not a single socialist party in the world, nor a single socialist leader of repute and responsibility, still adheres to the old formula of nationalizing *all* the means of production, distribution, and exchange. In July 1951 the Socialist International, speaking for more than 30 Socialist parties throughout the world, adopted a program that specifically rejected the older doctrine of total nationalization and conceded that socialist planning is compatible with private ownership in agriculture, handicrafts, retail trade, and small and medium-sized industries.

In 1959, the German Social Democratic party, the largest democratic socialist party on the European continent, adopted a new program in which freedom, justice, and respect for the individual are declared to be its highest values. As for nationalization, the program specifically states that "efficient small and medium-sized enterprises are to be strengthened to enable them to prevail in competition with large-scale enterprises." Only where competition is impossible for natural or technical reasons, does public ownership become a necessity. The following two general principles are included in the program: "Private ownership of the means of production is no longer identical with the control of power"; and "Every concentration of economic power, even in the hands of the state, harbors dangers."

In 1964, the Social Democratic party adopted a series of new resolutions spelling out its domestic and foreign policies in detail. This time, the word "nationalization" did not even appear, so dead an issue had it become. The economic policy was summarized as follows: "Only a combination of the market economy and monetary and fiscal over-all control and welfare policy can be the solution suited for our time." In its "Government Program" of 1969, the Social Democratic party spelled out its economic and social programs in detail, but again there was no mention or discussion of nationalization. The usual welfare and labor-union policies were advocated: secure employment, technological progress, regional planning, and tax reforms in favor of low-income groups.

The leader of American socialism over four decades, Norman Thomas, wrote in *Democratic Socialism: A New Appraisal* (1953) that "the state under the most democratic theory and practice will become too huge, too cumbersome, if it seeks to control directly all economic activity." Ten years later, in *Socialism Re-Examined* (1963), Thomas stated again: "American socialists nowadays generally accept, as they should, a mixed economy, controlled by the overall concept that production should be for the good of all. For the state, under any system, to try to own and operate anything, would deprive us of some of the important values of private initiative and responsibility." Thomas spoke of the dangers of statism inherent in total nationalization, and like many other socialists he stressed that the alternative to capitalism is socialization, not nationalization.

Individual freedom is inextricably linked to the diffusion of power. This truism has always been admitted by socialists to apply to political government. They are now coming around to the idea that in the economic realm, too, there can be no individual freedom unless there is diffusion of economic power. The fundamental importance of constitutional government to democratic socialism was stated by the German Social Democratic party in 1971: "The decisive difference between Social Democratic and Communist policy does not lie in the different attitude toward private property, as important as this is, but in the difference between constitutionality and arbitrariness, between liberal democracy and party dictatorship, between self-determination and determination from outside."

The concept of socialization implies the diffusion of publicly owned property. Property is owned and managed not by the state but by producer or consumer cooperatives, labor unions, churches, educational institutions, hospitals, and other organizations, and these organizations derive their powers from voluntary association rather than from the sovereign authority of the state.

This approach has been successfully tried in Scandinavia as well as in Israel. In Scandinavia, most public housing has been built not by the state, but by corporations that combine individual ownership and management with financial assistance from housing cooperatives and municipal agencies. In Scandinavia, too, as mentioned earlier, cooperatives are not confined—as they are in many countries—to the retail business, but are common in the fields of manufacturing and wholesaling. In Israel, the Federation of Labor, the main organization of labor unions, is the largest employer in the nation; it has a considerable share in the ownership and control of such basic industries as highway transportation, navigation, aviation, banking, building, heavy machinery, cement, glass, and rubber. A sizable proportion of Israel's agricultural production is in cooperative farm communities. In all, the "workers' sector" in the economy accounts for almost one-quarter of Israel's national product.

None of these solutions is final, and mistakes are constantly made, but these forms of socialization do seem to their advocates to avoid the worst evils of nationalization—monopoly and the resulting concentration of economic and political power. In a capitalist democracy, the economic power of private monopolies can at least be opposed by the political power of the state. *When the monopolist is the state itself, who will protect the citizen against the state?*

Today, then, no socialist party advocates any longer that all industries be nationalized; nationalization is recommended only for some industries. There seems to be universal acceptance among socialists of the idea that natural monopolies in the public utilities field should be publicly owned and managed. The concept of the "sick industry" and the criterion of the "key industry" have also been accepted as standards upon which nationalization may be based.

It appears that nationalization lends itself best to industries or services that are highly standardized—that is, where uniform rules of administration can be easily applied (this is the thesis of "gas and water socialism"). On the other hand, in industries that demand high adaptability to changing conditions—for example, industries that produce largely for export or industries that operate with a considerable element of risk—the case against nationalization or socialization is strong. The tendency of a bureaucratically run enterprise to put security above adventure and risk is incompatible with rapid industrial expansion. The automobile industry a generation ago and the photocopying industry today are the products not of preexisting giant enterprises, but of relatively small corporations that were willing to put capital into new and risky products.

It remains to be proved that this same spirit of adventure, risk, and experimentation can be shown by publicly owned enterprises. After all, it is one thing to risk one's own money; it is quite another thing to use the public treasury for questionable, though potentially profitable, ventures. Similarly, it has been argued that, under public ownership, declining industries (such as coal and railroads) are being artificially propped up by the government when, for economic reasons, they should be allowed to decline. "This has been a great shock," a former high British official writes, "especially for the workers in these industries, as it has always been assumed that the workers were to be the main beneficiaries of state ownership. They naturally demand, therefore, that the Government should take the strongest measures to arrest this decline—regardless of the effects on the national economy" (R. Kelf-Cohen, *Twenty Years of Nationalisation: The British Experience,* 1969, pp. 315–16).

The traditional concern of socialists has always been with distribution rather than production. The most creative contribution of socialism has, therefore, been its revision of the internal social structure of nations in the direction of equality. Many countries with strong socialist parties exhibit internal cohesion and unity, the direct result, according to socialist leaders, of a high degree of social justice based on the concept of "fair shares for all." In contrast, these leaders pointed out, where socialism has recently been weak, as in France and Italy, the people are torn and disunited, and there is a general feeling of alienation and resentment.

It has not been shown so far that publicly owned enterprise is any more efficient in production than private enterprise or that it has materially increased the people's standard of living. C. A. R. Crosland, a leading British economist and member of the Wilson Cabinet in the 1960s, made important concessions on both points. First, he admitted that the performance of nationalized industries in Britain has not been conspicuously better than that of private enterprise and that nationalized industries have been plagued by "bureaucratic centralization." Speaking of living standards, he also argues that further nationalization "cannot be said to be necessary to full employment and prosperity, for these exist already."

From the very beginning, public enterprise has found that three specific difficulties hamper its overall performance. First is the *managerial problem* of administering vast public enterprises with flexibility and initiative and at a low cost. The excessive tendency toward centralization and playing it safe is a serious matter. Moreover, it is not certain that the managerial situation will improve as nationalization continues. In the first phase of public ownership, the public corporation can draw upon managerial talent which has been trained in the tough environment of private competition, but if nationalization goes on, management of public enterprises will have to draw its top personnel from among its own ranks. It will then be seen whether persons trained and bred in the secure, sheltered atmosphere of bureaucratic monopoly will possess as great a capacity to operate large undertakings as is shown by graduates of the hard school of private, competitive business.

If the American experience can serve as a guide to managerial performance, the outlook for nationalized enterprise is uncertain. In American corporate business, industries that are near the bottom of the executive pay scale (and presumably attract less able executives) include regulated industries like insurance, savings and loan associations, banking, air transport, railroads, and public utilities. These industries are either monopolies (as in the case of the public utilities) or enjoy relatively little competition since their existence generally depends on a governmentally granted franchise. There is relatively little product innovation in such industries, operations are often highly routinized, and seniority is a determining factor in promotions. By contrast, the industries near the top of the executive pay scale (automotive, chemical, metals manufacturing, electronics, department stores) are characterized by creativity and product innovation under the pressure of substantial competition. Promotion is less influenced by seniority, outside executive talent is more frequently brought in, and there is therefore a greater turnover of executive personnel.

In nationalized industries producing standardized goods or services (such as public utilities) the management problem may not be too serious. But in competitive industries, where flexibility and innovation are essential, nationalized industries will find it more difficult to attract top-quality executives for two reasons. First, as an industry becomes nationalized, it automatically becomes monopolistic and routinized and allows for less creativity and executive initiative than are demanded under conditions of private, competitive enterprise. Second, national-ized industries—like regulated industries in a nonsocialist economy—pay lower executive salaries, and able executives prefer more challeng-ing positions that offer better pay to more routinized work at lower pay.

The problem of management in nationalized industries is closely connected with a second major problem. In private business, the *system of profits and losses* operates in a crude but effective way to keep efficiency at a relatively high level, and the threat of bankruptcy is always real. In a public enterprise, this system no longer operates to the same extent; if there are losses, no one goes bankrupt and the losses of one division can be passed on to the whole enterprise. Even if the whole enterprise or industry is in the red, management can either increase prices or receive cheap credits or subsidies from the government be-cause it has a monopoly.

Third, there is the *political difficulty*. How are public corporations to be related to the elected representatives of the people? If the public corporation is too closely supervised by Parliament or Congress, its management may become demoralized and lose efficiency. If parlia-mentary control is relaxed, on the other hand, up goes the cry that there is not much difference between the old and the new systems (since if management can do more or less as it pleases, what has nationalization changed?). After more than two decades of nationalization in Britain, experience has shown that whatever political control over nationalized industries is exercised, it is done by the executive branch, not by the legislators. A former undersecretary at the Ministry of Fuel and Power who observed the problem of democratic control of nationalized indus-tries from the inside for many years concludes that "public ownership and parliamentary procedure do not go well together" (Kelf-Cohen, *Twenty Years of Nationalisation*, p. 177).

Because of all these difficulties and complexities, many leading so-cialists are increasingly reconciling themselves to the virtually com-plete elimination of nationalization from the socialist program, emphasizing the concepts of equality and welfare instead. In his Fabian tract *Socialism and Nationalisation* (1956), Hugh Gaitskell, then leader of the British Labour party, concluded that "the most vital question is how far greater social and economic equality can be achieved without more nationalisation and public ownership." After Labour's electoral defeat in 1959, Gaitskell publicly advocated that the Labour party elim-inate from its constitution clause IV, which calls for common ownership of the means of production, distribution, and exchange.

A prominent spokesman of the right wing in the Labour party and minister of defense in the Wilson Cabinet, Denis Healey, went even further than Gaitskell. American writers like A. A. Berle had said that in the American capitalist enterprise the real power is in the hands of professional managers rather than of the shareholders who legally own it. This viewpoint is now increasingly recognized by socialists as being equally applicable to publicly owned enterprise. "Industrial power in every large, developed economy now rests with a managerial class which is responsible to no one. The form of ownership is irrelevant. State control over nationalized industries is as difficult as share-holder control over private firms" (Denis Healey, *The New Leader,* August 17, 1957). For a high-ranking socialist to say that the form of ownership is irrelevant marks a basic change of outlook.

More important than what socialist leaders and thinkers have said is the voters' clear and repeated expression of opposition to further nationalization. In the 1950s and 1960s, numerous polls were taken on this question, some by independent polling organizations and others by Labour organizations. In every instance, from 65 to 80 percent of the voters opposed further nationalization; more seriously, even among Labour party supporters the number of those who favored further nationalization was generally only one-third to one-half of those who opposed it.

In recent elections the Labour campaign has de-emphasized public ownership and concentrated on the topic of economic growth as Britain's number-one problem. Harold Wilson stressed the need for Britain to "move forward," to get out of the lethargy and stagnation which, according to him, were the result of 13 years of Conservative rule. In particular, Wilson promised that a Labour government would increase and strengthen higher education and scientific research and that the new opportunities in research would stop the "brain drain"—the emigration of British scientists to other countries, mainly the United States. In his devotion to scientific growth Wilson went so far as to say that "if there was one word I would use to identify modern Socialism it was 'science.' " While Wilson also promised social welfare improvements in all three campaigns the emphasis clearly shifted from accelerated social justice to accelerated economic growth. Because the rate of British economic growth since the 1950s has fallen way behind that of the other major economies, nationalization, whether commercially a success or a failure, has had little impact on the problem of British economic growth. By staking its future, at least for the next decade or two, on this issue rather than on the side issue of nationalization, the Labour party is aware of the fact that it will be judged by the people in the light of its record on restoring Britain to a position of economic leadership.

This economic challenge dominated the Labour government of

Prime Minister James Callaghan, which came to office in 1974. Instead of pursuing distinctively socialist objectives Callaghan was preoccupied with such problems as controlling inflation, reducing the balance of payments deficit, and maintaining industrial peace. By 1977 the bonanza of large-scale oil discoveries in the North Sea off the Scottish coast relieved British dependence on expensive imported fuel, but other economic problems were only exacerbated. Most important from the standpoint of a socialist government, the trade unions showed increasing reluctance to moderate their demands for higher wages and support policies designed to stimulate investment, improve productivity, and expand exports. Paradoxically, the main obstacles to Labour's program for strengthening the economy came not from embattled capitalists but from embittered workers. As Callaghan faced new general elections in 1979 his principal concern was less with opponents of socialism than with proponents of inflationary wage hikes.

Surveys in various parts of the world (including Western Europe and Britain) have shown that about two-thirds of those polled reject both capitalism—if capitalism means the exploitation of the many by the wealthy few—and socialism—if socialism means government ownership of the economy. Two-thirds of the interviewees favored social welfare and private property. More specifically, 70 percent of those polled stated that socialism meant to them "social welfare" rather than "government ownership" (Ralph K. White, *Foreign Affairs,* January 1966, p. 225).

A leader of the Labour party, Douglas Jay, succinctly stated the reason democratic socialist movements shifted their emphasis from nationalization to the welfare state, economic security, and social justice: "Modern experience has proved that although governments are not always very efficient at producing goods, they are highly efficient at redistributing income and wealth."

The Future of Socialism

WHY SOCIALISM HAS NOT SPREAD IN THE UNITED STATES

The question is often asked why socialism has not been able to gain a strong foothold in the United States. According to classical socialist writers, the United States as the world's leading capitalist country was bound to develop the "inner contradictions" out of which socialist mass movements would develop. Yet nothing of the sort has happened. Is it because socialism is European? There are strong socialist parties in

Canada, Australia, New Zealand, Chile, Japan, and other countries outside of Europe. Why the failure in the United States?

The Socialist Party of the United States was founded in 1901. In the presidential elections of 1904 and 1908 it polled about 400,000 votes. In the presidential election of 1912, it polled nearly 900,000 votes, or 6 percent of the total vote—the highest percentage ever polled by it in any election. It maintained its absolute voting strength of about 900,000 votes in the elections of 1920 and 1932, receiving much fewer votes in the intervening years of prosperity. The Great Depression of the 1930s filled the Socialist party with hope of further growth. Yet 1932 was the last election in which the party made any impact. In 1932, Franklin D. Roosevelt was elected president, and after four years of his vigorous New Deal policies, the Socialist party obtained only 187,000 votes. This downhill trend accelerated in subsequent elections, until it decided to stop putting up presidential candidates.

Even in the heyday of its popularity, in the election of 1912, the Socialist party was strongest in the agricultural states of the West, and not—as in Europe—in the industrial areas in the east. In these agricultural states—Arizona, California, Idaho, and a few other states of the West—the Socialist vote represented not the outcry of the "oppressed industrial proletariat" against capitalism, but the protests of farmers against low prices for farm products, high interest rates, and corrupt politics.

Socialism bases its appeal on two main issues: (1) social equality and (2) the abolition of poverty.

Social equality

One of the driving forces of European socialism has been the protest against the inequality of social classes that Europe (and part of the extra-European world) has inherited from its feudal past. By contrast, the United States is a nation without a feudal past and has therefore developed without the legacy of the legally recognized inequality of classes. Most Americans consider themselves middle class; there is comparatively little class consciousness in the United States. Social mobility is great, mainly because higher education is available to more persons than anywhere else in the world. An American is about eight times more likely to get a college education as is a Briton. A black American's chance for a college education is several times higher than that of a white Briton, German, Frenchman, or Italian.

Racial inequality has been the persistent and pervasive form of inequality that has characterized American society from colonial days. Unlike the inequality of classes which affects the majority of the people in other countries, racial inequality affects only 12 percent (about 11 percent blacks and 1 percent other nonwhites). Yet this comparative numerical advantage is more than compensated by the depth of racial tensions, since inequalities between social classes are generally not as strongly felt and resented as racial inequalities, particularly when they are historically based on slavery.

Whereas the issue of capitalism versus socialism is relevant to the problem of social inequality, it has little bearing on racial inequality. Some capitalist societies are more racist than others, and the same is true of socialist and communist states. Problems of racial harmony exist in all continents whether the majority is white, black, or brown, and in each case the degree of racial inequality is determined by many factors. In the United States, the main thrust of the black response to racial inequality has not been in the direction of socialism. A few black leaders, such as Bayard Rustin and A. Philip Randolph, are socialists and have favored a coalition between blacks and labor unions. In recent years, however, the influence of socialist opinion has decreased in the black community in favor of more militant leaders who stress black racial solidarity and black power rather than the ideology of interracial and international socialism. There is also a small minority of black revolutionaries who see in Fidel Castro, Che Guevara, and Mao Tse-tung the models of revolutionary warfare, but the overwhelming majority of blacks rejects Maoism and Castroism even more than democratic socialism.

Abolition of poverty

Socialist groups in the United States have not been able to make the second promise of socialism—the abolition of poverty—a major popular issue. Early in this century, Werner Sombart, the noted German economic historian, studied the American labor movement and predicted that socialism in the United States would founder on the abundance of "roast beef and apple pie." As the American historian Frederick Jackson Turner saw in the nineteenth century, the frontier provided the American poor with an escape from poverty and class war—a phenomenon which did not, and could not, exist in overcrowded Europe. When the frontier was closed around the turn of this century, economic opportunity in the expanding economy and the migration to the West replaced the agricultural frontier as the means of escaping poverty.

Poverty in the United States has substantially declined in recent decades. In 1947, 32 percent of the population were poor, as compared with 12 percent in 1976 (poverty being defined as an annual income of under $5815, at 1976 prices for consumer goods, for a nonfarm family of four). Yet there is the undisputable fact of growing concern about poverty in the United States. Suffering less from poverty than any other major country, the United States increasingly shows more concern about poverty than do most other countries. There are two reasons for this paradox. First, as the production of wealth increases and as poverty declines, the sensitivity to the still remaining poor segments of the population also deepens, since the ultimate goal of abolishing poverty altogether seems close at hand. In India, poverty is not news; in the United States it is. In the United States itself, poverty is more widely discussed today than it was 20 or 30 years ago when it was more wide-spread.

The second reason for the growing concern in American poverty is that poverty is closely tied to the issue of race. In absolute numbers, the number of poor whites is more than double that of poor nonwhites. But the *incidence* of poverty is much higher among nonwhites than among whites. In 1976, one-tenth of all white persons in the United States were poor as compared with about one-third of all blacks.

Incomes of blacks have risen at a faster rate than those of whites—but not fast enough to bridge the gap. Between 1950 and 1976, the proportion of white families with incomes of $10,000 or more (in constant, 1976, dollars) went up from 35 percent to 73 percent, or more than doubled; during the same period, the proportion of nonwhite families in the same income group rose from 8 percent to 39 percent, or almost fivefold. The relative improvement of nonwhite families with high incomes of $25,000 or over was particularly striking: The percentage of nonwhite families with such high incomes rose from 1.2 percent in 1960 to 8.3 percent in 1976, or about eight times, as compared with a threefold increase in that period for white families (from 6.5 percent to 19.1 percent). Yet, despite this faster relative improvement of nonwhite family incomes, the fact is that the percentage of white families in this high income group in 1976 was still more than twice that of nonwhite families.

Looking at the problem in a broader, international perspective, we find again that it is one of race and not of socialism versus capitalism. In 1976, among black American families the median income—that is, the level at which half had more and half had less—was $9821, which was higher than the median family income in Britain, one of the wealthiest nations in the world. Yet blacks in the United States are understandably more concerned with the fact that the median income of black families in the United States in the late 1970s was about 55 percent the figure for white families.

Intelligent foreign socialists are gradually realizing that the socialist-capitalist controversy is not very relevant in the United States. Thus a leading British socialist economist, C. A. R. Crosland, wrote in *The Future of Socialism* that in Britain a leftist would be a socialist, whereas in the United States his concern would be much less "to promote social equality or material welfare, of which plenty exists already, than with reforms lying outside the field of socialist-capitalist controversy" such as civil liberties, racial equality, juvenile delinquency, and foreign policy. With respect to inequality of wealth—a key theme in traditional socialist argumentation—Crosland pointed out that "in the United States, property is more equally distributed than in Britain." Despite 25 years of socialism, the top group of property holders in Britain still owns substantially more of the country's total wealth than the comparable group in the United States.

THE IMPASSE OF SOCIALISM TODAY

Today, socialists everywhere find themselves bewildered and uncertain of the future. For more than a half-century, the socialist movement was devoted to propaganda and organization outside the framework of governmental responsibility. Now that much of the socialist program has been realized, however, socialism faces a fate similar to that of organized political Liberalism.

Just as political Liberalism passed away largely because the causes it championed either died a natural death or were solved by conservatives and socialists along liberal lines, socialism too may gradually pass away, as far as its original program is concerned, even though political parties with the socialist label may continue.

In the field of international affairs, governmental responsibilities have modified the traditional socialist outlook. As long as socialist parties were in opposition and had to confine their political activities to propaganda and electioneering, they could steadfastly adhere to the classical socialist doctrine that capitalism was the root of all international tensions. From experience with both fascist and communist imperialism, socialists have learned that international affairs are much more complex and that the forces of imperialism can be tied to any system of economic organization. Moreover, once socialist parties assume governmental responsibilities in foreign policy, they tend to follow established national interests on the one hand and economic realities on the other. At times, the requirements of national economic planning under socialist governments have given socialist foreign policies an element of isolationism, which is in sharp contrast with the traditional doctrinal commitment to internationalism.

Thus the foreign policy of the Labor government during the years 1945–1951 was discouraging to all those, in Europe and America, who believed that Britain would be the natural leader in a movement for a united Europe. In fairness to the Labour government, however, it should be noted that the Conservative government that followed it vacillated for years on the issue of joining the Common Market.

Having liquidated its far-flung empire in the 1950s and 1960s, Britain adjusted to the fact that it was now basically a European, and not a world, power. Both the Conservative and Labour parties resigned to this new status, although the Conservatives found it somewhat harder to abruptly abandon the memories of Britain as a Great Power with worldwide interests.

National interest is also the primary factor in determining the foreign policies of other socialist governments. Norway, always looking toward the Atlantic rather than to the European continent, has favored the alliance with the NATO countries. By contrast, Sweden's socialist governments have followed a policy of maintaining strict neutrality and avoiding alliances, while keeping Sweden fully armed with the most modern weapons and ready for self-defense in case of attack. This Swedish policy is based not on socialist isolationism, but on the traditional Swedish policy—a policy that has worked for a century-and-a-half—of avoiding alliances and wars. In the Near and Middle East, the socialist-dominated government of Israel is strongly associated with the United States, but India's government, though strongly prosocialist, is pursuing a policy of nonalignment leaning toward the Soviet Union. All these policies have little to do with socialism and are based primarily on national interests, attitudes, and traditions. Looking at the picture as a whole, it can be said that the foreign policies of socialist governments have been no better and no worse than those of nonsocialist governments in the same countries. The quality of a particular government depended on how intelligent and farsighted that government was, rather than on whether it was socialist, liberal, or conservative.

At the first congress of the reestablished Socialist International in July 1951, more than 30 socialist parties committed themselves to support the rearmament of their countries for collective defense against the threat of communist aggression. Meeting again in June 1962 in Oslo, the Socialist International rejected the idea that the democratic nations should disarm unilaterally. As to the causes of the Cold War, the Socialist International stated that the "East-West rivalry has largely been imposed upon an unwilling world by the communist leaders." These resolutions are primarily of interest as a reflection of a marked change of socialist outlook on the nature of war.

The present difficulties of the economic program of socialism are not likely to be resolved so soon. One great objective of socialism, the *welfare state*—that is, the responsibility of the community for a minimum standard of social and economic security for every person—is no longer a monopoly of socialist parties. All other parties in democratic nations, with the exception of ultraconservative diehards, also favor the welfare state. Some parties are more warmly for it than others, and some parties recommend more benefits than others, but as a general principle the welfare state (in the minimum sense) is accepted by all parties and is no longer a matter of partisan controversy.

The concept of the welfare state no longer requires a separate political party. In fact, much of the welfare state in England was historically the work of the Conservative party, and the limits of the welfare state are increasingly set by the ability to pay for its benefits rather than by differences of ideology. Thus, the Labour government in 1968 and 1969 introduced 30-cent charges for prescriptions and fees of $10 for glasses and $15 for false teeth, thus breaching the principle of universal medicine without fees. It also overhauled the old-age pension system, so that contributions and benefits will be more closely correlated to earnings.

The principle of universality, under which the same benefits are given to everybody regardless of need or income, has been mainly defended by socialists on the ground that means tests are thereby avoided. Yet the experience of the welfare state has taught the Labour party that under this principle of universality the needy do not receive enough benefits. As a result, the principle of "selectivity" has been increasingly debated in Britain, with more zeal by Conservatives than by Labourites. Under the principle of selectivity, more benefits are provided for those who need them than for those who do not. But a welfare system using the selectivity principle cannot do without some form of means test. In the context of British social history, the very term *means test* evokes for many British reformers, socialist as well as nonsocialist, a long chain of abhorrent memories going back to the operation of Elizabethan poorhouses. Pragmatically, the Labour party is unlikely to switch from universality to selectivity in a wholesale manner, but the current thinking and policies are groping in the direction of more selectivity, since the British economy does not produce enough—not yet, at least—to provide universal benefits on a level which is so high that the needy will receive enough for an adequate standard of living.

The very fact that after almost two generations of socialist accomplishment the main principles of the welfare state have been accepted by all parties in democratic states has created a real dilemma for the future of socialism. If it keeps on trying to convert the converted, it will lose the old fire and enthusiasm that made it a distinctive movement in the Western world. If its leaders are unable to formulate a new program, adapted to the needs of the last decades of the twentieth century, the party may simply settle down to a fixed position slightly to the left of the conservative parties, separated from the latter not by a basically different economic or political philosophy, but simply by its own concentration on translating the conception of the welfare state into a reality at the earliest possible moment.

SOCIALISM IN DEVELOPING COUNTRIES

The distinction between socialism and communism is of particular importance in the developing countries. Poor nations desire to attain rapid economic growth. Without such economic progress, the newly emerging nations feel, there can be no genuine political independence or international leadership. Domestically, rapid economic growth is the only means to achieve better living standards, health, and education.

The history of the last two centuries has shown two methods of rapid economic development. The first is that of the advanced Western nations (northwestern and central Europe, North America, and Australia and New Zealand), in which the free market was the main instrument of producing rapid economic growth. While it is true that government greatly aided this process (tariffs for infant industries; land grants for railways and educational institutions; legislatures, executives, and courts favoring the employer rather than the employee), it is also true that private initiative and capital were primarily responsible for the economic progress of the Western nations. Without any government-sponsored five- or ten-year plans, private individuals decided how available resources—labor, capital, land, raw materials—were to be used, and individual consumers decided how much of their income was to be consumed and how much saved.

Economic growth in these Western nations was greatly favored by factors that are largely absent in developing nations today: a stable government, a fairly efficient civil service, relatively high levels of education, adequate means of transportation and communication (highways, canals), and—perhaps most important of all—a considerable level of technological and entrepreneurial skill and initiative. Some nations —such as Great Britain, the Scandinavian countries, and the United States—had developed democratic political institutions before rapid economic expansion took place. As Alexis de Tocqueville noted in his *Democracy in America* (1835), "democracy is favorable to the growth of manufacturing, and it increases without limit the numbers of the manufacturing classes."

The second historically proved method of rapid economic growth has been communism. In this method, the state owns the means of production and sets an overall goal—as in the Soviet five-year plans—

of what is to be produced and how the available resources of labor, land, and capital are to be employed. The freedom of the consumer, worker, and producer is replaced by the orders of the state. Because the communist state possesses totalitarian power, it can generally ensure that the plan is translated into reality. This may take a few decades, and millions of people may pay with their lives, but eventually a modern industrial economy does develop at a rapid pace. It is important to note that no nation has so far freely chosen the path of communist economic development: Communism has either been imposed by internal revolution or civil war (Russia, China, Yugoslavia, Cuba) or by external armed force (the communist states in Eastern Europe, and Tibet and North Korea in the Far East).

In facing the issue of economic modernization, developing nations today generally do not wish to imitate either the Western capitalist process of development or the communist path of complete state planning and ownership based on political repression. Nearly every developing nation likes to think that its economic and social problems can be solved through methods which are different from both Western capitalism and Soviet or Chinese communism. The label which is attached to this "third way" is that of socialism. Socialism means many things in the context of underdeveloped countries.

First, socialism in the developing world stands for the ideal of social justice. In developing countries, the differences between the rich and the poor are proportionately greater than in the wealthier countries. Socialism, then, stands for the commitment to raise the poor masses to a higher level and to narrow the gap between the thin upper class of the privileged and the vast mass of the dispossessed. Socialism means more welfare services for the poor, more schools for the uneducated, and more human dignity for the traditionally underprivileged. Where tribal organization of society is still alive, socialism is but a new term for traditional tribal loyalty and solidarity given universal application. Thus, African socialism was defined by a leading Tanzanian statesman:

> The foundation, and the objective, of African Socialism is the Extended Family. The true African Socialist does not look on one class of men as his brethren and another as his natural enemies. He does not form an alliance with the "brethren" for the extermination of the "non-brethren." He rather regards all men as his brethren—as members of his ever extending Family (Julius K. Nyerere, *"Ujamaa": The Basis of African Socialism*, 1962, p. 8).

When attacked for betraying socialism by encouraging private foreign investments in India's fertilizer industry, essential to its increased production of food, Prime Minister Indira Gandhi affirmed her government's commitment to both socialism and democracy in a nationwide address on April 24, 1966. Then she gave her definition of socialism: "What we all want is a better life, with more food, employment, and opportunity in conditions of economic justice, equality, and with individual freedom."

Second, the term *socialism* in developing countries often stands for the ideal of human brotherhood and world peace through law. As a result, socialists in developing nations frequently advocate nonalignment between the two sides in the Cold War. Even where, as in India, nonalignment has been difficult, socialists still cling to it as a hope for the future. In Africa, the view is held that the world is divided, not between capitalist and communist countries, but between rich and poor countries, and the poor countries, in the words of Nyerere, "should be very careful not to allow themselves to be used as the 'tools' of any of the rich countries of the world," whether such rich countries are capitalist or communist.

The third meaning of socialism in developing countries is the commitment to planning. Because developing countries look upon economic growth with a sense of urgency, they feel that the functioning of the free market may not ensure the kind of rapid economic expansion and growth that are called for. Some basic elements of a modern economy—highways, means of transportation, hospitals, housing, schools—cannot, in the very nature of things, attract private enterprise, since they are the framework within which private enterprise and profits can be generated but which in themselves usually do not create such profits. Also, there is the kind of basic enterprise, such as the manufacture of steel, for which there is either not enough private capital available or which cannot hope to compete with established foreign enterprises. Only the state can build the foundations of a modern economy (highways and the like), and only the state can assume the risks of profitless enterprise over a number of years, if such enterprise is necessary for the economy as a whole. In 1963, for example, India had five steel plants, of which three were state-owned. With a population at the time of over 460 million, India produced only 5.6 million tons of steel in 1962, as compared with about 100 million tons produced in the United States. Yet even at her low level of development, India needed to produce annually at least 10 million tons of steel. As a step toward this goal, she asked American aid for the building of a sixth steel plant, to be state-owned, which would eventually produce about 4 million tons of steel. After several years of negotiation, the United States finally turned India down, largely because the projected plant would be state-owned. Indian businessmen, opposed to socialism as a general principle, publicly regretted the U.S. position, because the refusal was bound to hurt the private sector of the economy which needs steel.

Shortly after India was turned down by the United States, the Soviet Union offered to build the needed steel mill—one of the great Soviet propaganda triumphs of the 1960s. Although India has a predominantly private property economy, the Soviet Union was able to overcome ideological inhibitions more effectively than was the United States. Soviet aid to India in increasing the production of steel turned out to be a profitable political and diplomatic investment. Throughout the 1960s, Soviet-Indian relations grew consistently warmer, and in 1971 these ties were formally expressed in a 20-year treaty of cooperation between the two countries.

The need for planning, to which all developing countries are committed, does not imply overall or even large-scale nationalization of the means of production. India again provides a good illustration, as she is committed to the general idea of socialism. India has much public enterprise in heavy industry, coal, electric power, rail and air transportation, chemicals, and communications. In 1969, the Indian government also nationalized the 14 largest banks so as to gain a controlling financial leverage over the whole economy, particularly in foreign trade and over investment priorities. In 1971, India nationalized over 100 domestic and foreign insurance companies as a step toward eventual nationalization of the insurance business. After the nationalization of the major banks in 1969, the nationalization of the major insurance companies came as no surprise, since the government seemed determined to acquire control over the whole financial sector of the economy. The Indian government has sought to strengthen the public sector of the economy by allocating for its development two dollars for every one dollar in the private sector. Thus, the government seeks to increase the proportion of public enterprise mainly by creating new productive facilities rather than by nationalizing existing ones. As a result, public and private companies often compete in the same industry. Where the competition is with foreign companies—as in the case of Air India— public companies do well. Where the competition of public enterprise is with domestic Indian companies, public enterprise does less well, and where it has a monopoly its performance has been least impressive and is vigorously criticized in India itself.

Indian economic policies follow a pragmatic course rather than a rigid ideology of public enterprise for the sake of public enterprise. The differences between Indian economic policies and those of advanced Western nations are due to the different stages of economic development rather than to abstract theory. Where rapid development was necessary in the United States—as, for example, in atomic energy, jet aircraft, and space technology—the planning and financing have come almost entirely from the government, since in each of these areas the initial job was too big, too costly, and too profitless for private enterprise or initiative. What atomic energy and space technology in their beginning stages are for the United States, steel and railroads may be for India or any other developing country.

In the economic field, socialism in developing countries means an economic structure in which some industries are completely private (such as farming, handicrafts, and small business), others have both a private and a public sector (as in heavy industry), and, finally, still others are dominated by the public sector (for example, transportation and public utilities). While this is the general meaning of socialism in the economic sphere in developing areas, the practical application varies in different countries. In general, it can be said that nationalization has gone furthest where political democracy is weak or nonexistent, as in Egypt, Algeria, or Burma. Where constitutional government is a reality (as in India, Israel, and Uruguay), private enterprise is encouraged or at least tolerated.

Thus, we see that the meaning of socialism in developing countries differs from that in the wealthier countries, because the historical situation is different. In the West, socialism has meant, not how to industrialize an undeveloped country, but how to distribute the fruits of a wealthy society in a more equitable way. As a result, the concept of the welfare state has virtually absorbed the idea of socialism. By contrast, socialism in developing countries is confronted with the task, not so much of distributing the fruits of an industrial economy which hardly exists, but of building an industrial economy so as to raise the economic and educational level of the masses of the people. For the same reason, while socialism in Western countries has generally developed best within a framework of established constitutional government (as in Britain or Scandinavia), socialism in developing countries frequently develops with a burdensome tradition of authoritarian rule by foreign imperialists or native power holders. It is therefore to be expected that socialism in some developing countries will show a greater tolerance for authoritarian practices than has generally been true of Western socialism.

Yet, in the final analysis, socialism in the developing countries tries to imitate neither the Western capitalist pattern in toto nor the communist pattern. From communism, the developing nations (regardless of their commitment to socialism) have borrowed the idea that economic development can be planned, and in some cases must be planned, by the state. However, most developing countries have decided that they want planning without the police state of communism. The developing countries, and especially the socialist elements in them, greatly admire the technological efficiency of the capitalist West. Nonetheless, the great disparities of wealth as produced by the relatively freely functioning capitalist economies seem a less worthy object of imitation in developing countries. The aspect of Western nations that most appeals to developing nations is political democracy based on the rule of law. Whether the developing nations will be able to merge, under their concept of socialism, the Western political idea of liberty with the economic concept of planning, largely borrowed from the practice of communism, still remains to be seen. If the developing nations should fail in their attempted synthesis of constitutional government and economic planning (including partial government ownership of industry), there is the possibility that they may consider constitutional government expendable, but not rapid economic development through full-fledged planning and public ownership of industry.

For Further Reading

ATTLEE, CLEMENT R., *As It Happened.* New York: The Viking Press, 1954.

BUBER, MARTIN, *Paths in Utopia.* Boston: Beacon Press, 1960.

COATES, DAVID, *The Labour Party and the Struggle for Socialism.* Cambridge: Cambridge University Press, 1975.

CROSLAND, C. A. R., *The Future of Socialism.* New York: Macmillan Publishing Co., Inc., 1956.

CROSSMAN, R. H. S., *The Politics of Socialism.* New York: Atheneum Publishers, 1965.

EBENSTEIN, WILLIAM, "Democratic Socialism and the Welfare State," in *Great Political Thinkers* (4th ed.), Chap. 24. New York: Holt, Rinehart and Winston, 1969.

FREID, ALBERT, ed., *Socialism in America: From the Shakers to the Third International—A Documentary History.* New York: Doubleday & Co., Inc., 1970.

HANCOCK, M. DONALD, and GIDEON SJOBERG, eds., *Politics in the Post-Welfare State.* New York: Columbia University Press, 1972.

HARRINGTON, MICHAEL, *Socialism.* New York: Saturday Review Press, 1972.

HAYEK, FRIEDRICH A., *The Road to Serfdom.* Chicago: University of Chicago Press, 1960.

HEILBRONER, ROBERT L., *Between Capitalism and Socialism.* New York: Random House, Inc., 1970.

HOWE, IRVING, ed., *Essential Works of Socialism.* New York: Bantam Books, Inc., 1971.

LANE, DAVID, *The Socialist Industrial State.* Boulder: Westminster Press, 1976.

LASCH, CHRISTOPHER, *The Agony of the American Left.* New York: Vintage Books, 1969.

LICHTHEIM, GEORGE, *A Short History of Socialism.* New York: Praeger Publishers, Inc., 1970.

MYRDAL, GUNNAR, *The Challenge of World Poverty.* New York: Pantheon Books, Inc., 1970.

PRYKE, RICHARD, *Public Enterprise in Practice.* London: MacGibbon and Kee, 1971.

RANIS, GUSTAV, ed., *Government and Economic Development.* New Haven: Yale University Press, 1971.

SCHUMPETER, JOSEPH A., *Capitalism, Socialism, and Democracy.* New York: Harper & Row, Publishers, Inc., 1962.

SIGMUND, PAUL E., ed., *The Ideologies of the Developing Nations* (2nd rev. ed.). New York: Praeger Publishers, Inc., 1972.

THOMAS, NORMAN, *Socialism Re-Examined.* New York: W. W. Norton & Co., Inc., 1963.

WILSON, HAROLD, *The Labour Government, 1964–1970.* Boston: Little, Brown & Company, 1971.

Index